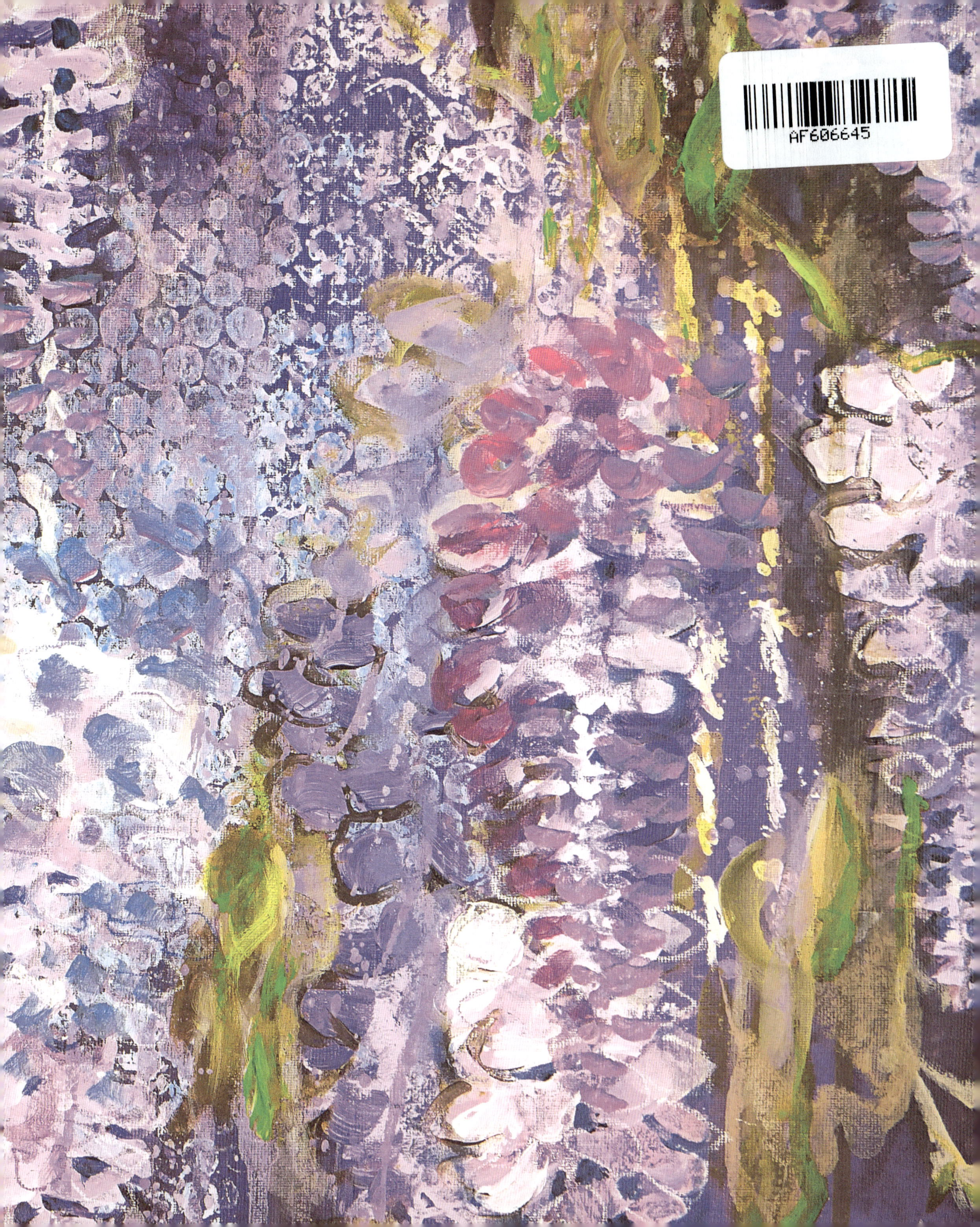

Fabulous Flowers *with* Acrylics

Paint 22 Blooms from Delphiniums to Dandelions

RUTH ALICE KOSNICK

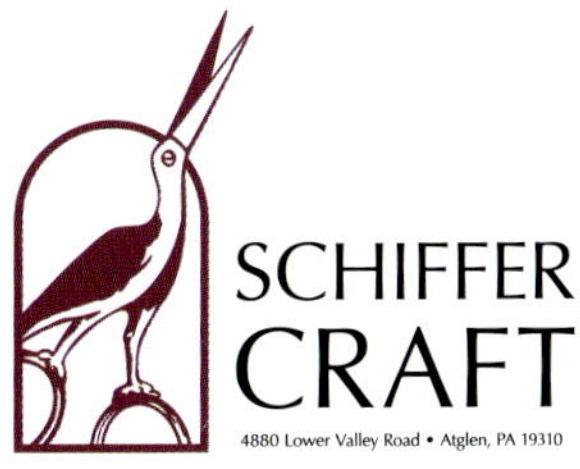

Contents

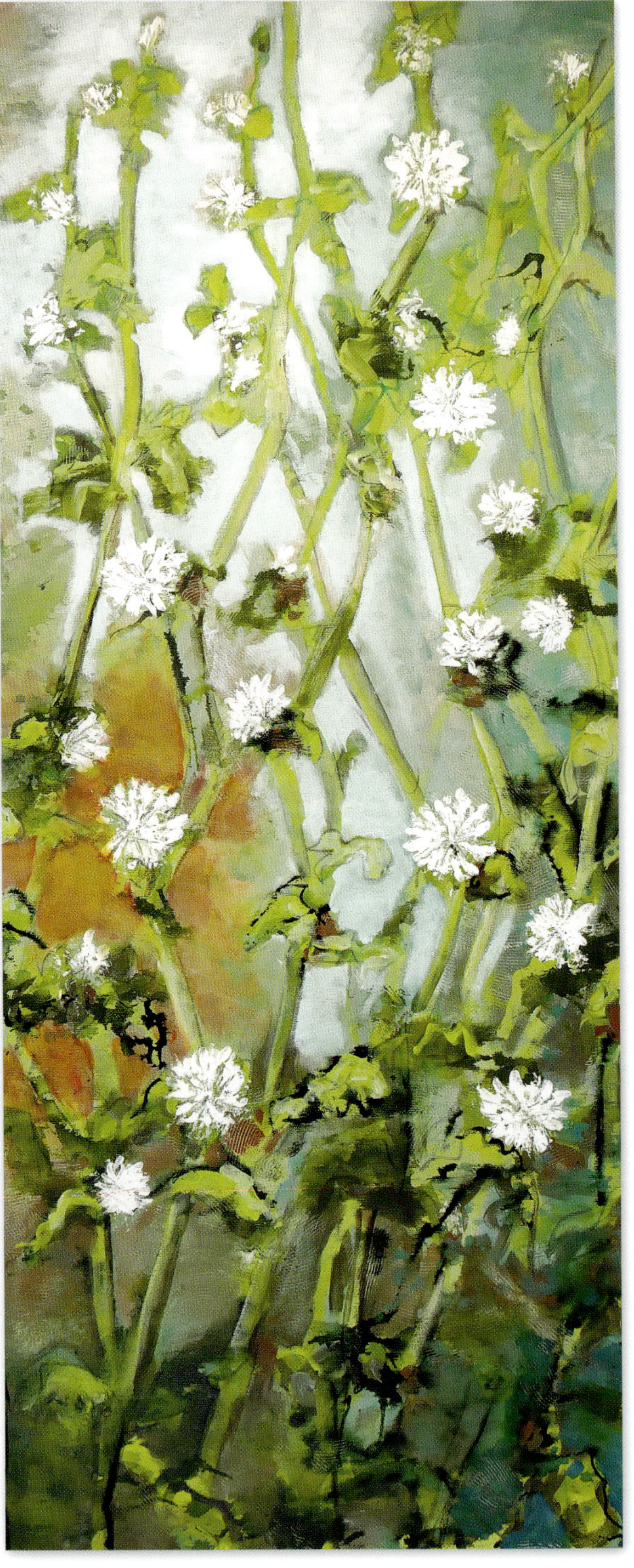

Foreword

It's wonderful and inspiring to engage with nature. When observing plants closely, you'll see small details that have previously gone unnoticed. When I paint, I create an island of peace, a brief pause, and a journey into the world on the other side of the front door. The majority of the flowers in this book grow in my garden. In the summer, I place my easel right in front of the buddleia or the peonies. Or I discover something on my travels like the phenomenon of lemon blossoms, which grow on the tree at the same time as the fruits. When I look at the flowers, stems, and leaves of plants, I try to capture their nature. The choice of media and technique is heavily influenced by the character of the plant species in question. In this book, I want to take you on a journey through the seasons in my garden. I have limited myself to one plant per picture and haven't combined any species in order to achieve a uniform design. This allows the uniqueness of each individual plant to be better revealed. I love experimenting, using different materials and techniques, and combining acrylic paints with other media. This book includes a broad range of methods for combining materials, techniques, and tools. Acrylic paints form the basis. Their wonderful flexibility and ease of use means that they can be combined with nearly all other media.

With a loose painting style and an ample dose of coincidence, I wanted to capture the vitality and movement of nature and, at the same time, leave room for the observer's imagination.

My painting style is loose and deliberately unprecise. I let paint drip and allow glazes to run, then I go over them in the next step. In this way, many layers are frequently created during the painting process, which provide a contrast to the completely untouched areas of the first application of paint. When these layers are still partially visible, unplanned elements are often created that I find very attractive. I frequently add quick, bold accents, which are fast movements that add a powerful dynamic to the subject. In combination with the most-varied media and techniques, a style of painting comes about that I call "dynamic acrylic painting." The basics of composition and design techniques presented in this book have, over the years, proven to be helpful. They can also be used on other subjects. In this book, I would like to show you how you can achieve vivid picture composition with simple materials and equipment. I hope that I can inspire you to try out the diverse media and techniques of acrylic paining and that you let yourself be enchanted by the magic of flowers.

I wish you a lot of enjoyment with dynamic acrylic painting.

Ruth Alice Kosnick

Basics of Painting Composition

Knowledge of the rules of composition is a necessary part of laying out every picture. In painting, you differentiate between static and dynamic as well as between harmony and tension. Too much static and harmony has just as much of an unpleasant effect as too much dynamic and tension. Too much harmony creates stiffness and boredom, while too much tension brings about chaos and confusion. Knowing the basics of picture composition allows you to deliberately deploy the respective devices.

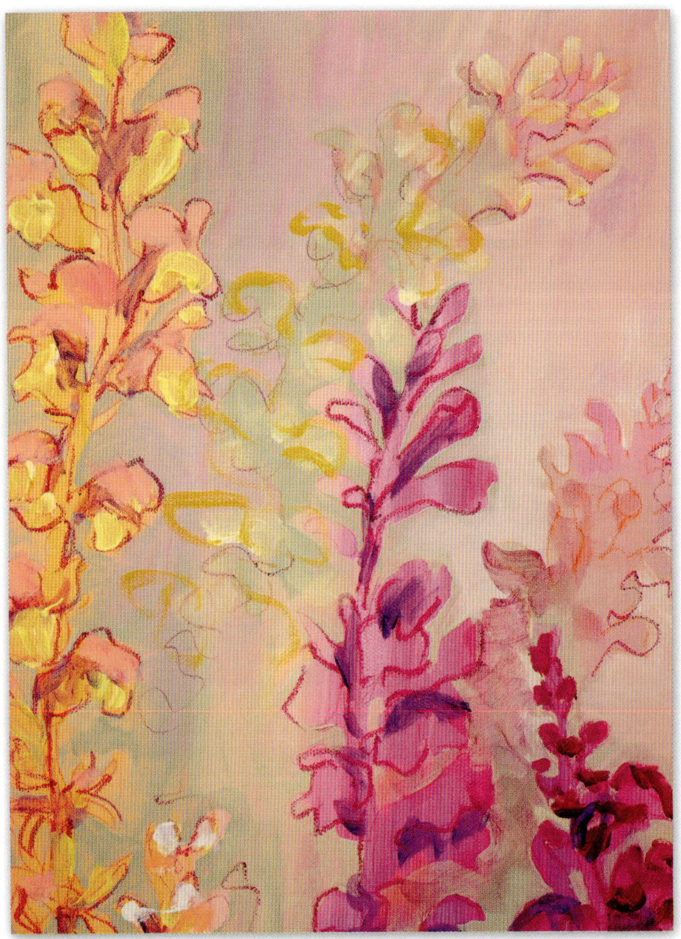

Cutting off shapes on the edges of the canvas gives the impression of abundance. By overlapping and reducing the color of the flowers in the background, an impression of depth is created.

Picture Shape and Size

Shape and content are inextricably linked to each other. Every shape, even just an unworked canvas, is already making a statement. People experience the most-varied effects when looking at different shapes and sizes. Portrait orientation is perceived as active, powerful, and dynamic, while landscape orientation feels static, peaceful, and harmonious. In the case of extreme shapes, whether portrait or landscape, the effect is tension filled. Square shapes appear balanced, neutral, and calm. However, they're also sometimes perceived as being bland and expressionless. Since the shape adds to the picture's statement, that statement should be considered when selecting the shape.

Extending Beyond the Frame and Overlapping

In painting, selecting where to cut off the image is of considerable importance because the subject creates a connection to the background and, as a result, influences the picture's statement. The surrounding frame and the object enjoy the same importance. Floral subjects are generally a composition of several flowers. In this regard, the topics of extending beyond the frame and overlapping are of particular importance. A subject where the petals are cut off at the edges gives the impression that the subject is just a section of an abundance of blooms. It looks as if the flowers extend far beyond the edges of the picture. When cutting off, you should ensure that the flower heads are not cut directly through the middle and are not positioned exactly in a corner, because it creates an unsettling optic. Overlapping creates an impression of depth, which can be increased by the restrained use of colors for the plants in the background. Thanks to these two composition elements (overlapping and extending beyond the frame), the subject gains depth and expanse.

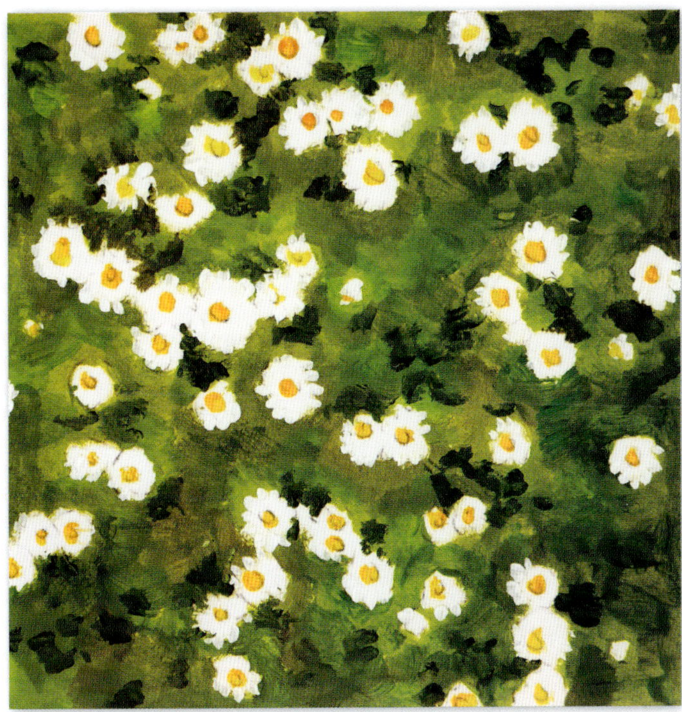

The distribution of the daisies in a meadow illustrates the random formation of groups. An empty space has been selected for the center of the picture.

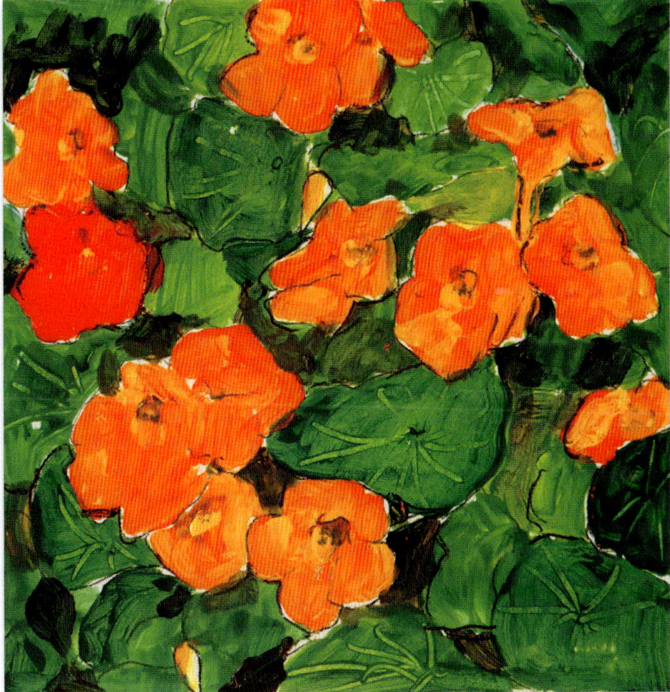

Not only the size but also the color choice influences the formation of the focal points. The individual red flowers are more prominent than their centrally placed orange neighbors.

Center of the Picture

Due to the way we generally view things, picture elements positioned in the center of the shape or on the halving main axes are ascribed a particular importance. Therefore, focal points should not be placed on the axes or right in the center, since this overemphasis makes the picture appear stiff. For this reason, the focal-point selection is an important design criterion used to create an interesting tension. The focus, also known as the center of the picture, is the area that attracts the eye of the beholder—for example, the face of the person when illustrating people or the center of a flower when painting florals. In addition to shape, the color scheme is also an important criterion when creating the center of the painting. The eye is attracted to the darkest areas and the strong reds.
If the picture center is configured according to the golden ratio, which is calculated at an approximate ratio of 1/3 to 2/3, then it's generally experienced as a pleasing harmony. In general, there are several primary and secondary centers for floral subjects, whereby it should be ensured that the distribution is uneven because equal distances between the centers could appear unnatural and lifeless. For some florals, no specific centers arise due to the abundance of flowers. In this case, different contrasts could be deployed to enliven the subject.

Tip: For a composition with several flower heads, the largest flower should not be positioned in the center.

Design Techniques

Acrylic paints are extremely versatile. Their uses range from heavily water-diluted glazes similar to watercolors through soft, creamy paints and very thick paints that are applied with a palette knife like oil paints. One advantage to acrylics is that they dry quickly, and once dried, they are no longer water soluble, meaning that they can be easily painted over. Even very dark colors can be fully covered with light colors, which is simply not possible with many other media.

All tools can be easily cleaned with water, so looking after them is easy. Acrylic paint can be easily combined with other media. Since they are produced on a resin base, they also have adhesive powers—something that's very handy when using collage paper or other additional materials. In the following pages, you'll become acquainted with a few of the basics of composition and some design techniques that will facilitate your use of this versatile media and help you create dynamic compositions.

Negative Space

On a white base, the color intensity of acrylics is particularly vibrant. For this reason, I often cover the canvas with the colors of the petals as the first layer of paint. It allows for flowing color gradients within a flower. Often, it doesn't correspond to the real color of the flowers, but it's very picturesque. In the second step, I use a watercolor pencil to draw the shapes of the flowers, stalks, and leaves. If you need to correct it, the watercolor pencil can easily be wiped off with a damp cloth. Then I create the background space by painting everything around the outlines and filling the background. This technique is called "painting the negative space." As a result, the colors of the flowers keep their vibrance. This technique is particularly attractive if the stems and some leaves also keep the colors of the flowers. During the painting process, the negative space is worked over several times with slightly varying tones. I like to allow some of the underlying layers to show through subsequent layers. In this way, diverse background spaces are created that correspond to each other in terms of color.

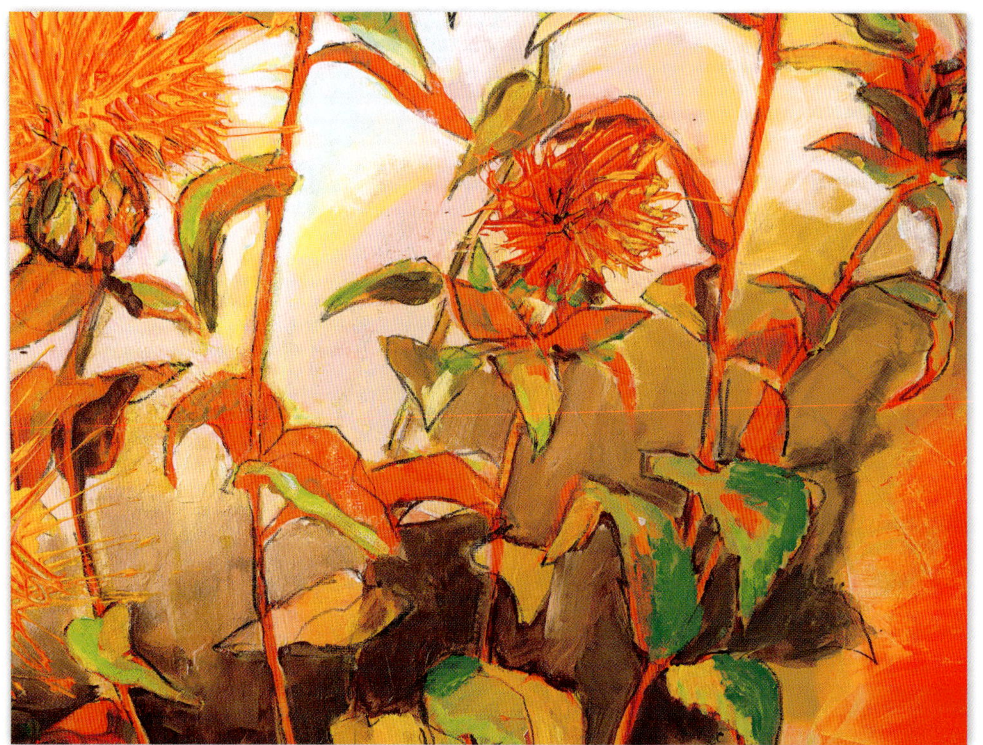

When painting over negative space, some stalks and leaves remain in the color of the petals.

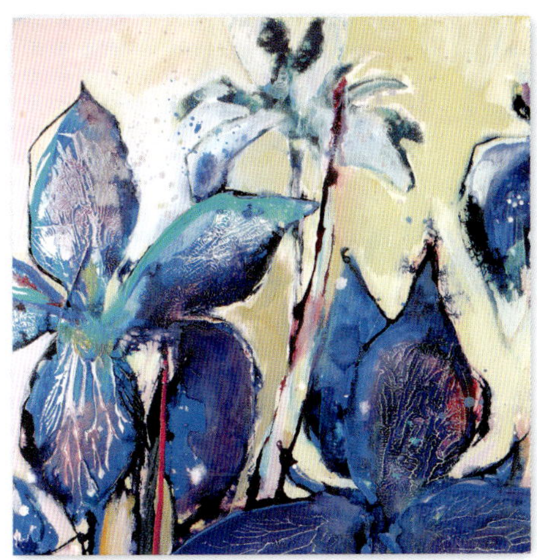

By reducing the size of the shape, an optical spatial depth is created.

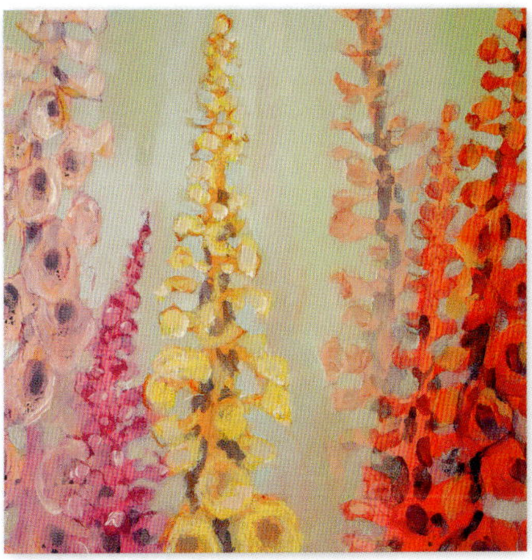

A depth effect is created by using vibrant colors at the front and paler colors behind them.

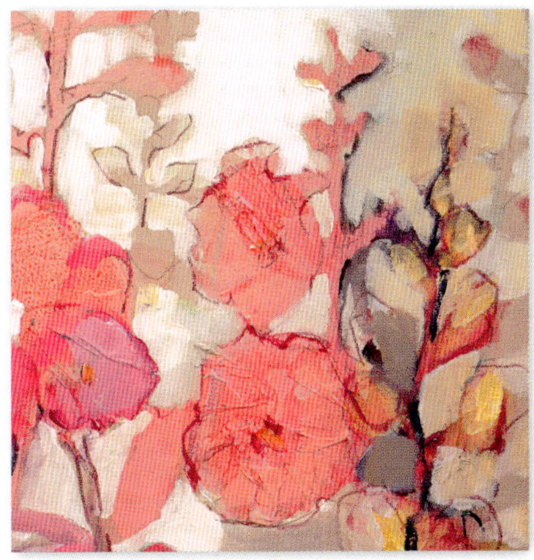

Painting a second level of plants over the negative space creates a very strong depth effect.

Depth

The simplest way to create the effect of depth is to make the shapes in the background smaller. Optically arranging the flowers behind others so that they overlap increases the depth effect. Depth effect can also be produced though the choice of color, with the dominant shade in the foreground and the softer colors in the background. The background colors may additionally be blurred using a glaze. Another method is to paint over the negative space by sketching a second level of flowers and leaves on the first layer of paint of the background. Then the negative space is once again painted over to create a second foggy level of plants with fragmented colors that produces a strong depth effect. This technique does not reflect reality, because in nature, distance does not change the color so drastically. However, when painting, we have all kinds of freedom and may divorce ourselves from the existing reality.

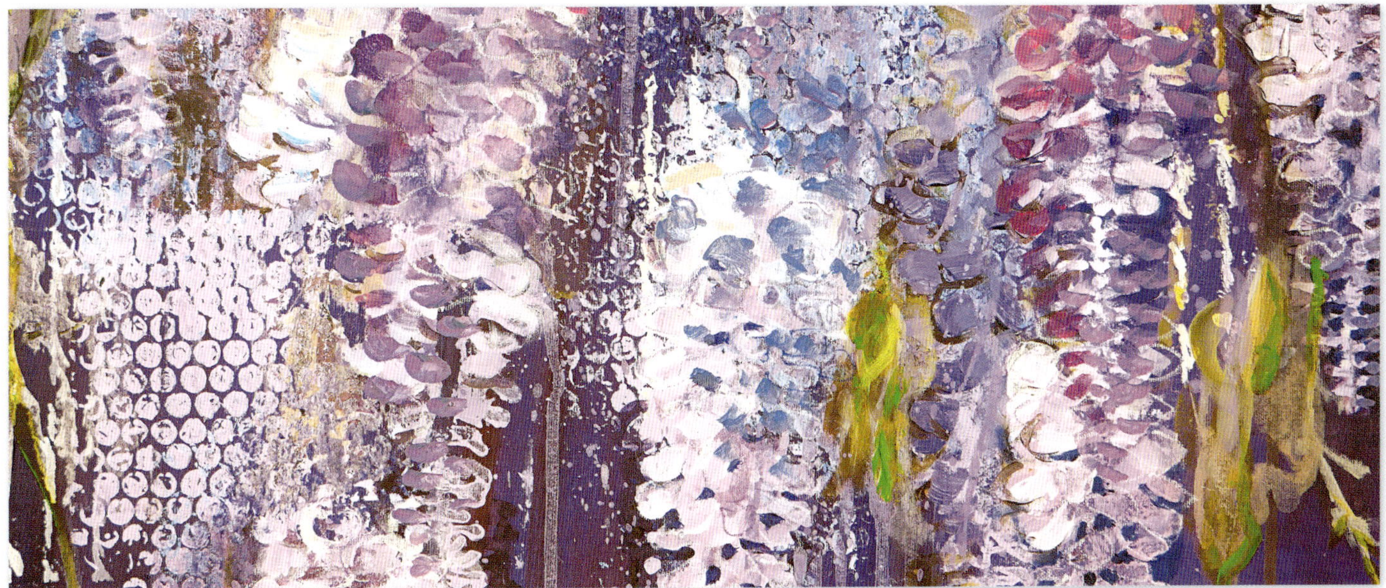

An optical depth effect is created by overlapping shapes and positioning vibrant colors at the front.

Color

Color plays an important role in floral painting. For this reason, I spread the main colors of the flowers over the whole surface to be painted. Although many areas will be covered in the painting process, small patches of it will still show through.

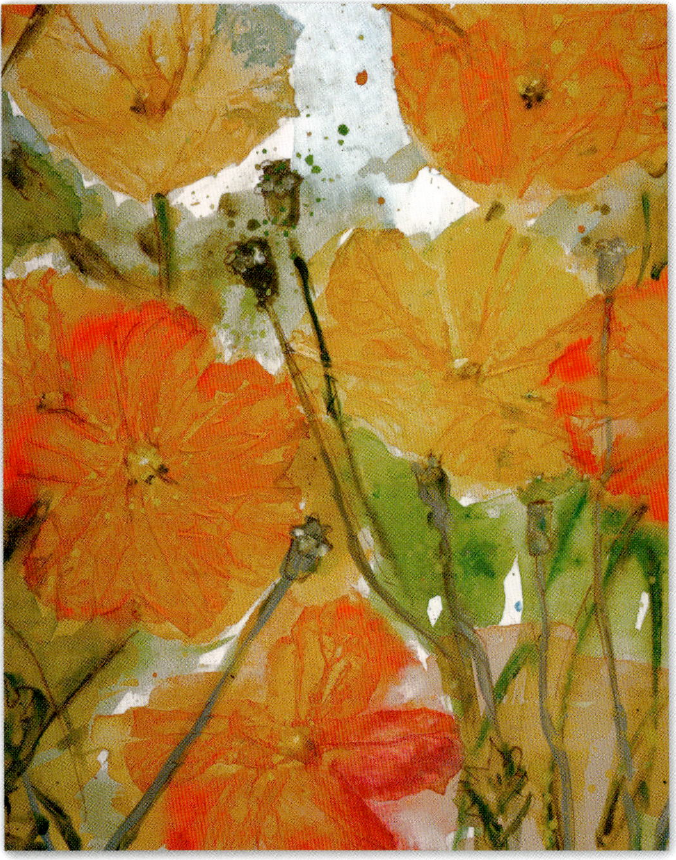

This subject has been painted with a limited color palette. There are no blue or violet shades.

This effect is known as "allowing the color to show through." In contrast to nature, in painting every flower is given an individual hue. Often, the shades from the neighboring plants also influence the color of the flowers. As a result, there is more tension, and at the same time, there is an overarching connection. Another artistic technique to make the subject appear vivid is allowing the paint to run, so that the color of the flower partially runs into the background or vice versa. Using impure shades when working on the negative space is a further technique to create exciting contrasts. Impure colors such as beige, light umber, or warm light gray allow the pure colors of the flowers to shine. This combination of pure and impure shades is known as "quality contrast." An interesting effect is created by using a limited color palette (i.e., just using a few primary colors). Since the majority of flowers already have strong primary colors (e.g., red, orange, or violet shades), then many green or blue shades can be heavily reduced or even completely excluded. As a result, the painting doesn't appear too colorful but pleasantly harmonious.

Tip: The intensity of the pure flower colors is increased by using an impure color in the background. Suitable impure shades are created by mixing all colors on the palette and then lightening with white. In this way, impure shades such as sand, light umber, or greenish brown are created.

Outlines

In real life, there are no outlines. However, the way we're used to looking at and drawing things breaks down all filled shapes into outlines. When painting, I enjoy mixing in elements of sketches, which are primarily done using outlines, alongside painted in shapes. Fragments of draft elements remain unfinished beside the fully painted areas. They overlap and permeate each other. Leaving traces of sketching and sometimes emphasizing them combines painting with graphic elements. The outlines are sometimes closed, are sometimes left open, don't completely touch the shapes, have different widths, or stand alone without being filled with paint. This mixture of a draft sketch and completed painting gives the work a loose, unfinished, and hence vivid character.

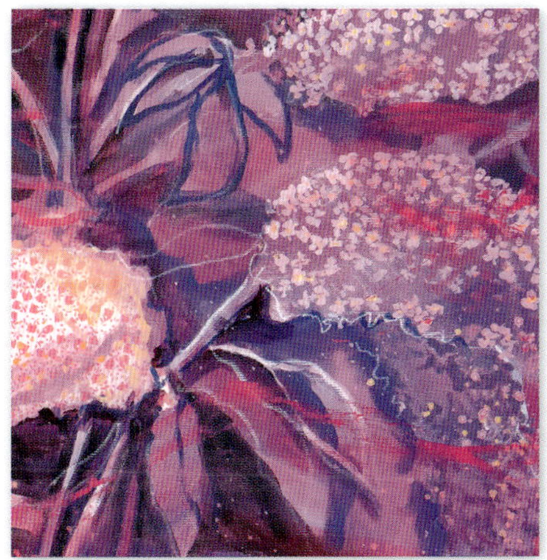

Elements of sketching and painted outlines overlapping filled leaves increase the impression of a sea of leaves.

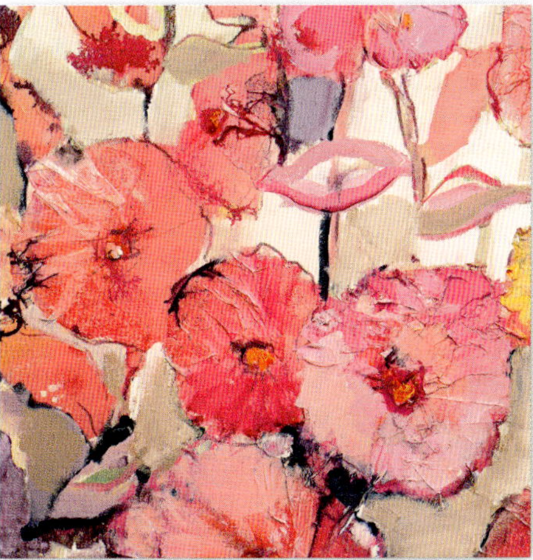

A painted outline that isn't filled in appears like an "empty leaf" and loosens the picture style.

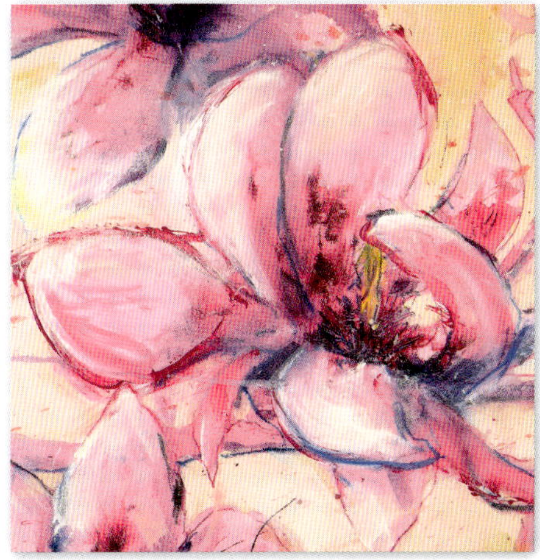

Drawing the outlines in different line widths and colors, breaking them up, or not following the shape exactly enlivens the subject.

Shape

The picture composition creates an important artistic contrast. With floral subjects, we're used to looking at the plant in full bloom, presenting the observer its opened flowers. However, the stages of the unopened flower or the bud are just as important for the picture composition, not forgetting the flowers that are just starting to wilt. An opened flower clearly turning away or overlapping and side views of some flower heads contribute to a design full of contrast.

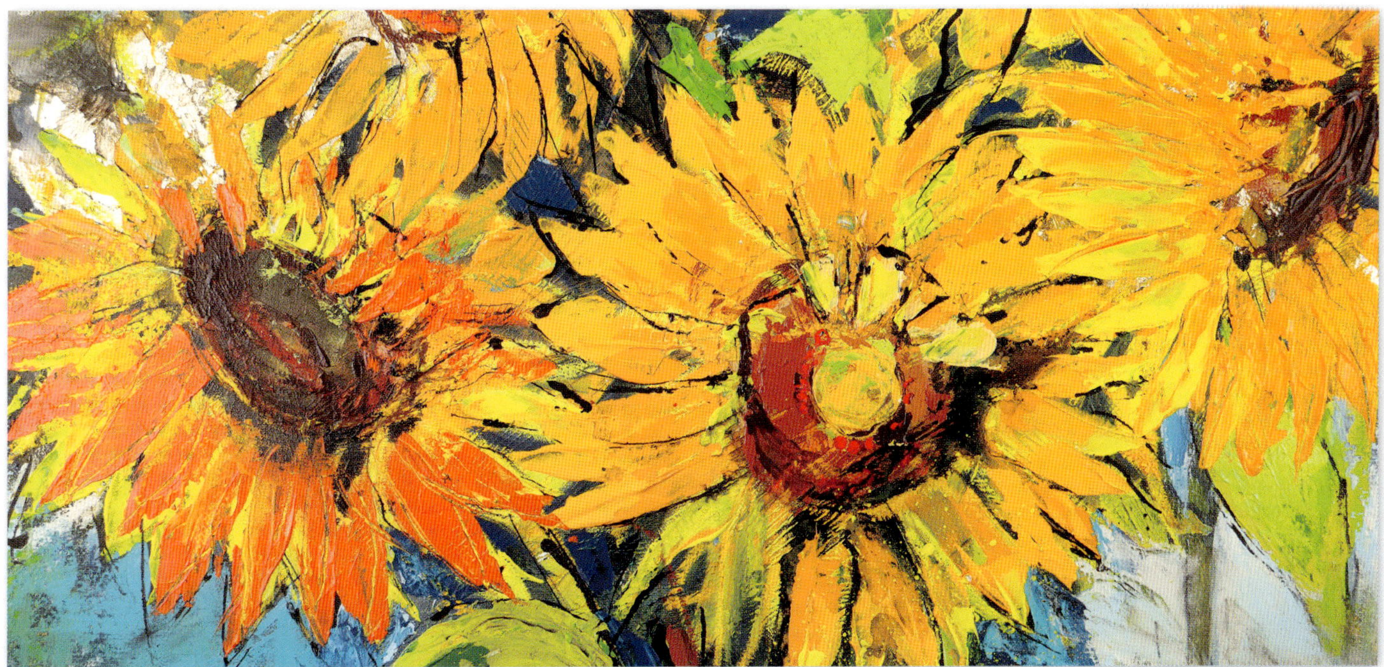

Some flowers facing away from the observer enliven the general composition.

Contrasts

Creating contrasts in a picture is very important. In addition to the well-known contrasts such as complementary or light-dark contrasts, it's important that individual sections of a picture contrast. For example, detail-rich and loosely painted picture elements can sit alongside each other. Through a different application of paint within a subject, the tension can also be increased. Alongside covered, half-covered, and glazed sections of the picture, a completely untouched section of canvas may show through. Furthermore, if you use putty or the impasto technique, this contrast is increased. The quality contrast between pure and impure colors has already been explained in the section about color. The unknown quantity contrast often creates a surprising effect. It describes the size relationship between two or more areas of color. The more tension increases, the bigger the difference in sizes. For instance, if one shade that isn't present in the rest of the image is added to a small area, then a quantity contrast full of tension is created. This term can also refer to shape contrasts such as a contrast of large and small, long and short, or narrow and wide, or even of plenty and empty.

Tip: During the painting process, it's helpful to frequently gain some distance to the picture in order to better see the contrasts. Another trick is to turn the picture upside down or to look at it through a mirror toward the end of the picture design or when the process has entered into the tough phase.

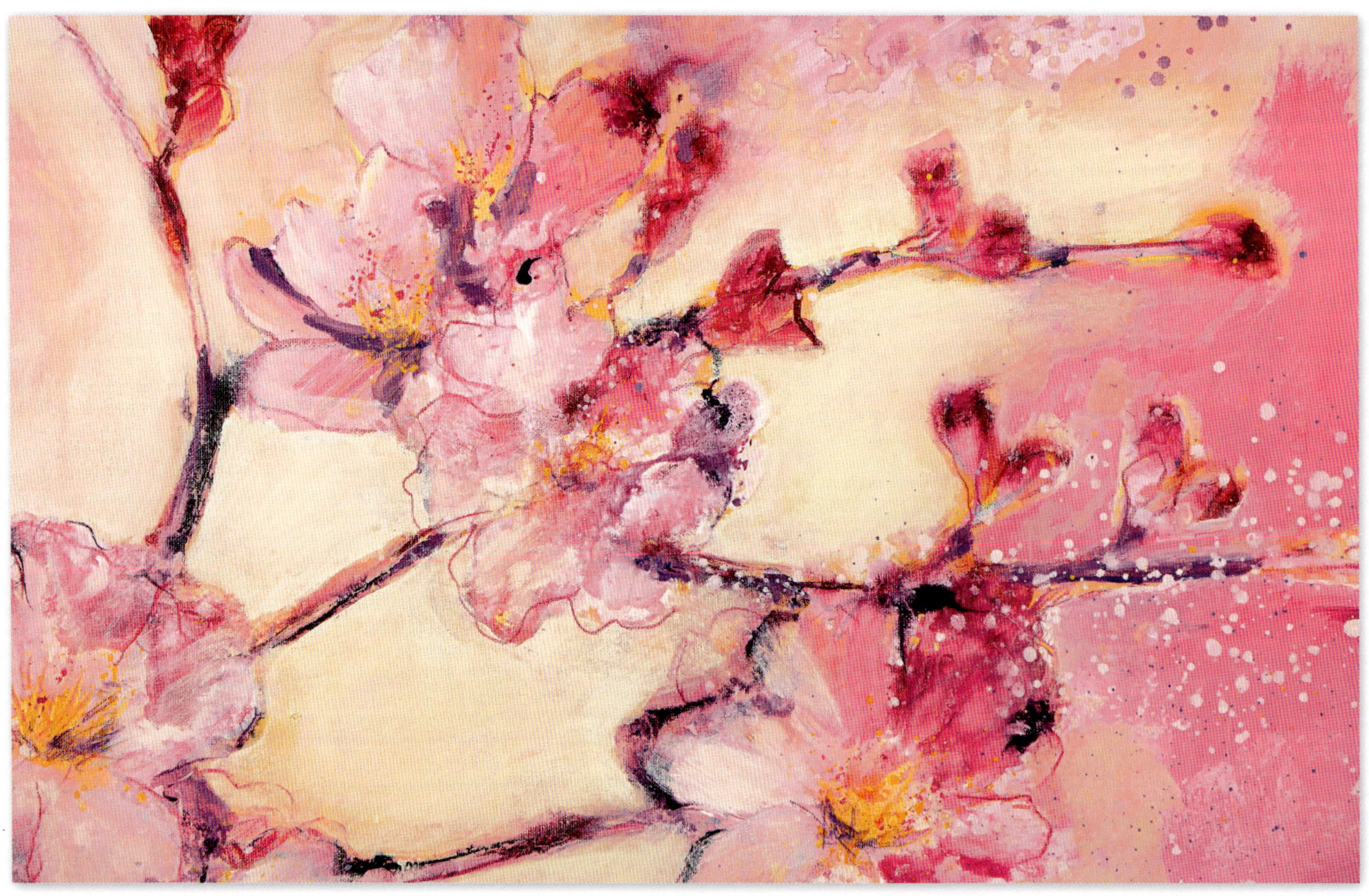

The buds next to the opened blossoms create an important pictorial design element.

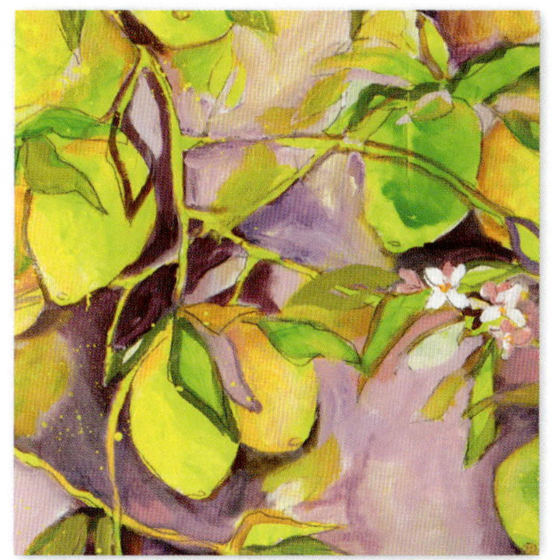

Complementary contrast: the shadow areas around the yellow lemons are painted in violet.

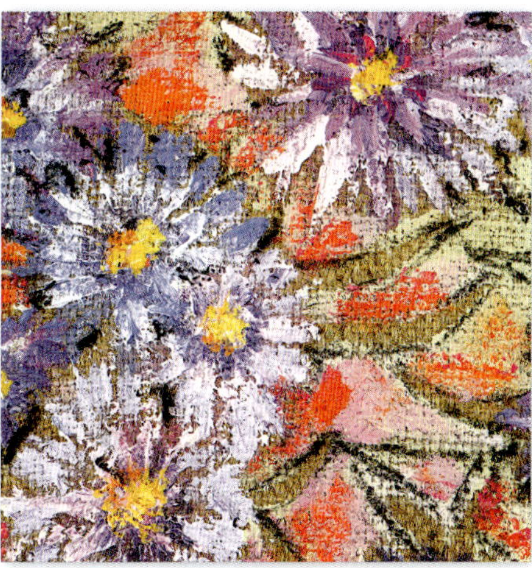

Contrasting application of color: putty sits alongside covering and glazing paints as well as unpainted canvas.

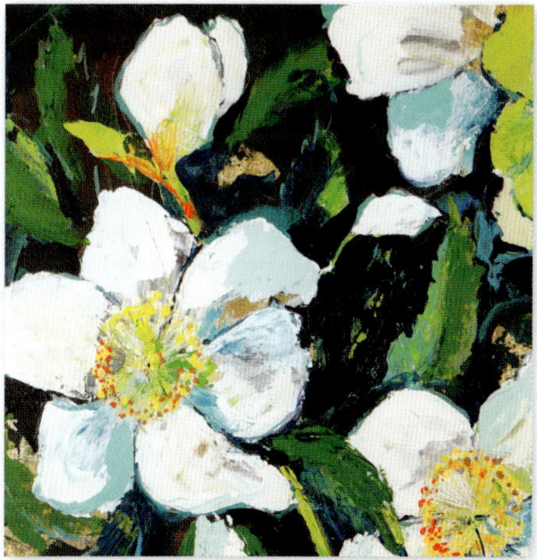

Quantity contrast: the minimal red-orange accents stand out against the different-colored surroundings.

Material and Style

Material and style are inextricably linked with the effect of the picture. A quickly drawn outline or a swiftly placed brushstroke allows the observer to feel the lightness and dynamic that the painter deployed when working. Together with unusual materials and techniques, the multi-layered acrylic pictures become full of life and tension. The options to combine acrylic paints with other media are unlimited. Experiment and let yourself be surprised by the results.

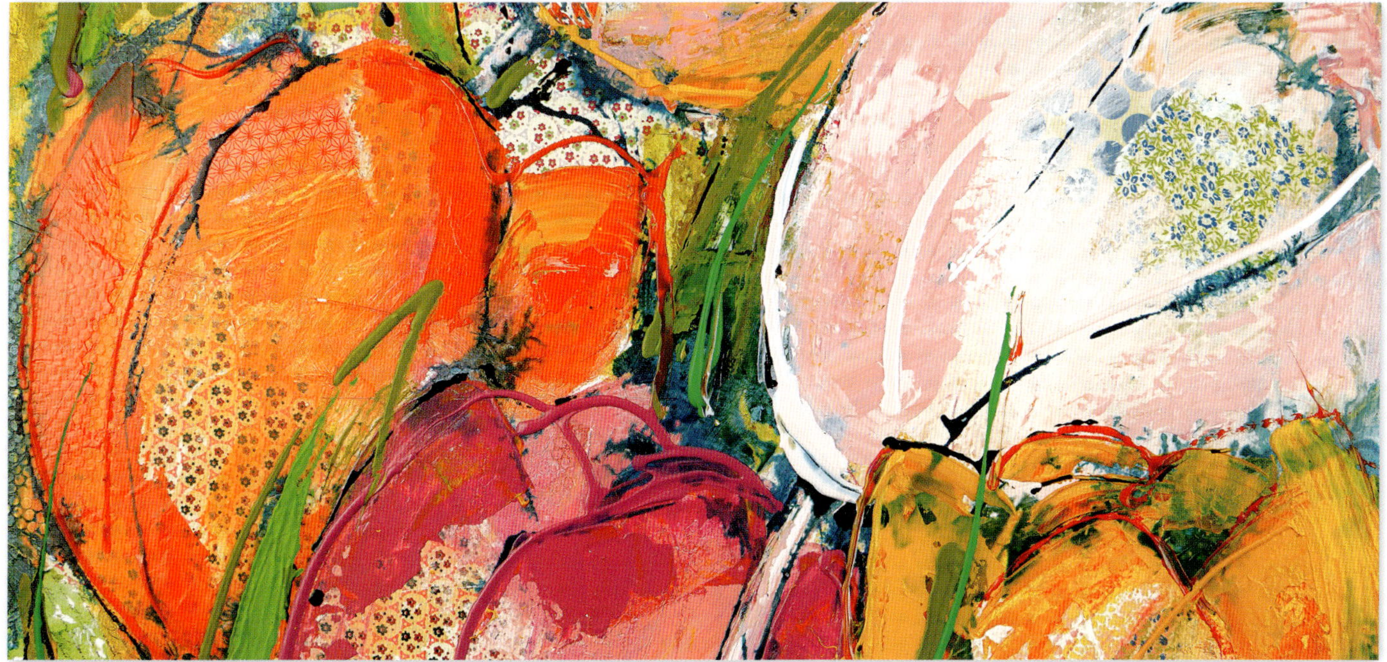

Unusual materials together with a bold style create a dynamic effect.

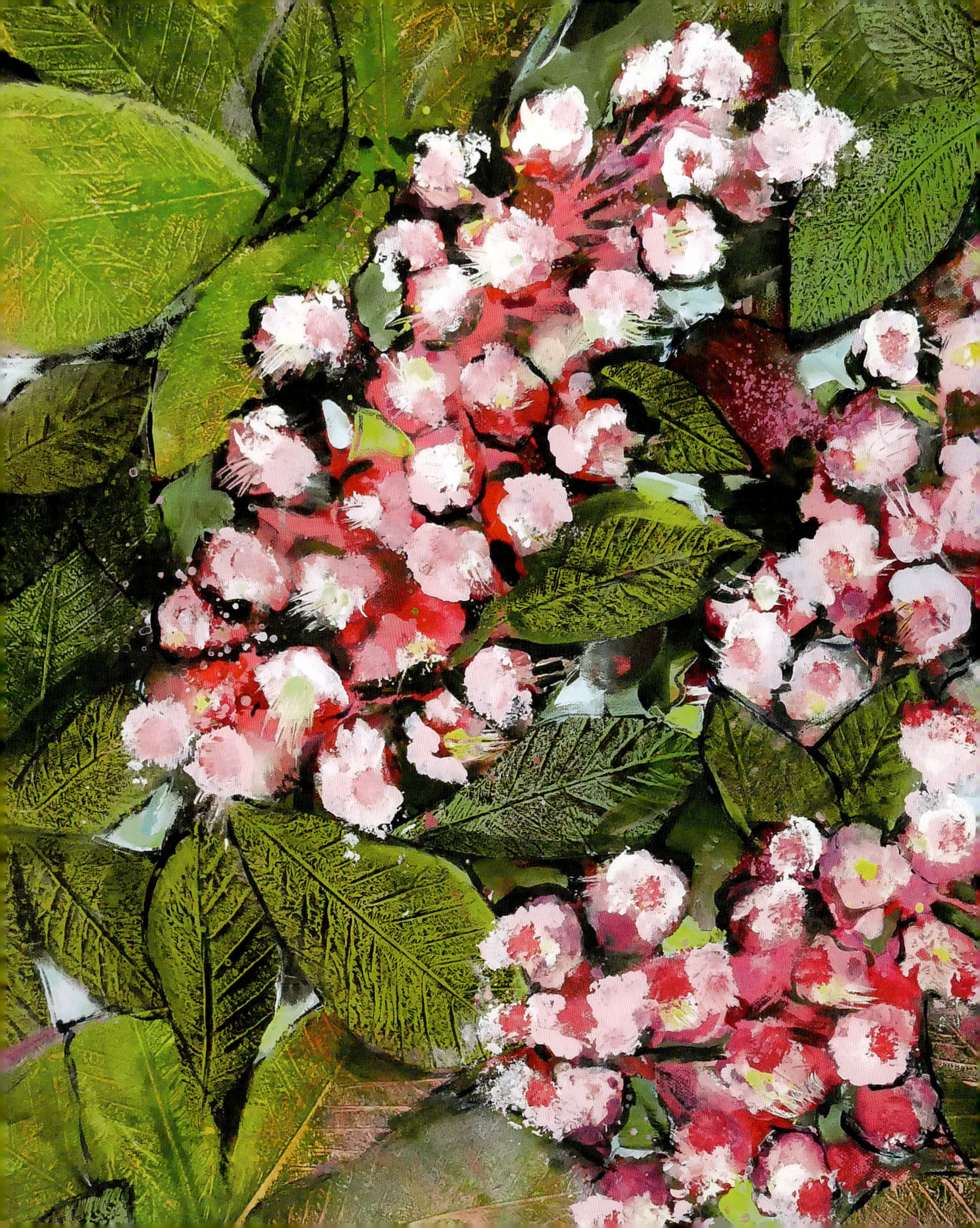

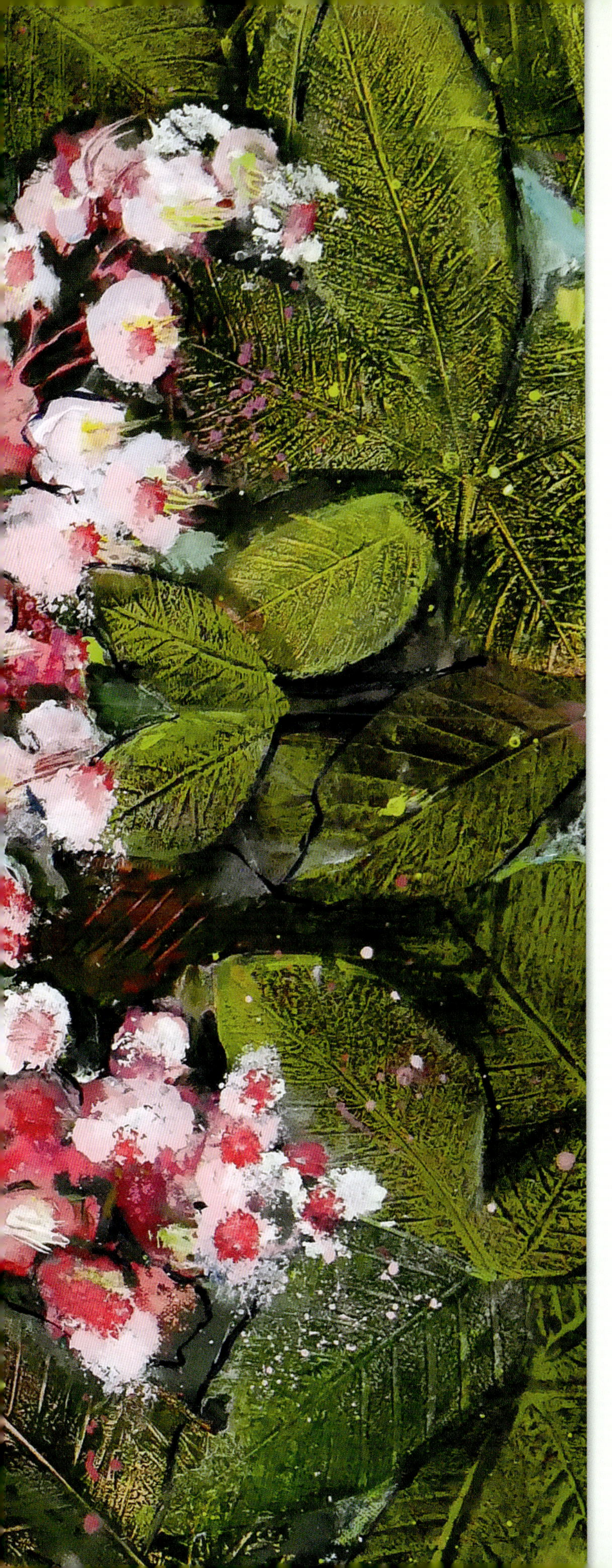

PAINTINGS

Hellebores

Materials:

- Canvas, 24 x 24 in.
- Acrylic paints in titanium white, cadmium yellow, orange, cyan blue, light green, grass green, chrome green, turquoise, Prussian blue, natural umber, and burnt umber
- Round natural hair brush, size 2
- Flat natural brush, sizes 10 and 50
- Japanese spatula, 4 in.
- Watercolor pencils in white and dark blue
- Binder and container
- Palette knife with long and short blade
- Gold metal leaf
- Cardboard, thin
- Painter's palette

As the garden sleeps away the deep winter, the radiant white flowers of the hellebores bloom in spite of the frost and snow. Hellebores, also known as Christmas roses, flower in the coldest months of the year. Their ever-green foliage is a real eyecatcher in the flower beds.
As is appropriate for the darker time of year, the white flowers appear against a dark background. This effect, combined with the gold leaf, increases vibrancy. The paint mixed with putty and applied using the impasto technique highlights the unusual strength of this special plant.

Step 1
Place the thin cardboard between the stretch frame and the canvas so that the wood does not leave marks when using the palette knife. Squeeze chrome green, turquoise, natural umber, and burnt umber directly out of the tubes onto the canvas. Use a Japanese spatula to spread the paint. Work in scratch marks. Leave some areas unworked at the edges of the picture. Place a few pieces of gold metal leaf on the wet paint and lightly go over them with a broad brush. Let dry.

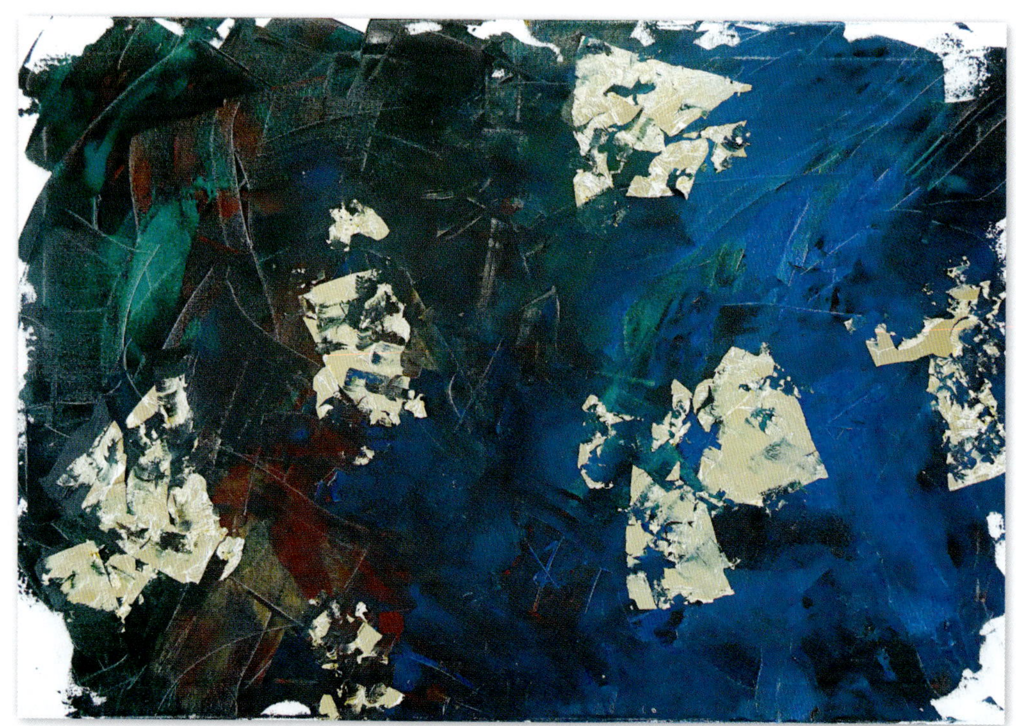

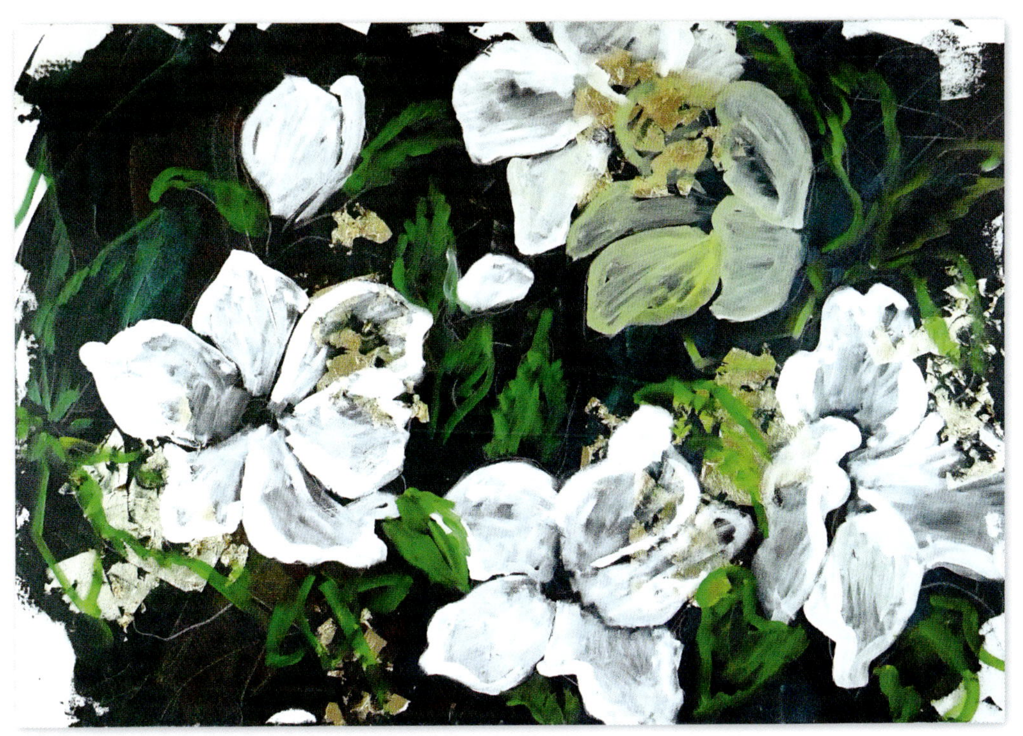

Step 2

Using a white watercolor pencil, sketch the flowers. Use a brush to shape the petals. The darkness of the background shows through the white, producing a white-gray mixed color. In the areas with the gold leaf, use only a small amount of titanium white. The small pieces of gold that will ultimately remain visible serve as a reminder of the dark time of year when Christ was born and give the plant one of its names. Use light green and grass green to paint the suggestion of leaves.

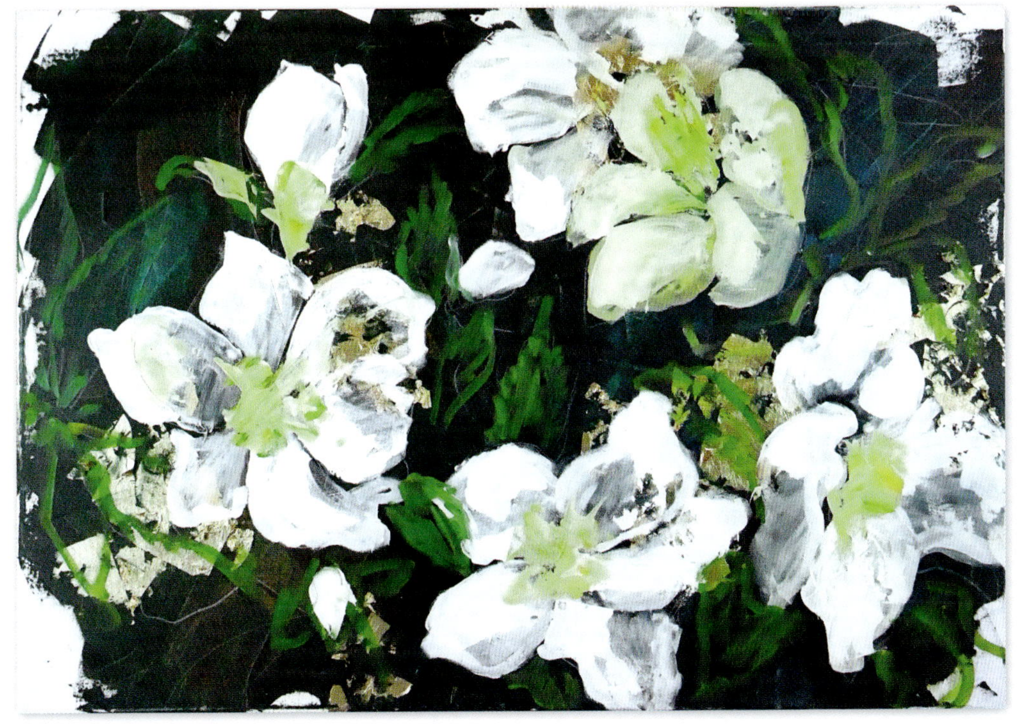

Step 3

Use a palette knife to intensify the white on the edges of the petals by applying the paint thickly and gently teasing it to achieve a fragmented layer of paint toward the center of the flowers. Fill the centers of the flowers randomly with a light yellow mixed from titanium white and cadmium yellow with a little light green. Paint in one flower toward the top of the picture so that it is clearly more of a light green. This special flower will later form the seed head and therefore has a different appearance from the flowers with stamen.

Step 4

Use a dark-blue watercolor pencil to roughly trace the outlines of the petals. The outlines can often be inside or outside the drawn shape. Dip the watercolor pencil into the binder before starting each petal. It gives the outline a more intense color and, at the same time, fixes it in place. Use the palette knife to fill the leaves with different shades of green. Use a brush to add detail to the white and yellow stamen. Use the back of a brush to scratch the filaments into the wet paint.

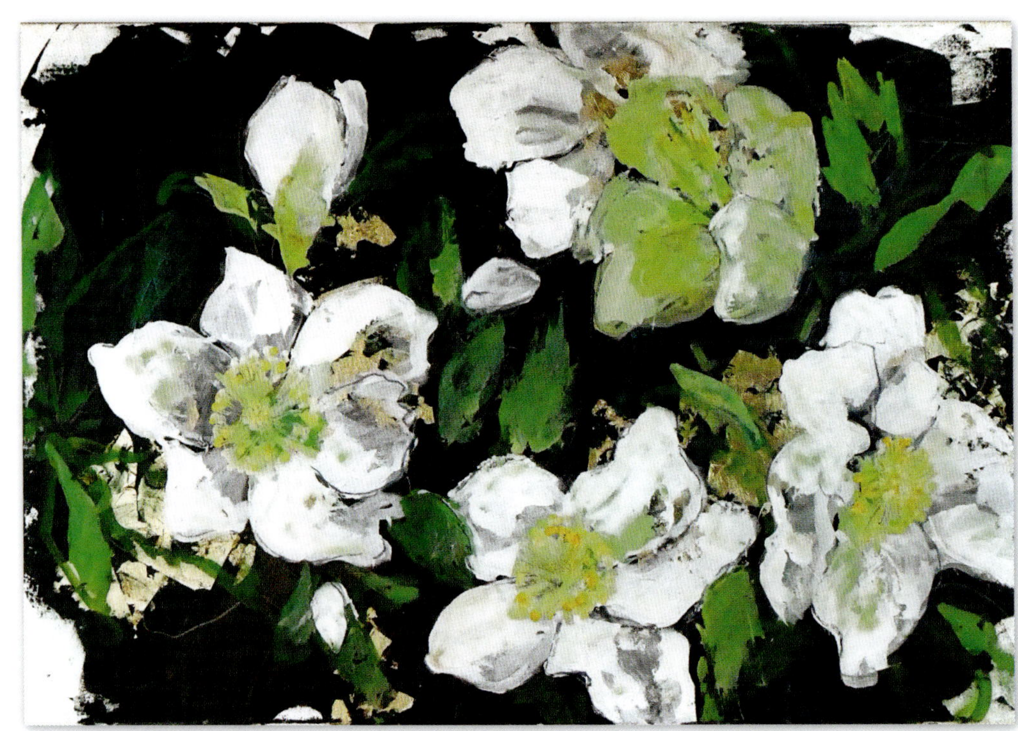

Step 5

Develop the leaves further by using the palette knife to give some of the leaves the jagged edges typical for hellebores. In the top right-hand corner, add a strong cyan blue to the background. Work over some outlines by using a fine brush and a light green as well as a light turquoise mixed from titanium white and turquoise. Ensure that the outlines are not closed, but rather that they are broken or just sketchily suggested to keep the loose feeling. Also vary the widths of the outline lines.

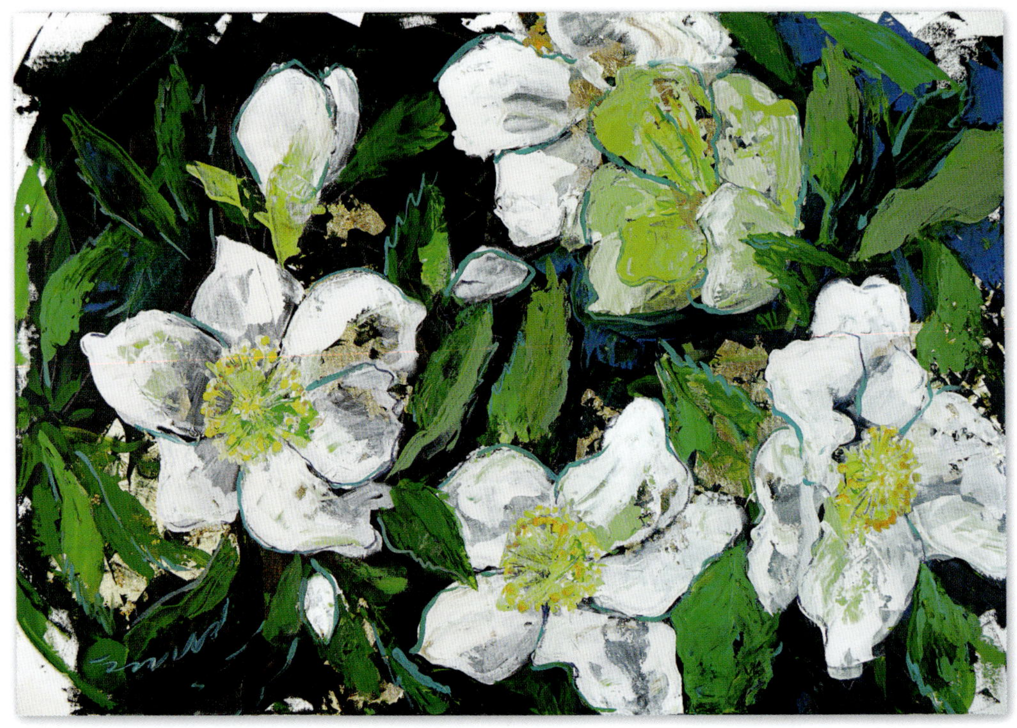

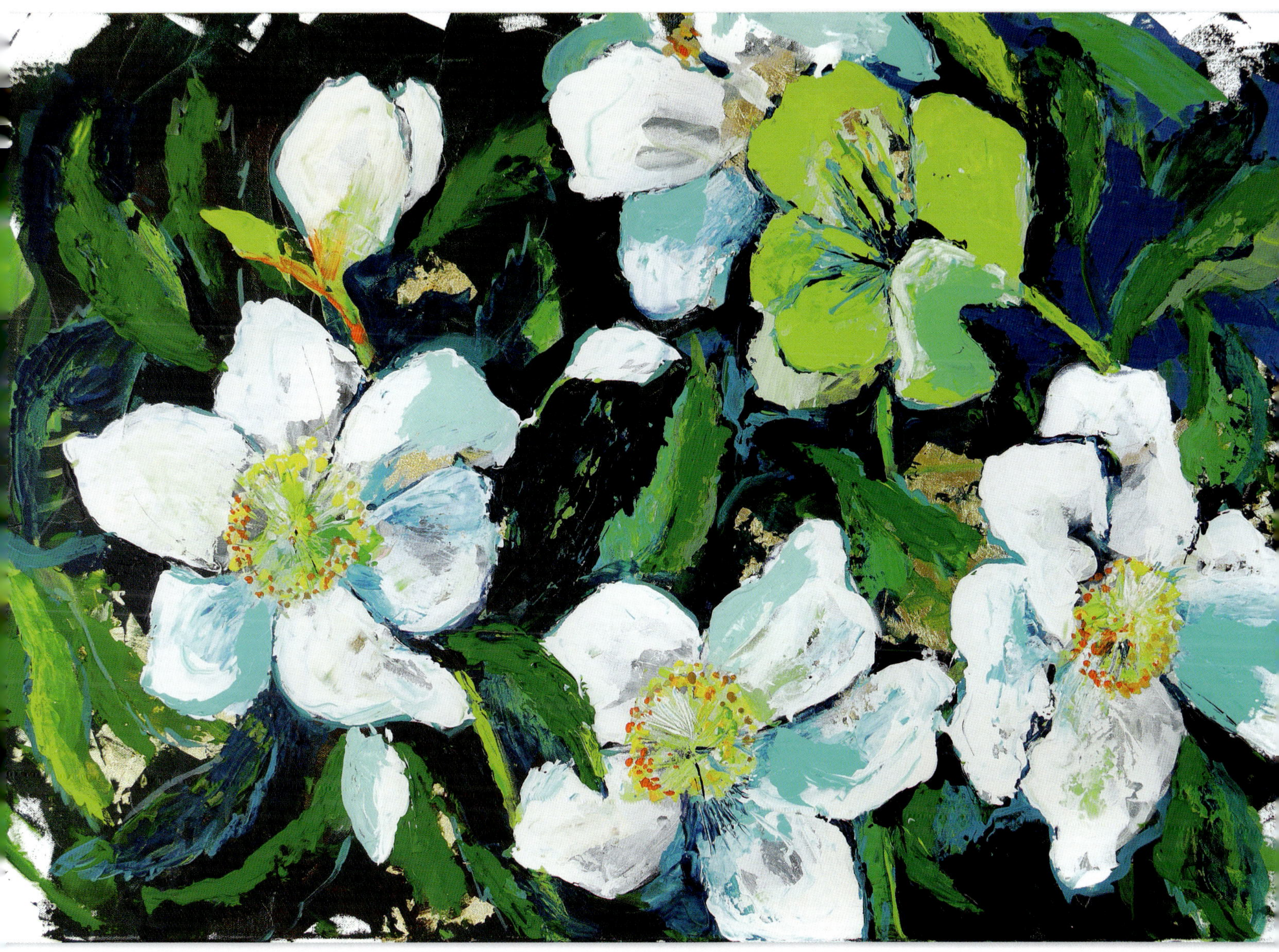

Finished Painting

Work over the leaves with further shades of green. Add a couple of light-green stalks. Use orange to dab small dots around the stamen and to add an accent on the left side of the picture. They are the only red tones used in the whole subject (quantity contrast). Mix various shades of turquoise, using titanium white, cyan blue, and turquoise, and add random areas of shading to the petals. The cool turquoise adds to the winter ambience. Use the short palette knife to develop the stems, leaves, and outlines. Finally, use Prussian blue to pull together areas in the background and to add small accents to the flowers.

Crocuses

Materials:

- Canvas, 32 x 40 in.
- Acrylic paints in titanium white, cadmium yellow, Indian yellow, orange, carmine red, magenta, olive green, and dark violet
- Flat synthetic bristle brush, sizes 30 and 120
- Flat natural hair brush, sizes 12 and 18
- Plastic wrap
- Watercolor pencil in dark gray and dark violet
- Binder and container
- Drawing ink in yellow and dark violet
- Pipette
- Water spray bottle
- Painter's palette

When the snowdrops and crocus bravely brace the cold and poke their heads through the covering of snow, the days become noticeably longer. Crocuses are one of the early bloomers and are not only the harbingers of spring but also attract bumblebees and honeybees with their vibrant stamen and pistils.

The complementary colors of yellow and violet contrast with the snow-white background. The gently drifting snow is represented by white paint splats that lend the picture the characteristic mood of a day in late winter.

Step 1

Use water to dilute Indian yellow and violet and apply to the canvas with a wide synthetic bristle brush. Cover the canvas completely with the wrap so that it forms crinkles. You can use the plastic wrapping from the canvas for this step. Leave for around two hours. Then remove the wrap and once again place it over the slightly wet paint. In this way, a second layer of crease structures is created. Let dry.

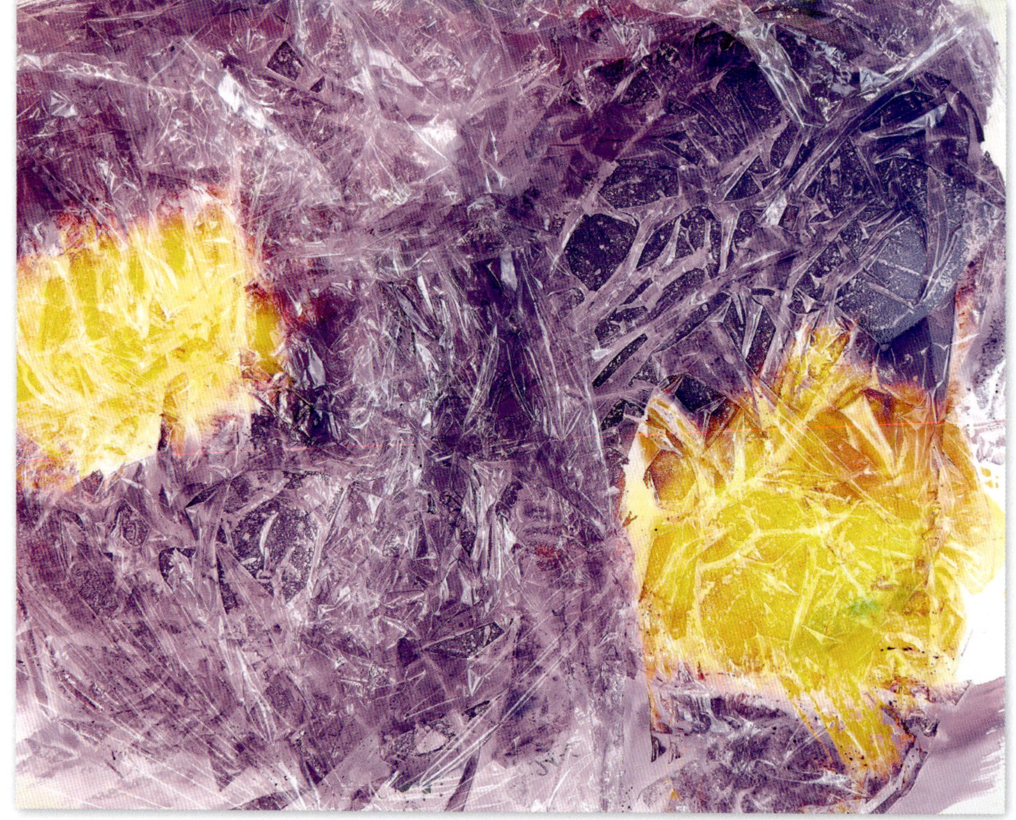

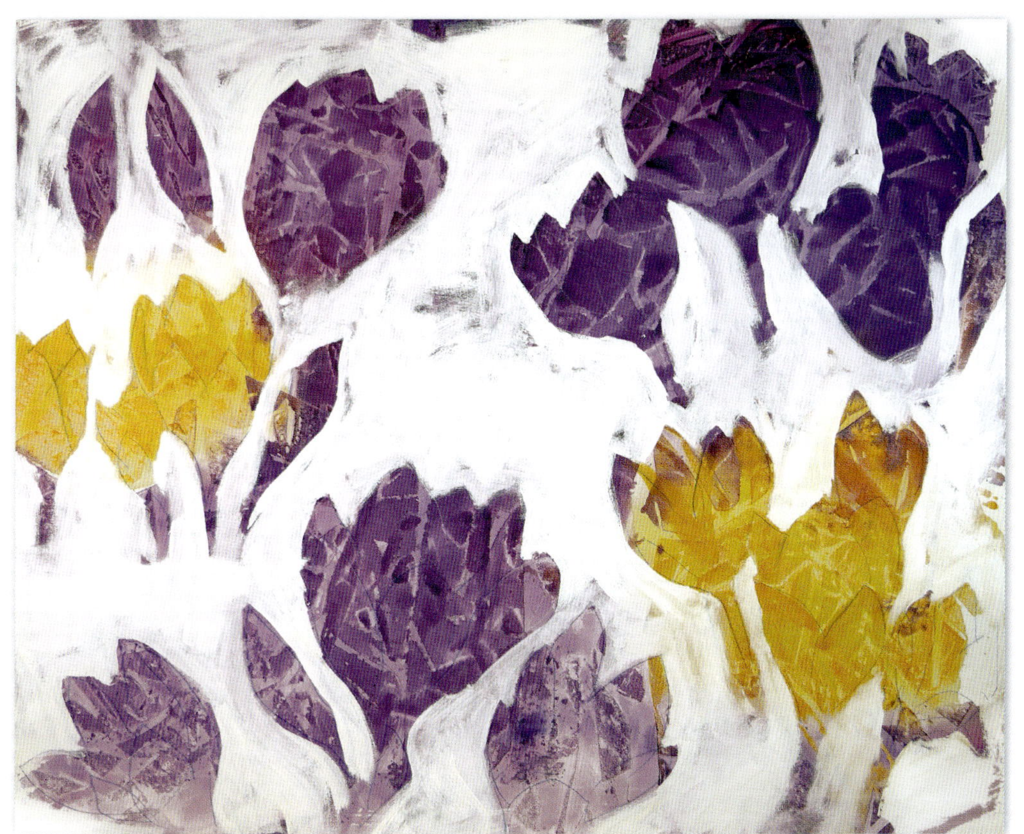

Step 2

Use a dark-gray watercolor pencil to sketch out the shapes of the crocus flowers. Do not yet add the shape of the leaves. Use a broad synthetic bristle brush to paint titanium white on the background. Work loosely so that some areas are fully covered, some are just glazed, and others are completely unpainted. Around the shape of the flowers, the paint layer is largely covering the background. Leave some unpainted areas at the edges.

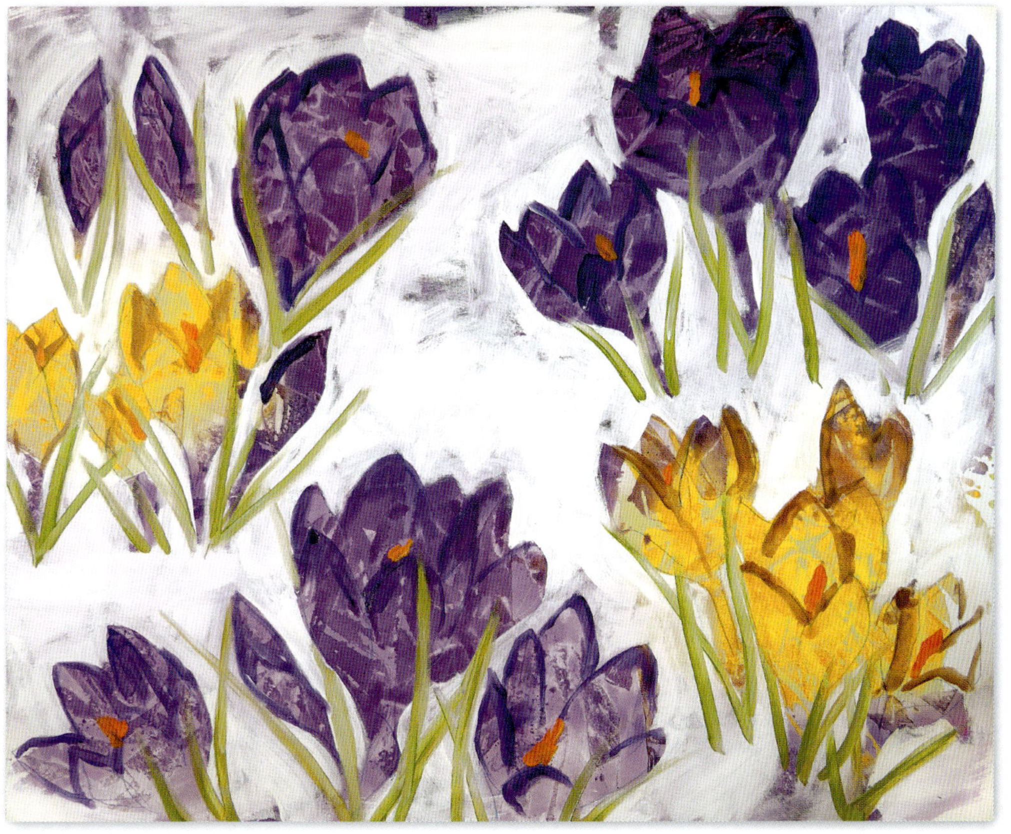

Step 3

Use a flat natural hair brush to paint the leaves in olive green. When doing so, paint some leaves over the petals. Ensure that the leaves are in groups and break through the snow where the flowers are. Separate the individual petals in the flowers from each other by using darker tones to paint the outlines and to create shade within the individual flowers. Add orange pistils of different sizes to every flower.

Step 4

Mix a shade of brown from dark violet and Indian yellow and use it to add accents to the yellow crocuses. Dip the dark-violet watercolor pencil into a mixture of binder and water and use it to draw outlines. As more pigment dissolves, the lines become more intense and, at the same time, are fixed in place. Draw the outlines unevenly. In places, intentionally cover the shapes. Add some leaves that are not painted in green but that enrich the composition as empty outlines.

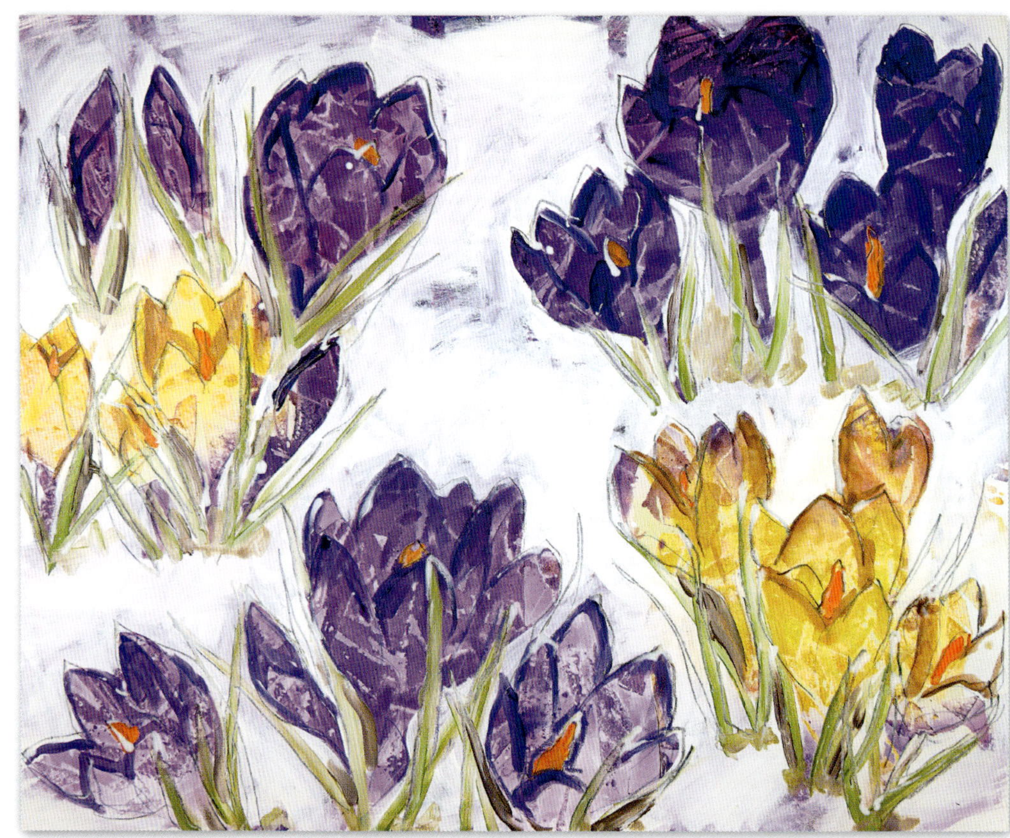

Step 5

On the large empty areas in the background, use a broad synthetic bristle brush to thickly apply undiluted titanium white. Cover the outlines in part and then reveal them again with scratch marks made with the back of the brush. Add accents and splatter marks to the yellow flowers with orange and Indian yellow. Work some dark violet into the purple flowers. Add some splatters to them too.

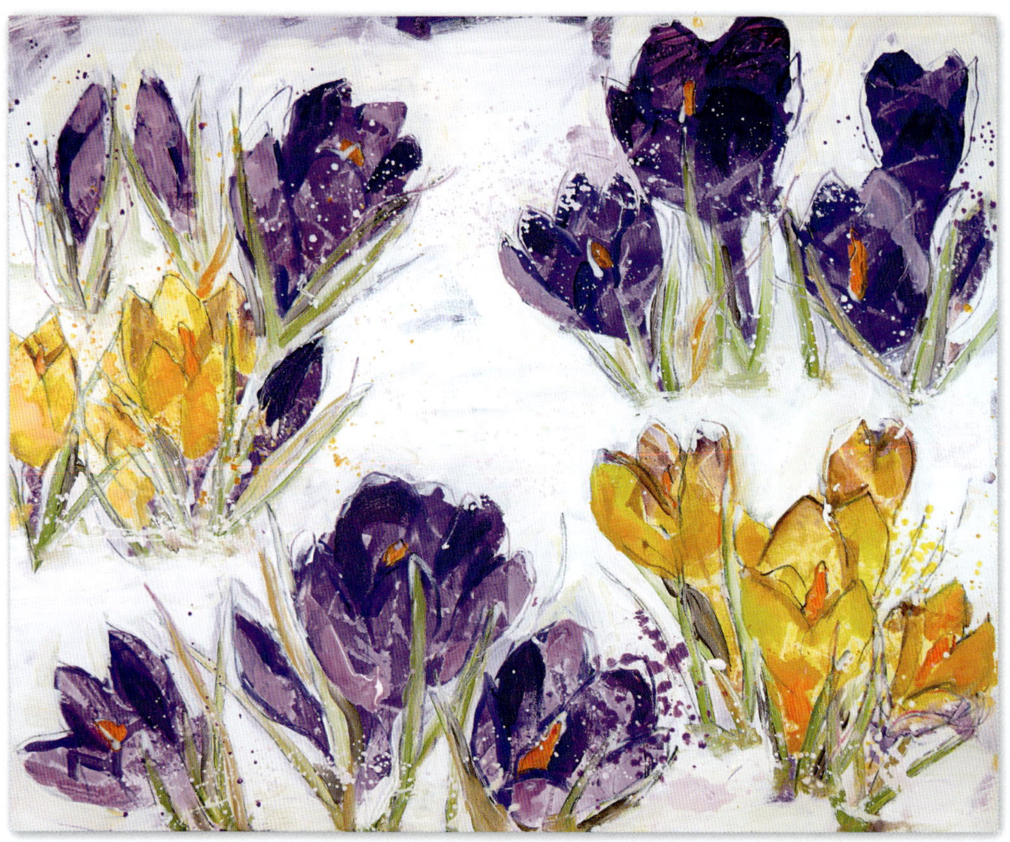

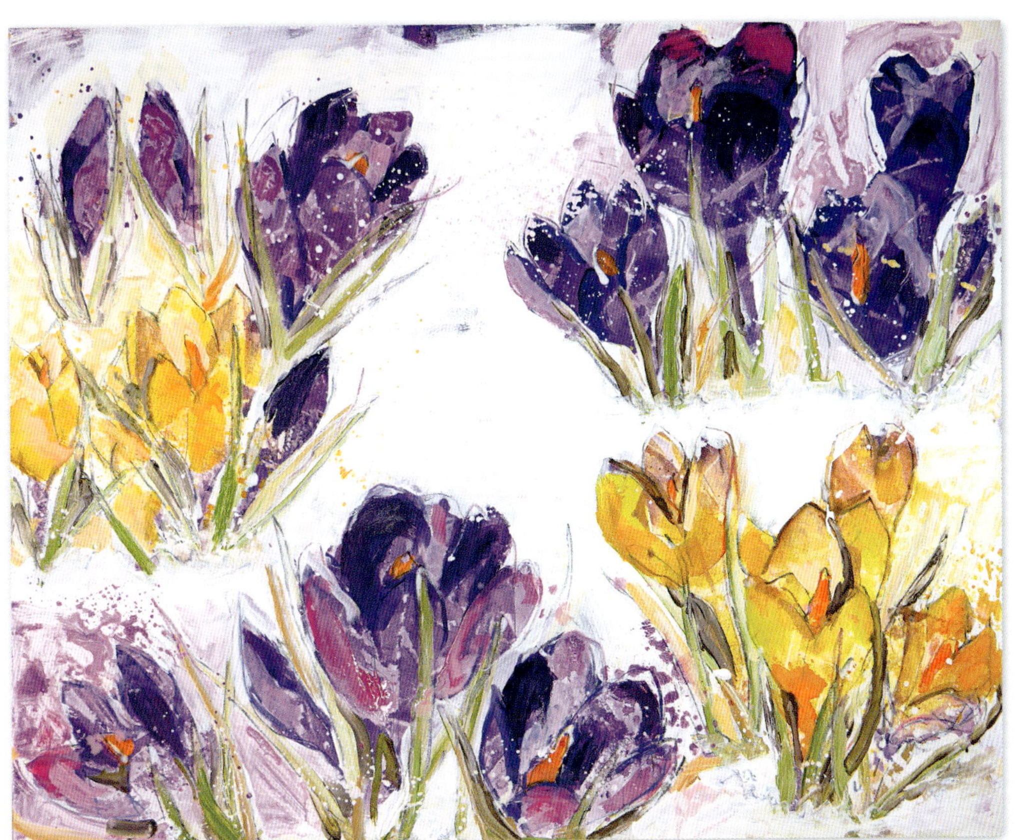

Step 6

Use magenta to add some accents to the purple flowers. Make a diluted watery glaze with titanium white and dark violet. Apply and allow it to run in the left-hand bottom corner and in the top right corner. The watery glaze forms a shiny surface on the well-dried underlying layers. Also add glazes made of titanium white and cadmium yellow to the yellow flowers. Do not allow these glazes to dry; they are needed for the next step.

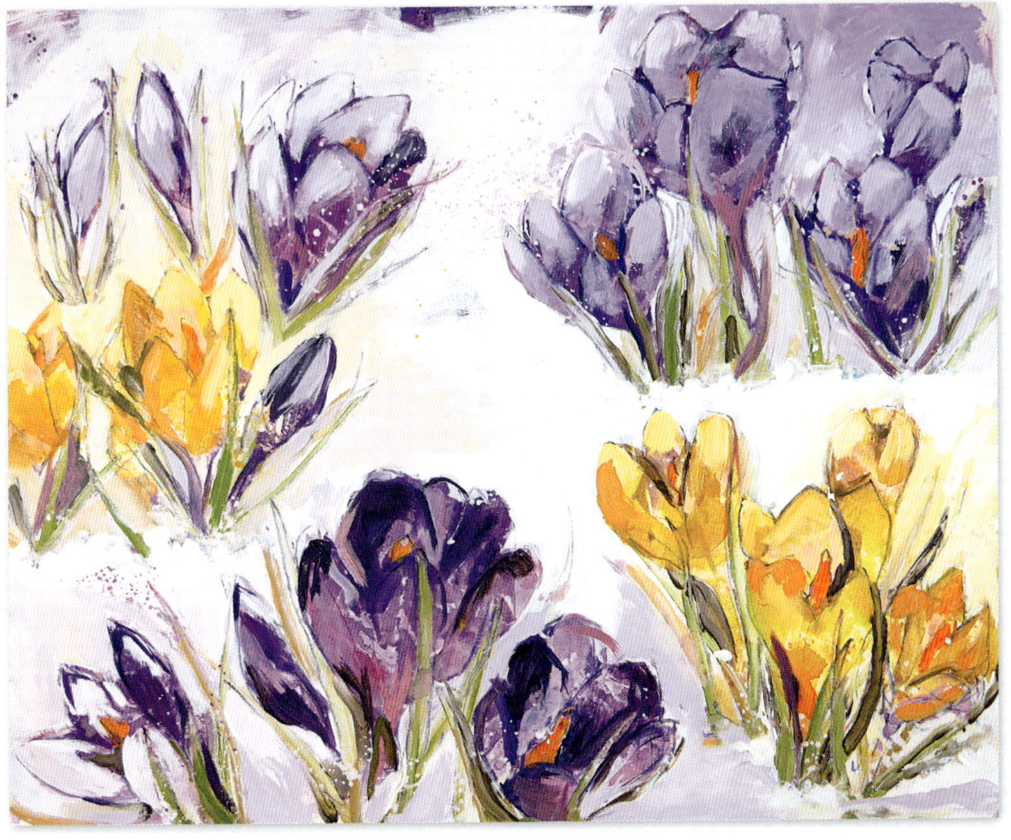

Step 7

Once again, go over the background with titanium white. In doing so, work in the wet paint so that shades of pale yellow and violet are created, which sometimes become impure tones due to mixing titanium white with cadmium yellow and dark violet. Use these mixed colors to highlight the tips of the flowers. The upper flowers should be lighter to create an effect of depth. On the left-hand side of the picture, add a light brown-gray made of titanium white, orange, and dark violet.

Step 8

Add more orange to the yellow flowers. A few carmine red nuances increase the vibrancy of the orange pistils. Use a pipette with the yellow and dark violet drawing ink to trace around the outlines of some flowers in the corresponding colors. Use a water spray bottle to create the runs in a few places. Allow the color intensive ink to run into the white background, where it creates random shapes.

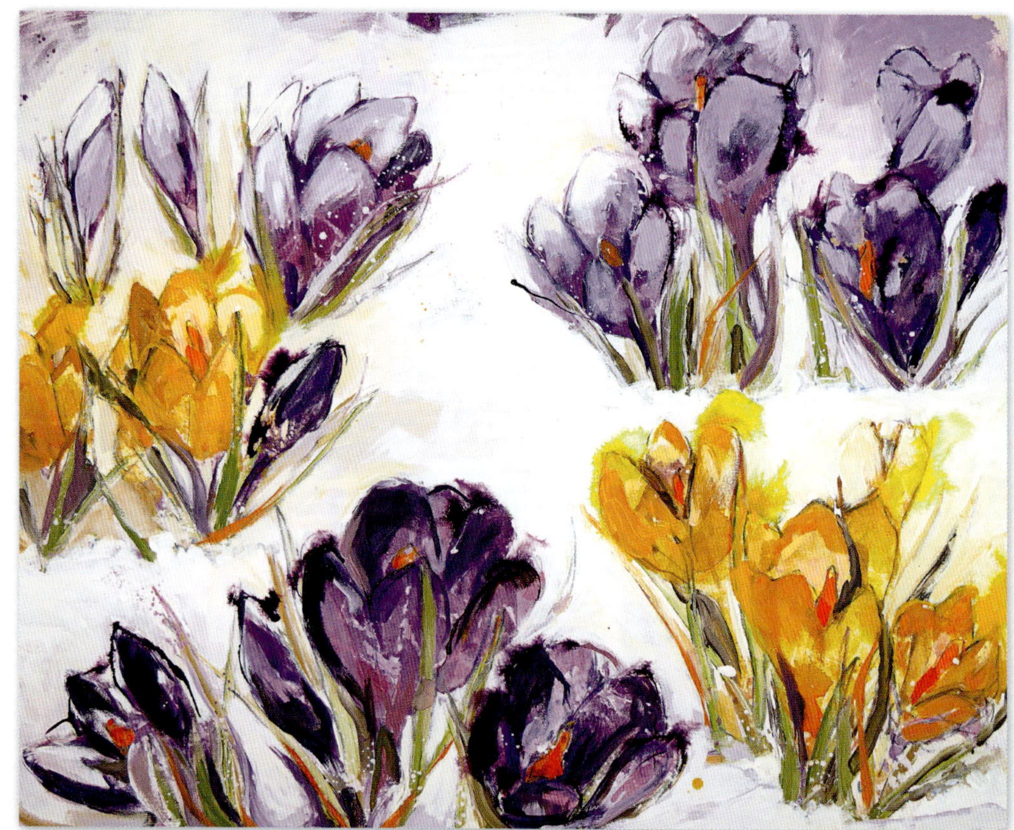

Close-Up

Even though many areas have been covered during the painting process, the crumpled texture from the wrap is still visible in some places. This texture sits alongside the covering brushstrokes. The change in the thickness of the paint layers generates a tension, which is accentuated by further painterly contrasts; for instance, in the different ways that outlines have been depicted—e.g., full covering, glazing, or as sketched, sometimes wider, and sometimes narrower.

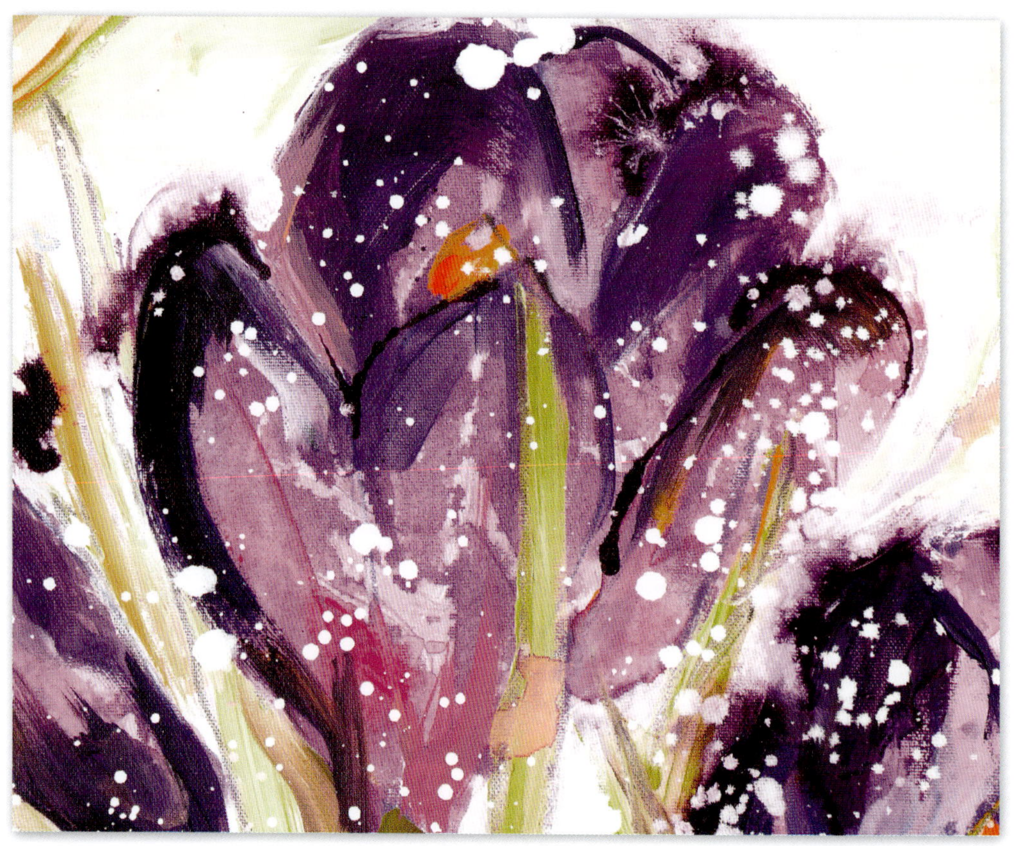

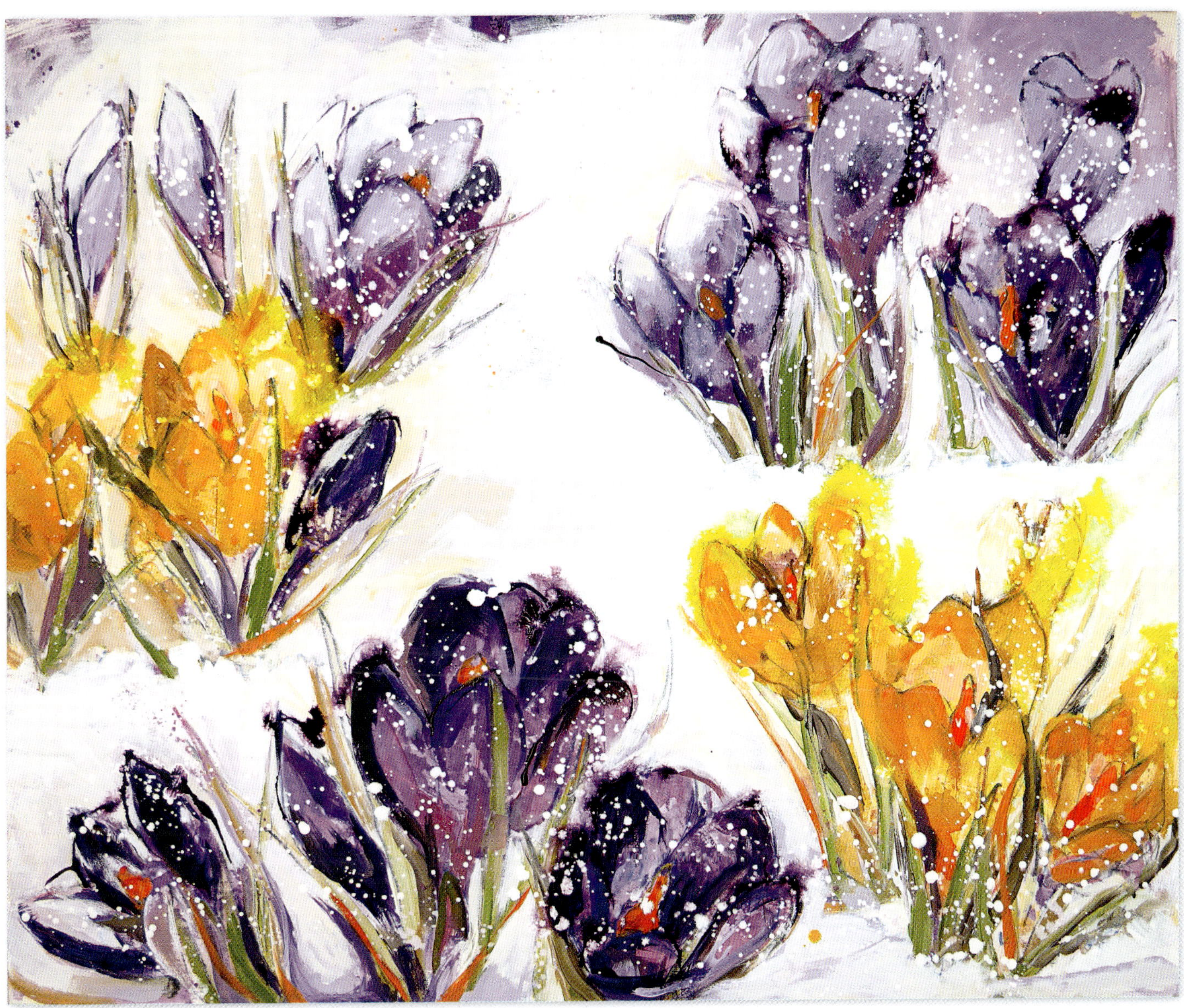

Finished Painting

Finally, add white splatters, allowing them to combine with the wet ink. To do so, pick up some slightly diluted titanium white with a flat natural hair brush and then tap the brush against the fingers of your other hand. The less paint and water you have on your brush, the finer the drops will be. For this step, ensure that the distribution is random. Splatters of different sizes form dense and less dense areas.

Tulips

When sunshine breaks through April showers and the first green buds emerge on twigs and bushes, the first tulips bloom and their abundance of color combines with birdsong to add to the richness of spring. They grow larger and more magnificent each day and turn toward the sunlight.

This dense tête-à-tête composition is supported by a sublayer of floral-patterned collage paper that demonstrates the variety of flowers at this time of year. The thick layers of paint are applied with a palette knife. The final outlines are squeezed directly from the tubes onto the canvas and create an energetic, powerful style, which suits the season.

Materials:

- Canvas, 32 x 32 in.
- Acrylic paints in titanium white, cadmium yellow, Indian yellow, cadmium red, orange, magenta, olive green, and dark green
- Broad synthetic bristle brush, size 35
- Flat natural hair brush, sizes 12 and 18
- Watercolor pencils in white and dark magenta
- Finishing spatula
- Small palette knife with a long blade
- Binder and container
- Wrapping paper or Nepalese Lokta paper, preferably with a flower pattern
- Putty, fine
- Net for structure
- Drawing ink in dark blue
- Pipette
- Water spray bottle
- Painter's palette

Materials for the homemade paper

- Glass or acrylic sheet
- Cooking oil
- Paper towels
- Tissue paper

Step 1

Glue ripped-up pieces of wrapping paper, Nepalese Lokta paper with flower pattern, and homemade patterned paper to the canvas, using a broad brush. Stick them in place in a random fashion with some overlapping. Position a few of the pieces of paper so they extend beyond the edges. Fill the gaps with putty. Place the net on the putty and stroke over it with the finishing spatula. Then remove the net again, so that its prints create texture. Allow to dry well.

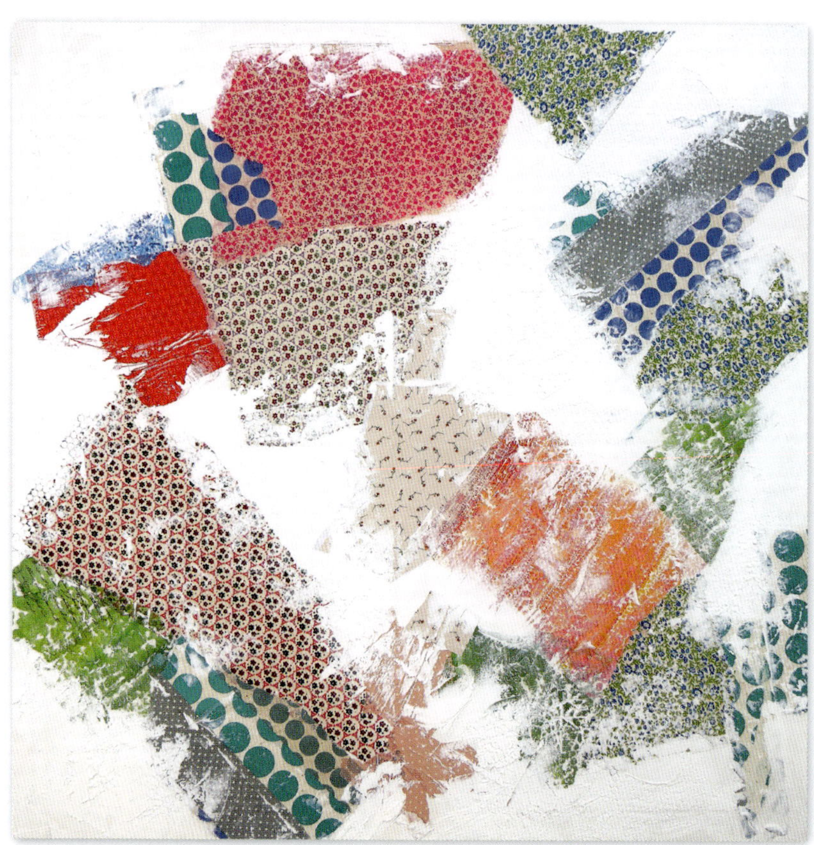

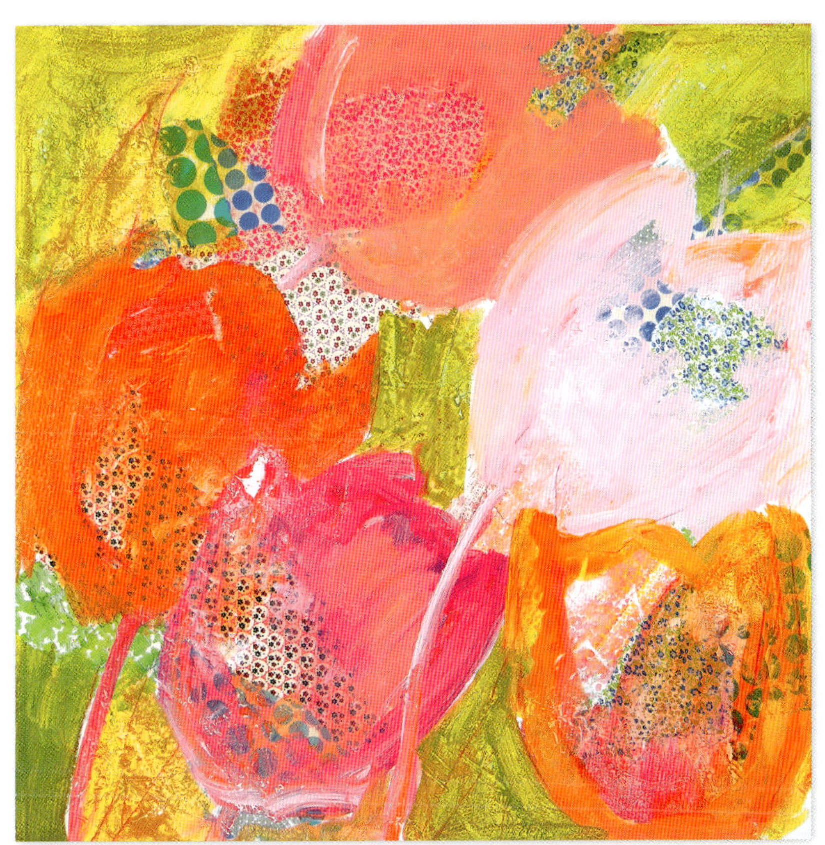

Step 2

Sketch out the tulip heads, using a watercolor pencil. Use a broad synthetic brush to paint the colors of the flowers. In doing so, give each tulip its own shade, borrowing from the main colors of the scraps of paper that are the base layer. Work in slight variations in shades. Partially paint over the paper scraps and create transitions by applying the acrylic paints as glazes. Leave partial areas unpainted so that parts of the paper scraps remained untouched. Cover the background with a glaze of light-green shades made from a mixture of olive green and cadmium yellow. Thanks to the glazes, the texture from the putty has a vivid appearance.

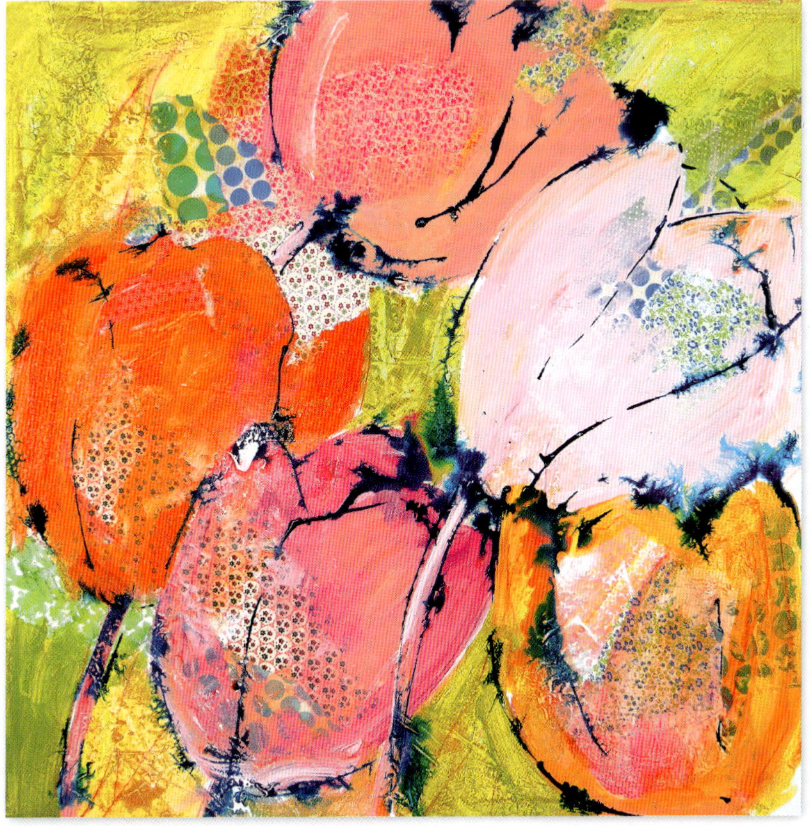

Step 3

Use the pipette to draw over some of the outlines in the dark-blue drawing ink. Also add outlines to individual petals in the flower heads. The loose and patchy application of ink from the pipette, including lines of various widths, is desired. Use a water spray bottle to spray some ink outlines so that uncontrolled ink feathering occurs. This lack of control blends in well with the painterly style of the picture.

Step 4

After briefly allowing the ink to dry, add a second layer of ink. Add further ink lines for the typical pointed shape of the tulip petals. Spray with water. Over the light color of the pink tulips, the ink turns into a turquoise blue. On the green background, it looks like grass green. Combined with the magenta, it has a violet tinge. The structured background appears especially textured thanks to the dark drawing ink. Feel free to apply the drawing ink copiously because it becomes significantly paler once dry. Allow to dry well.

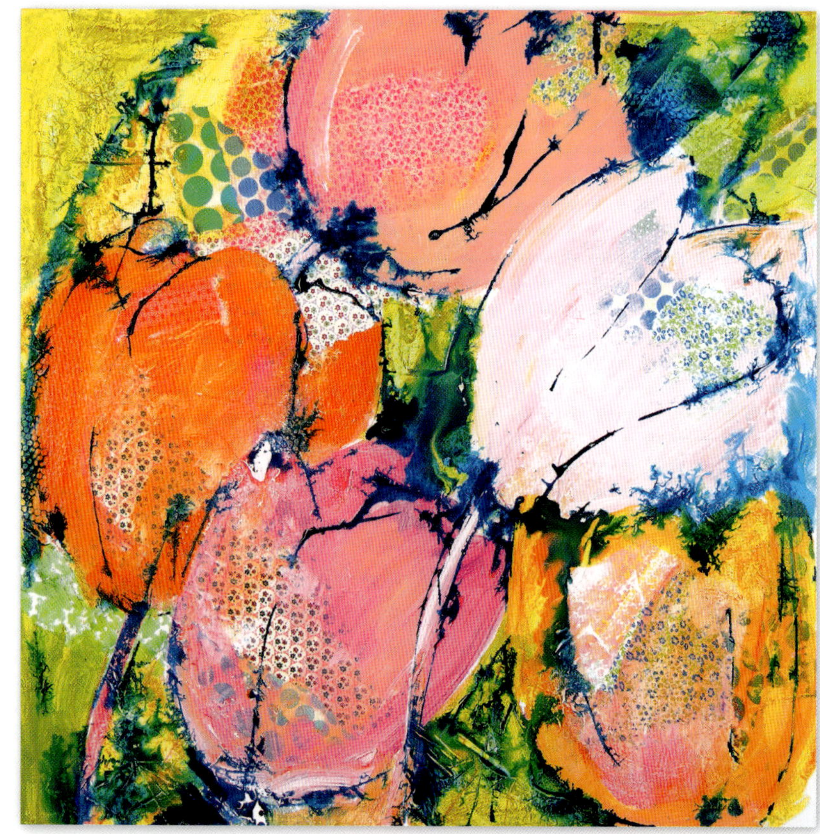

Step 5

Use a palette knife to apply a thick layer of undiluted acrylic paint in the color of the flower to the petals. Emphasize the tips and edges. Work in slight color variations. Use the palette knife to fragment the paint and reveal the layers below. Apply cadmium yellow and olive green to the leaves, using the tip of the palette knife to create the tip of the leaves. Once again, use the dark-blue drawing ink to go over some outlines. Allow to dry.

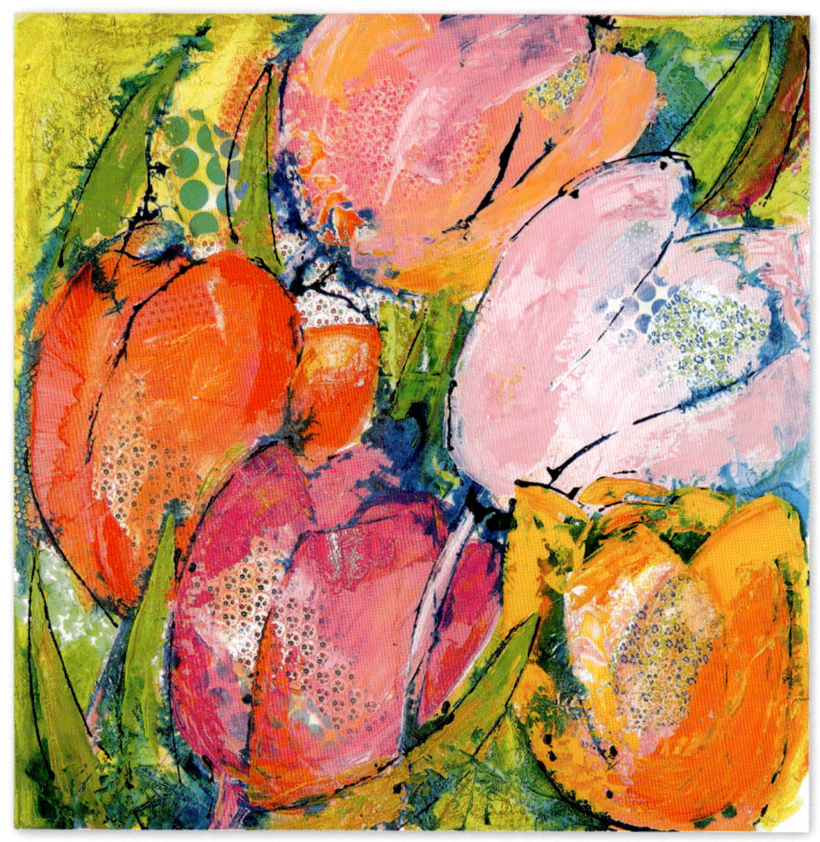

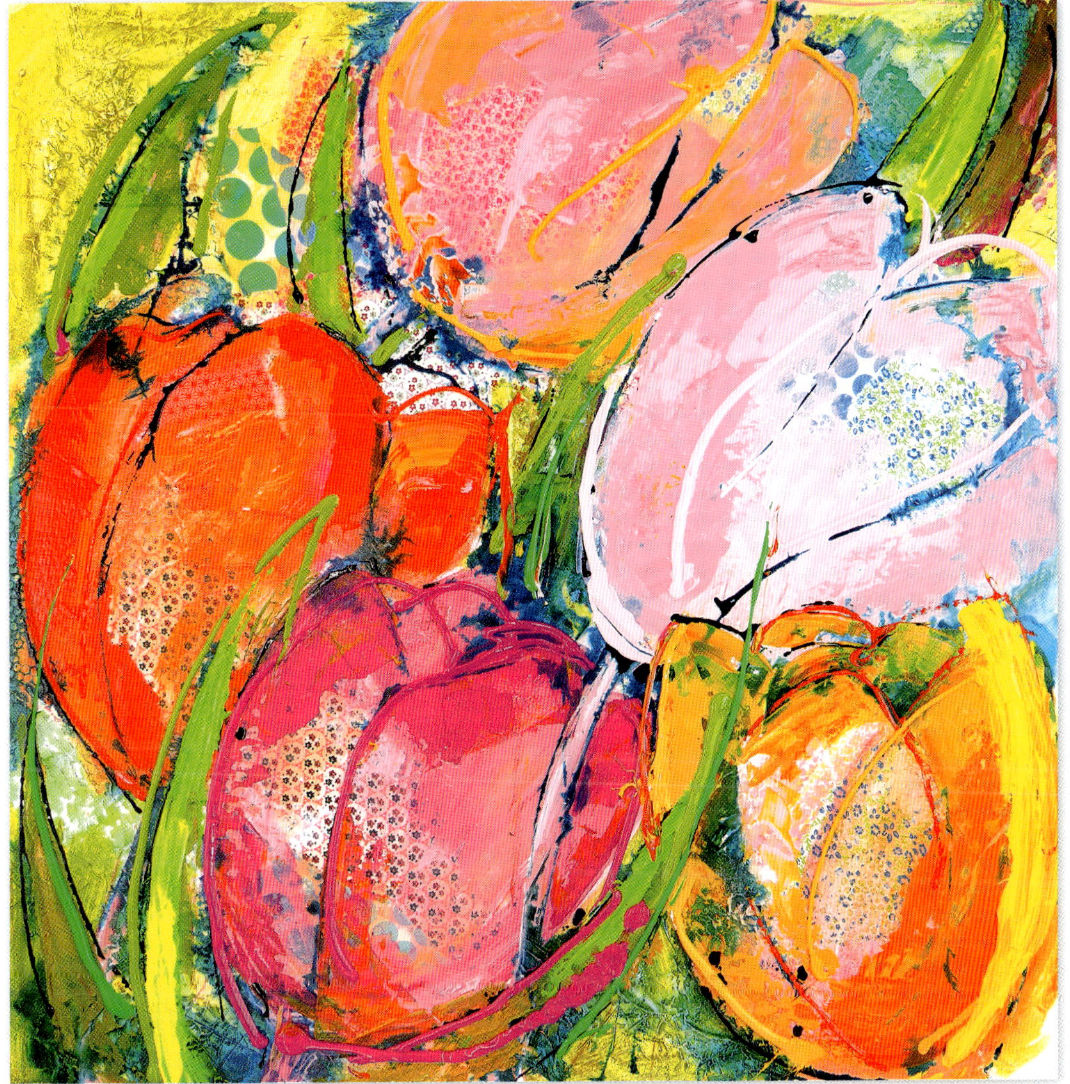

Finished Painting

Use a synthetic bristle brush to add some light-green accents to the leaves, using a mix of olive green and cadmium yellow. Squirt the final layer of colored outlines directly out of the tubes and onto the canvas. Small acrylic paint tubes are particularly well suited for this step. The outlines do not always follow the shape of the petals and sometimes go over the flower heads. The individual and textured character of these outlines adds to the richness and wealth of paint layers and materials in this subject.

Tip: It's a good idea to collect a stash of paper in order to fill you own treasure trove of collage paper. In this example, paper is created with a bubble-like texture by using paper towels and cooking oil to grease a smooth base (e.g., a sheet of glass). Water-diluted acrylic paint is applied with a wide synthetic bristle brush for a bubble-like drip pattern. The droplets are absorbed by the tissue paper.

Magnolia

Materials:

- Canvas, 24 x 36 in.
- Acrylic paints in titanium white, cadmium yellow, rose, magenta, dark violet, steel gray, and light umber
- Flat synthetic bristle brush, size 30
- Angular brush, size 12
- Watercolor pencils in dark magenta, dark blue, and dark gray
- Drawing ink in magenta
- Pipette
- Water spray bottle
- Foam paint roller, 2 in.
- Rags
- Painter's palette

As the magnolia opens its beautiful, delicate flowers and the green of the leaves is still in bud, then spring has arrived. The magnolia flowers are shaped like tulips and bloom in magnificent pastel pinks and whites. To keep from distracting from the delicacy of the flowers, the branches are painted in shades of magenta and rose. In this painting, the acrylic paints are used very fluidly so that when combined with the drawing ink and the highly pigmented watercolor pencils, they reveal a beautiful delicateness.

Step 1

Use the foam paint roller to apply magenta, titanium white, and rose mixed with water to the canvas to achieve light and hazy color gradients. Let dry. Sketch the outlines, using a magenta watercolor pencil. Paint in the background area in a mixture of light umber, rose, and titanium white. Allow the base colors to show through.

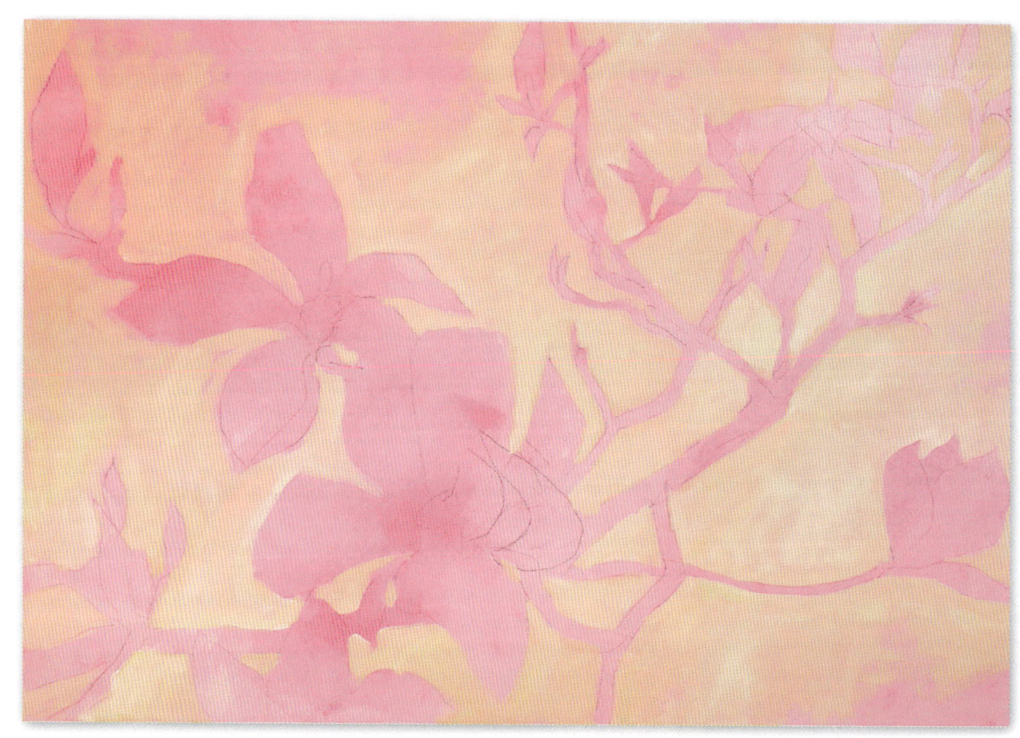

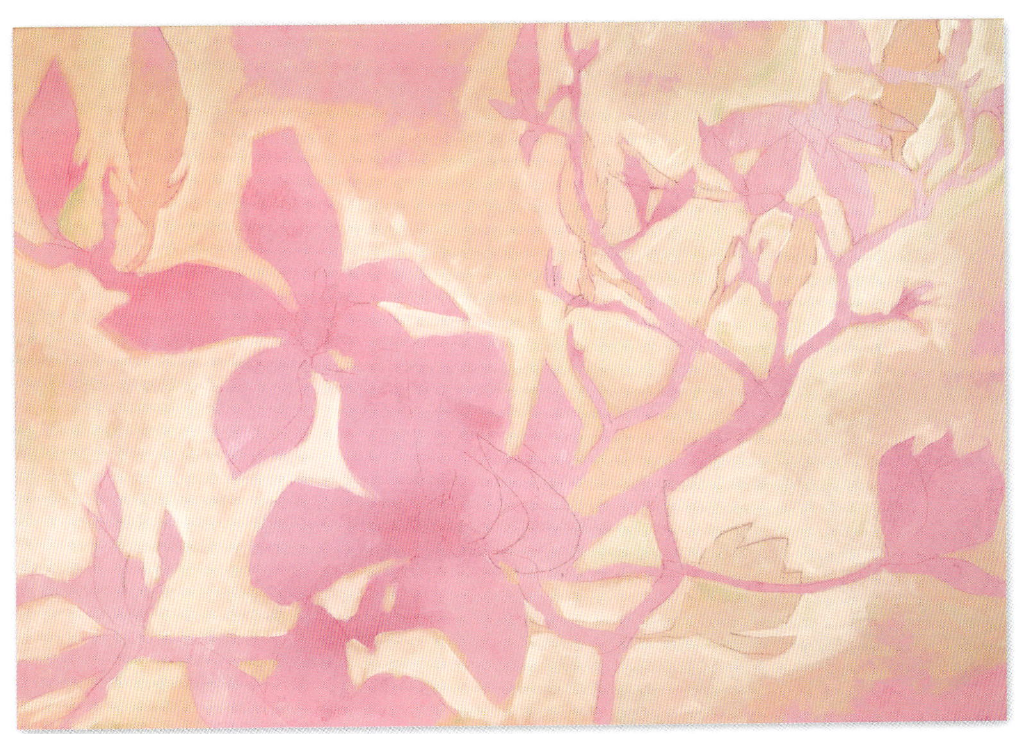

Step 2

Once again, use the watercolor pencil to add branches, flowers, and buds behind the ones already in the picture, so that they overlap. Paint over the background with a pale mixture of titanium white and rose. In this way, shapes are created and appear to be in the background, thanks to their subtle coloring. Leave a small gap around the first shapes so that the lower layer of paint remains visible as a small border.

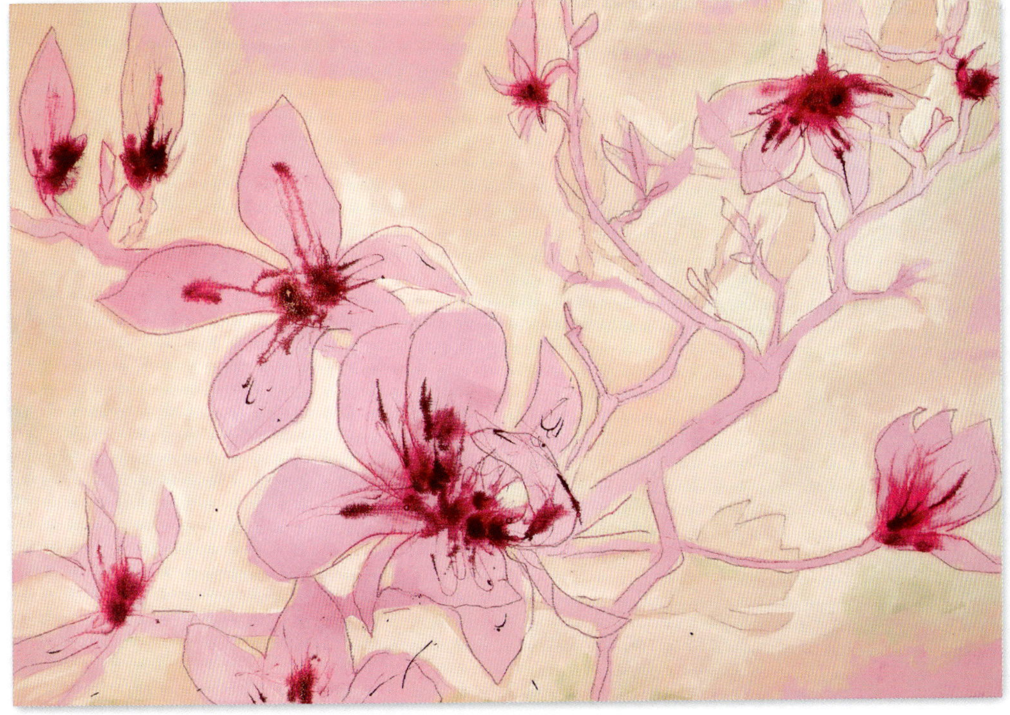

Step 3

Trace bold outlines with a magenta watercolor pencil. Consciously work loosely so that the outlines do not touch the shapes in many places. Apply lines to the flower centers and the leaves with a thin pipette and magenta drawing ink. Spray with a water spray bottle. Thanks to the fine pigment in the drawing ink, delicate veins are formed that resemble the character of the petals.

Step 4

Use a flat brush to paint the shadows, using very watery steel gray and dark blue. In this step, the acrylic paint is used like watercolors. As a result, the watercolor pencil outlines are partially dissolved. Due to the moisture, the lines drawn by watercolor pencil become more intense. Some of the still-wet drawing ink combines with the watery glazes so that the colors mix. Set an accent on the tips of the flowers with titanium white.

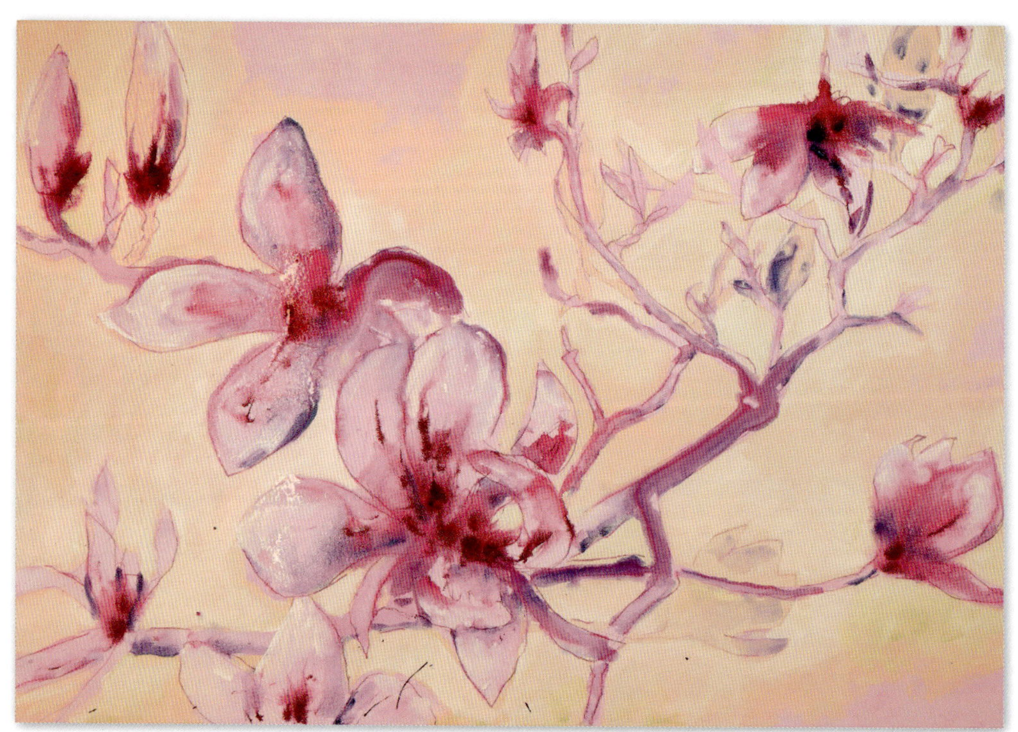

Step 5

Use gray and dark-blue watercolor pencils to intensify parts of the outlines. Spray with the water spray bottle to allow the colors to run more. If necessary, mop up any excess water with a rag. Paint cadmium yellow mixed with a little light umber in the centers of the flowers. Add a delicate yellow-green, mixed from titanium white, cadmium yellow, and a little steel gray, to the left section of the background. Finally, splatter a little paint on the canvas. Let dry.

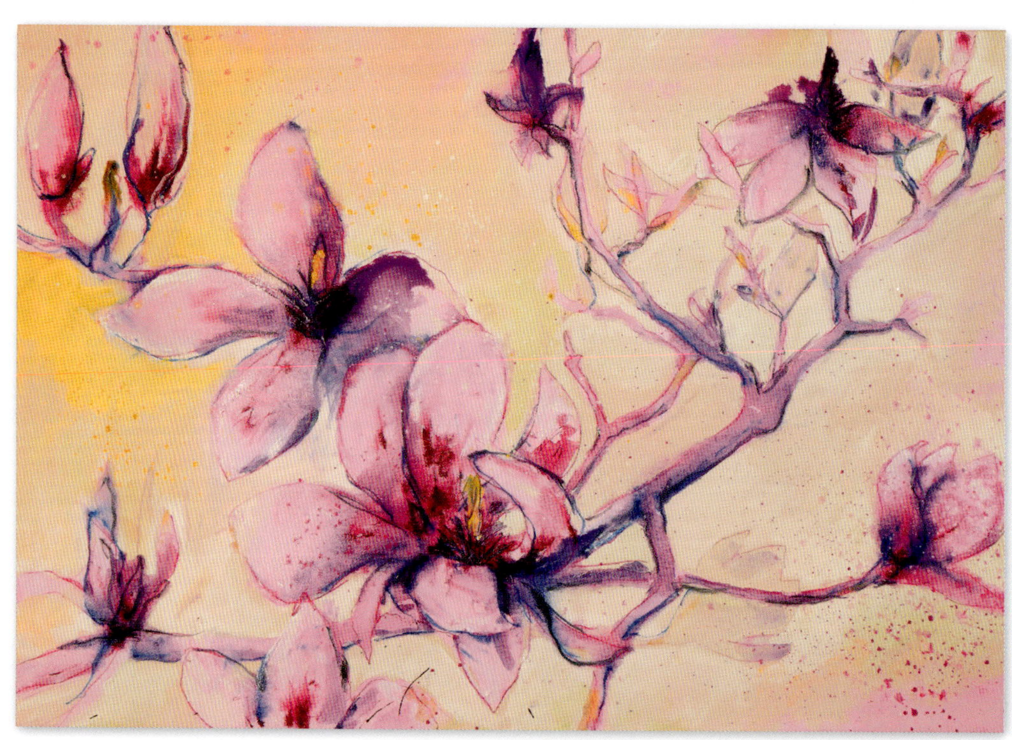

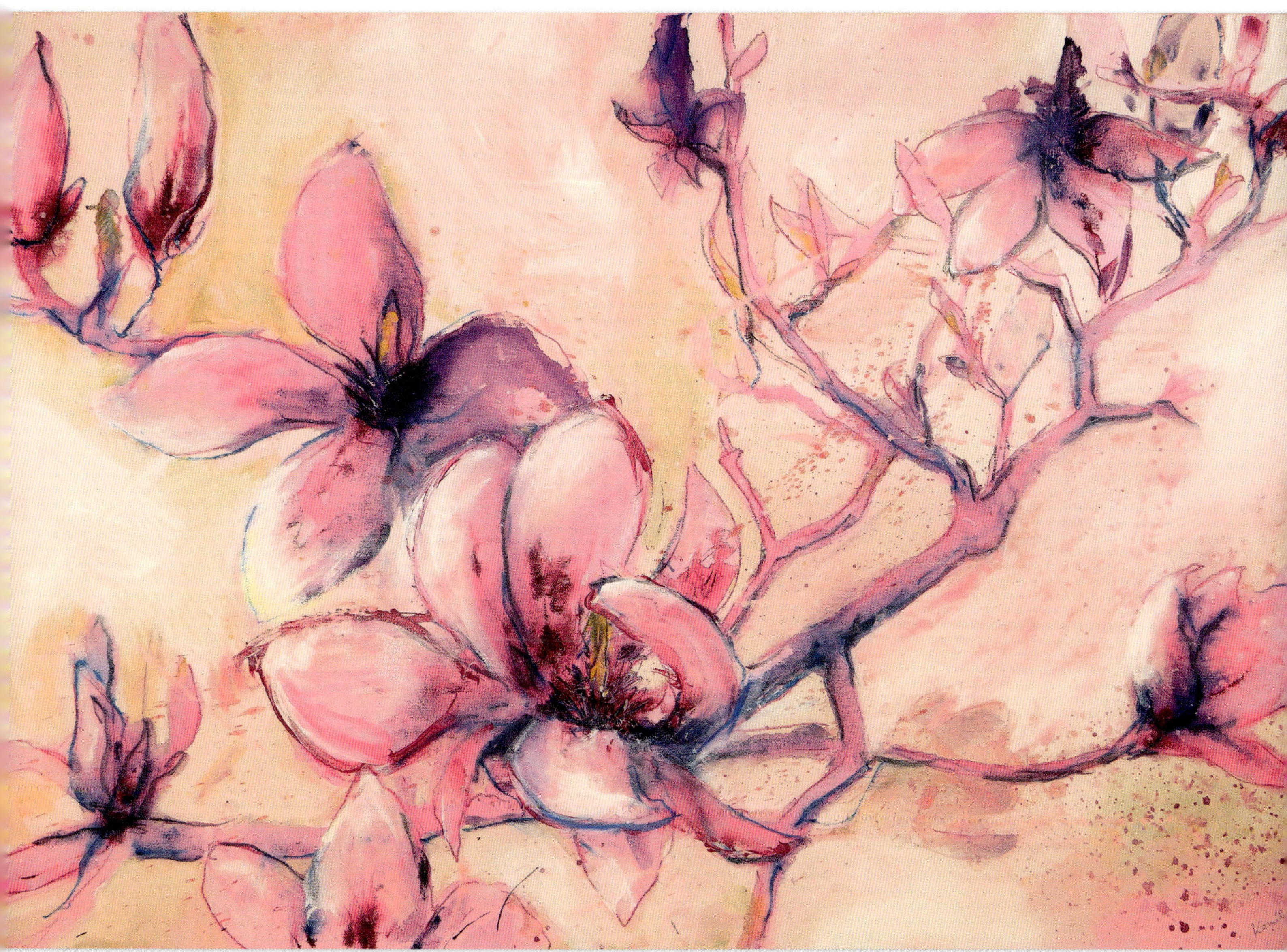

Finished Painting
Apply heavily diluted glazes to the background of the right section of the picture. Small drips should form as you do this. Use a broad synthetic bristle brush to paint slightly diluted titanium white on the background areas with random brushstrokes, applying paint only to the centers of the areas. Emphasize the central flower by painting a few outlines in magenta acrylic paint directly from the tube and blurring them slightly.

Peonies

Materials:

- Canvas, 24 x 28 in.
- Acrylic paints in titanium white, cadmium yellow, rose, magenta, cyan blue turquoise, dark violet, light green, grass green, and dark green
- Flat synthetic bristle brush, sizes 12 and 30
- Round natural hair brush, size 3
- Watercolor pencils in magenta and dark blue
- Oil pastels in white, rose, and magenta
- Drawing ink in white, magenta, and red
- Pipettes
- Water spray bottle
- Painter's palette

Peonies are a garden classic whose magnificent large flowers transform any garden into a spectacle of scent and color. Their dark, palmate leaves stand stark contrast to their soft and full pink flowers.
How opposites of form and color attract is shown in the delicate flowing colors set against the bold fingers of the leaves.

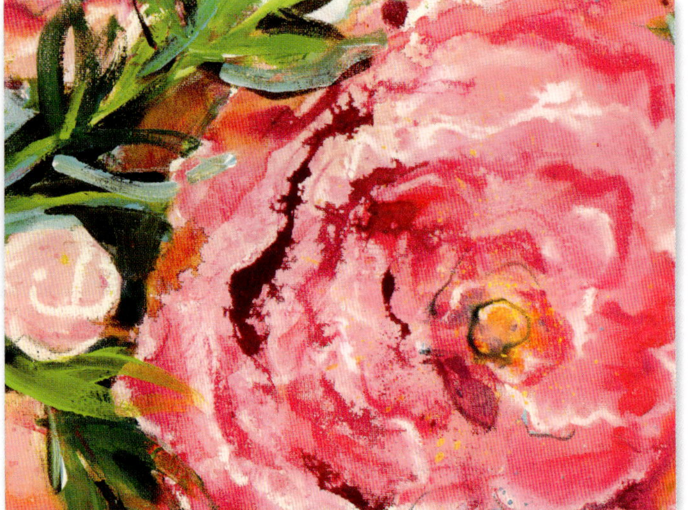

Section 1

Just like waves, the different outlines of the petal edges wind around each other. The shades mixed from white, rose, and magenta appear to melt into each other. The drawing ink feathers and adds a veining pattern to this flowing harmony. The bold-green pointed leaves form a stark contrast to the flowers.

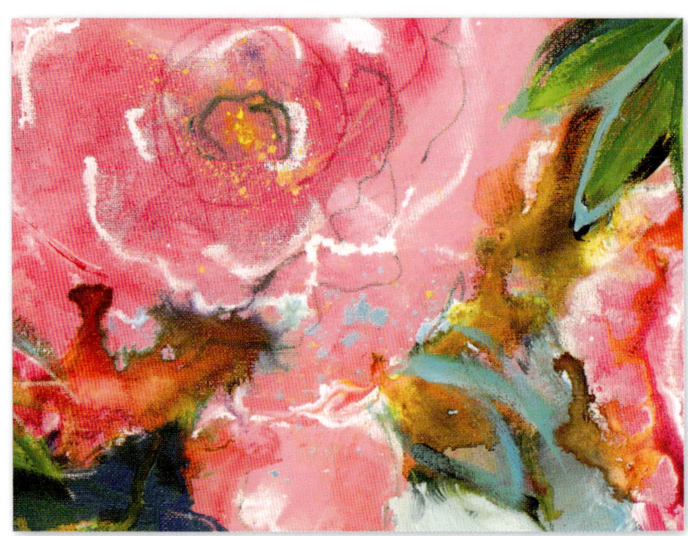

Section 2

Some accidental greenish-brown veining on the edge of a petal is kept, since it appears like natural wilting. The acrylic painting is enriched by its watercolor-like color gradients. The use of different media enlivens the composition.

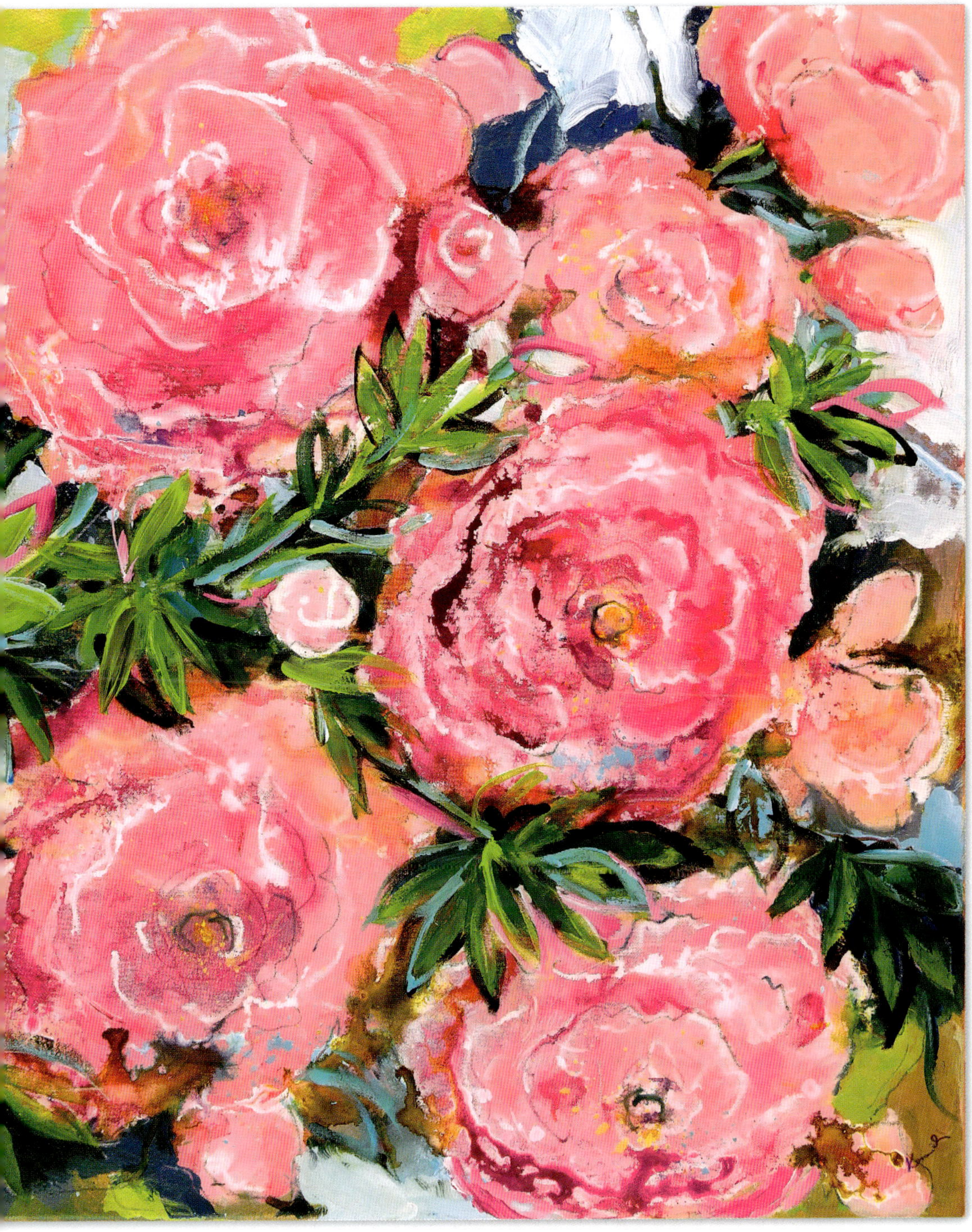

Instructions

Use a broad brush to paint filled circular shapes on the canvas with shades of acrylic paints mixed from titanium white, rose, and magenta. Use different-colored watercolor pencils to sketch the flowers. Apply magenta and white drawing ink to parts of the flower heads, and spray with a water spray bottle. Fill the background areas with shades of green. Allow to dry. Use various-colored oil pastels to outline the edges of the petals and smudge slightly. Splatter the centers of the flowers with cadmium yellow. Add to the background with shades of blue mixed from titanium white, cyan blue, turquoise, and dark green. Add splatters by using a turquoise lightened with titanium white and light green. Fill the picture with green foliage, which sometimes overlaps the flowers. To do so, use acrylic paint in various shades of gray and add accents in titanium white and turquoise.

Apple Blossom

Materials:

- Canvas, 28 x 40 in.
- Acrylic paints in titanium white, pastel yellow, Indian yellow, rose, magenta, and dark violet
- Flat synthetic bristle brush, sizes 30 and 120
- Fan brush, size 10
- Angular brush, size 12
- Watercolor pencils: in light blue, magenta, dark magenta, and dark violet
- Binder and container
- Drawing ink in white, magenta, and dark violet
- Pipettes
- Water spray bottle
- Paper towels
- Terry cloth towel
- Painter's palette

In autumn, apples from your own garden are like a gift from heaven. The foundations of a good harvest are already laid in spring. After the first warm days in May, as the trees and bushes are revealing the tender tips of their leaves and buds, the apple trees are slowly transformed into a magnificent sea of blossom. The whole garden breathes in pink.
Spring is brought to life using flowing colors, running splatters, dabbed transitions, and delicate pale shades.

Step 1
Use a broad brush to give the canvas a base coat of water-diluted acrylic paint in light magenta and pastel yellow. Occasionally shake out the brush so that there are many droplets on the canvas. Use a light-blue watercolor pencil to sketch the outlines of the branches and blossoms. Paint the background with a mix of mainly titanium white and a little Indian yellow.

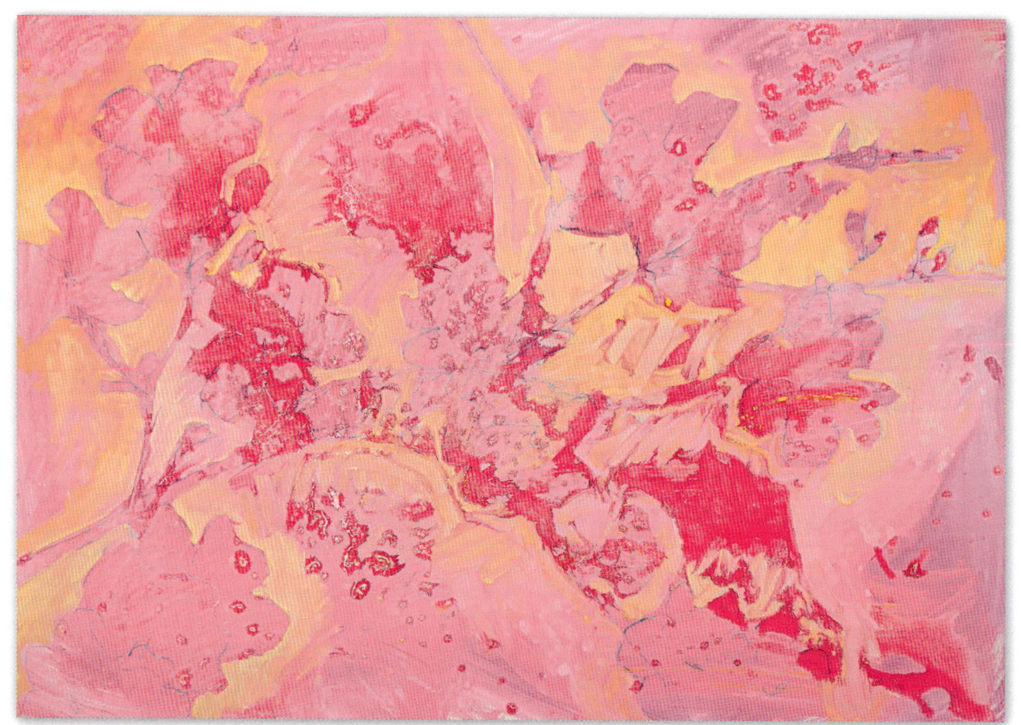

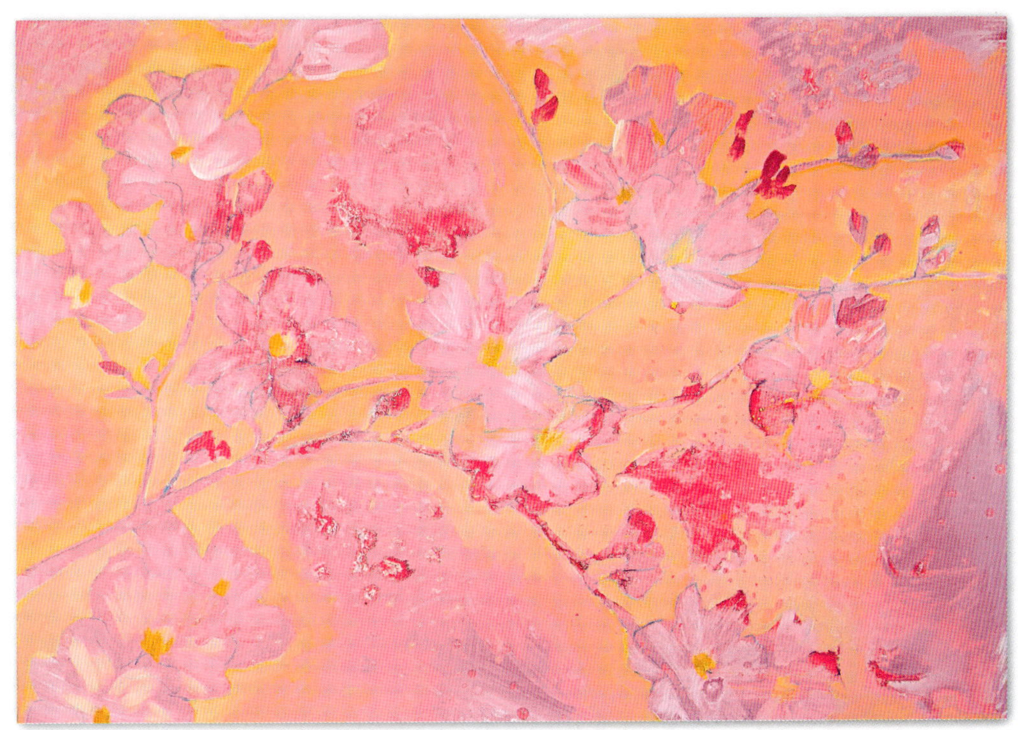

Step 2

Intensify the Indian yellow on the right and left edges of the picture, so that the center of the subject will later appear to be lighter than the outer sections. Apply pastel and Indian yellow to the center of the blossoms. Using a fan brush, emphasize the blossom petals. This brush should leave fine, frayed lines that highlight the character of the delicate blossom petals. Occasionally shake out the wet brush to create tiny splats.

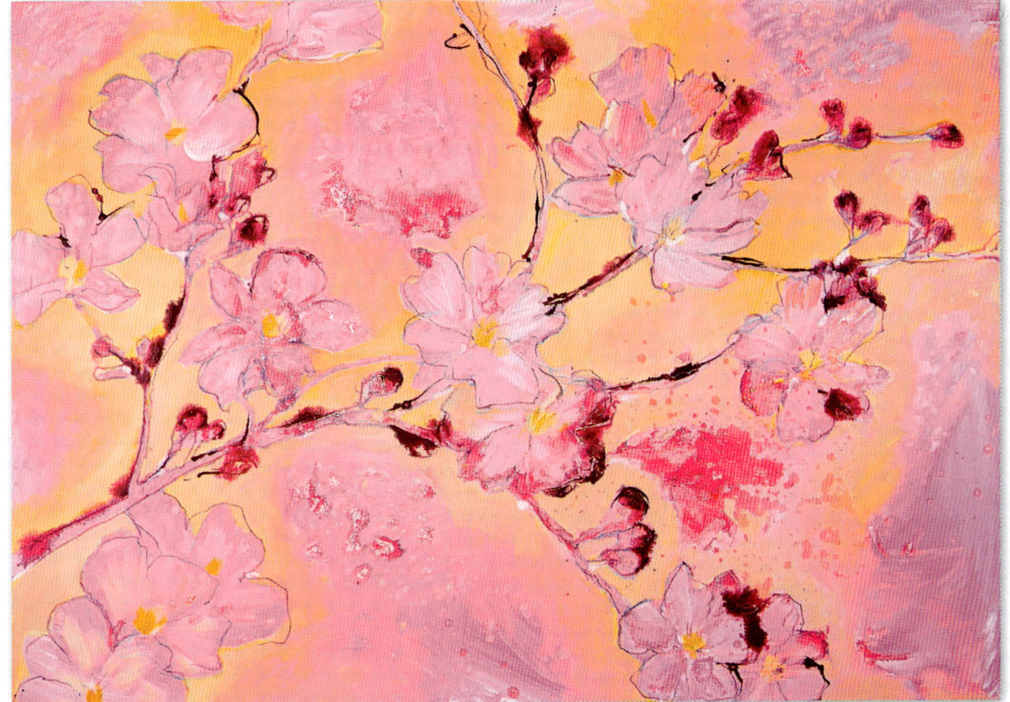

Step 3

Use a dark-magenta watercolor pencil to go over the outlines again. In the wet areas, the pencil will leave more pigment. As a result, the outlines will have different widths. Use a pipette to apply magenta drawing ink along the branches and on the buds. Use a water spray bottle to lightly spray. As a result, the ink will run fanlike and form unique vein patterns.

Step 4
Use white and magenta drawing ink to trace around the edges of a few blossom petals and then lightly spray with water. Allow the two inks to run into each other so that there are random streaks in the shades of pink. Use a dark-magenta watercolor pencil to draw fan-shaped lines in the centers of the blossom to indicate stamen. Add tiny splats in magenta. Use a brush to apply dark violet to the branches and to add some shadow on the blossoms.

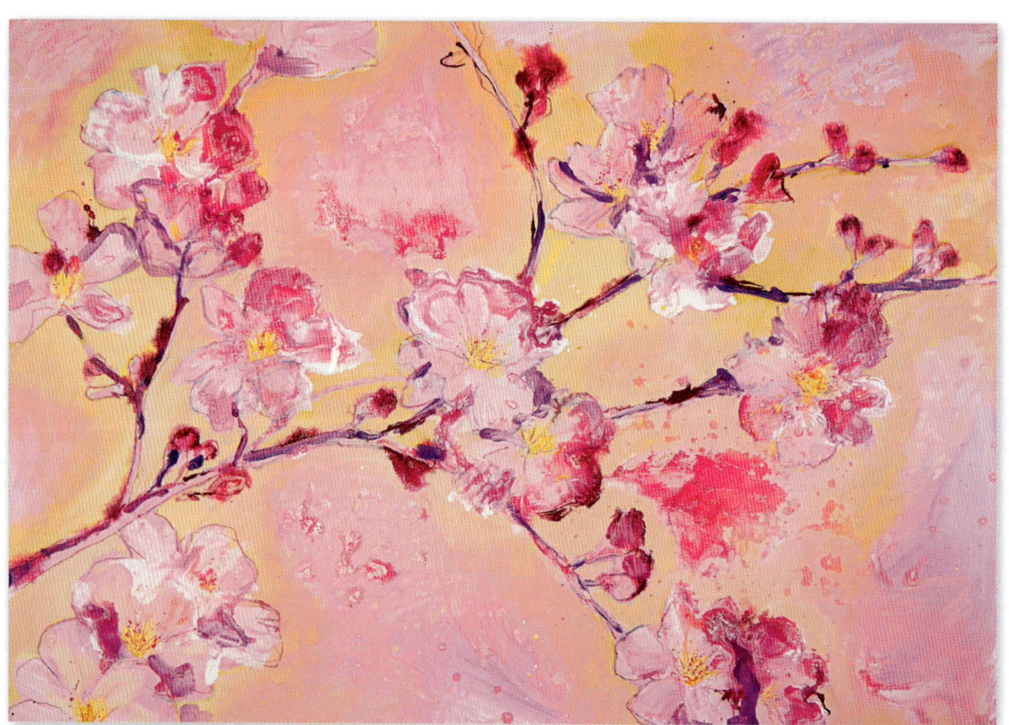

Step 5
Use a broad synthetic bristle brush to go over the left and right side of the background in a violet that has been mixed from dark violet and titanium white. Use the terry towel to dab the edges so that the paint gently flows into the other colors. Add some splats and spray some with water. Use the pipette to apply the dark-violet drawing ink to some of the outlines, and spray with water. Soak up the moisture, using paper towels if large paint puddles form. Let dry.

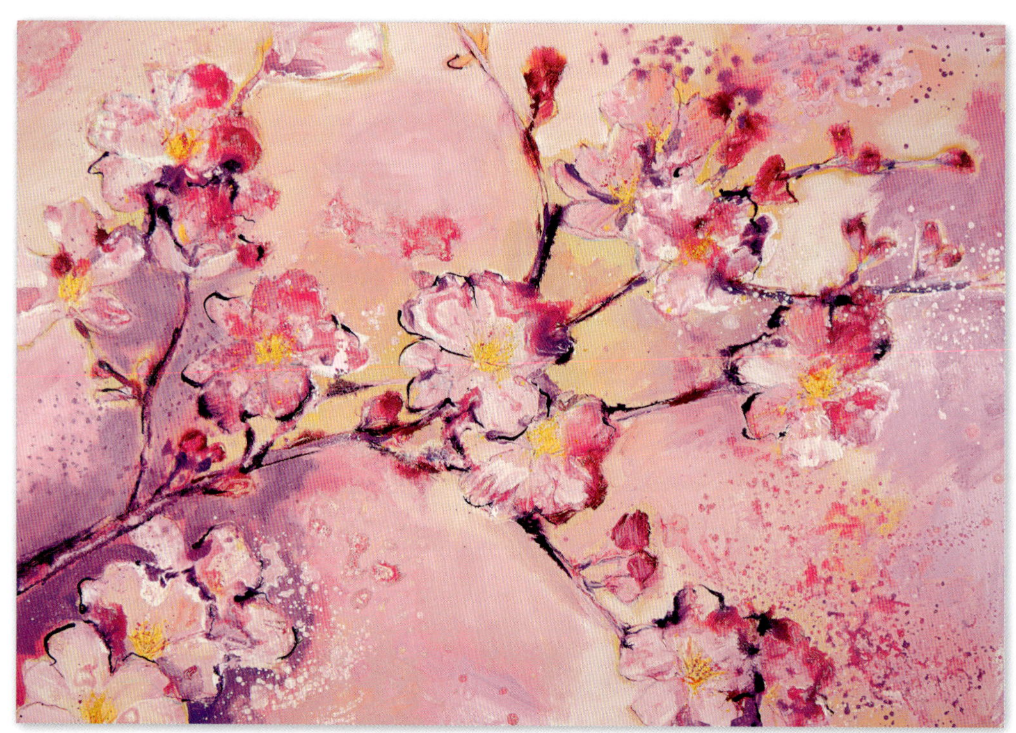

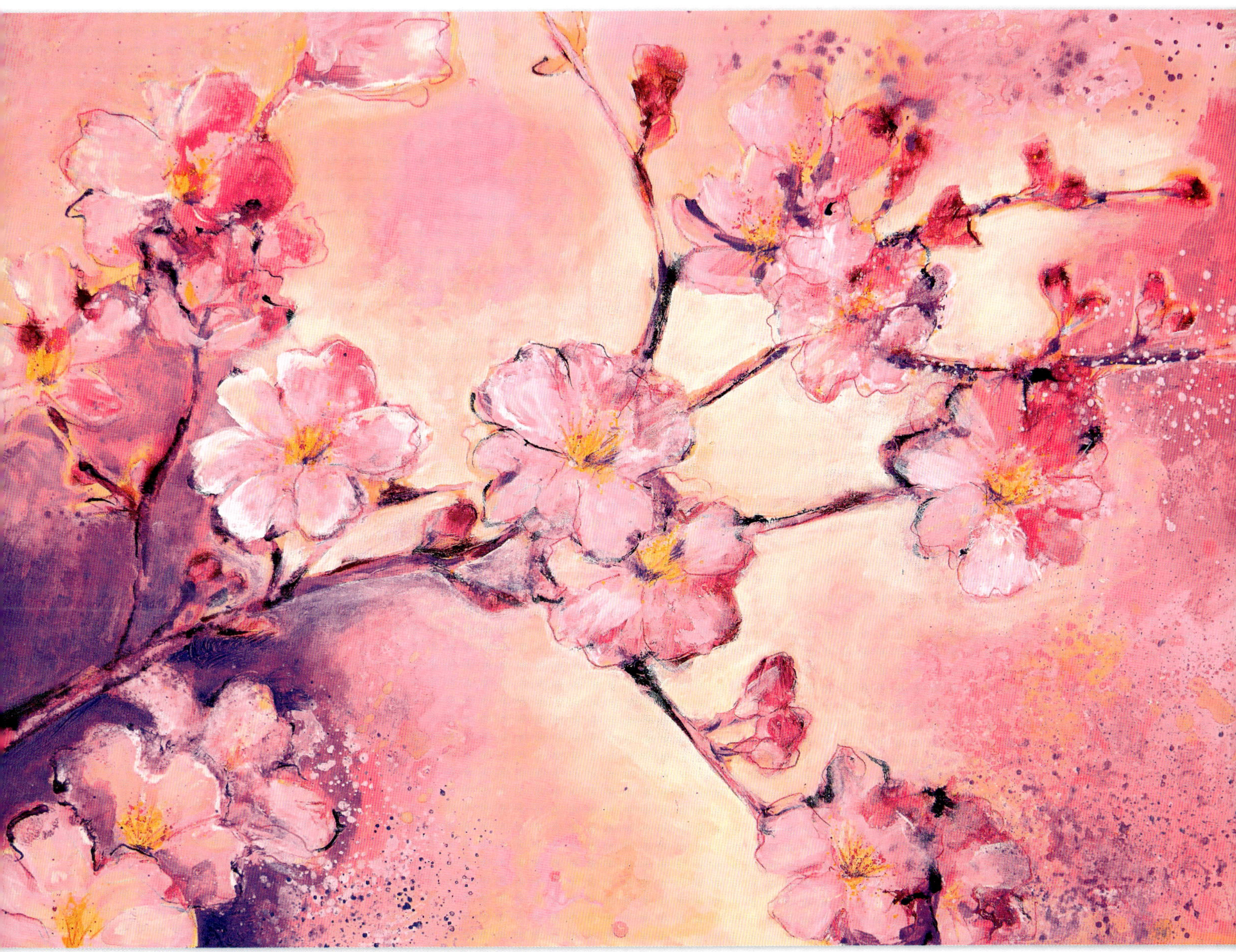

Finished Painting

Lighten the central areas of the picture, using titanium white and pastel yellow. Fill a small container with binder and dip a magenta watercolor pencil in the binder. Use the pencil to trace around some outlines. Add slight waves on the edges of the blossom petals. The lines do not need to follow the shapes exactly but can run beside them. Intensify the dark violet in the lower section of the picture. Dab the color transitions with a terry cloth towel. Use a fan brush to intensify the titanium white on the edges of some petals.

Wisteria

Materials:

- Canvas 28 x 40 in.
- Acrylic paints in titanium white, magenta, dark magenta, cerulean blue, dark violet, light green, grass green, and dark green
- Round natural hair brush, size 1
- Flat natural hair brush, sizes 10 and 18
- Watercolor pencils in white, violet, and blue
- Tissue paper
- Stamp that prints text
- Black ink pad
- Text stencil
- Binder and container
- Bubble wrap with small and large bubbles
- Lino roller, 4 in.
- Scissors
- Book for counterpressure
- Painter's palette

To make the stamp:

- Foam rubber
- Small pair of scissors
- Pen
- Wood glue
- Polystyrene or wood

Every year without fail, the wisteria with its hanging bunches of large blue flowers runs riot over my carport. The splendid ocean of flowers looks just like a pattern. The subject is printed using bubble wrap and a home-made stamp. Words appear to hang in the flowers. The text awakens lyrical and poetic associations, and at the same time, it's reminiscent of the delicate branches of the flowers before they wilt.

Step 1

To reduce the amount of work, it helps to make a stamp out of foam rubber that depicts the small tips of a group of flowers. Use a pen to draw the shape on a piece of foam rubber. Make sure that it's not symmetrical, so that it appears natural. Use the small scissors to cut it out. Cut a piece of polystyrene or wood and use the wood glue to glue the foam rubber to it. Allow to dry well.

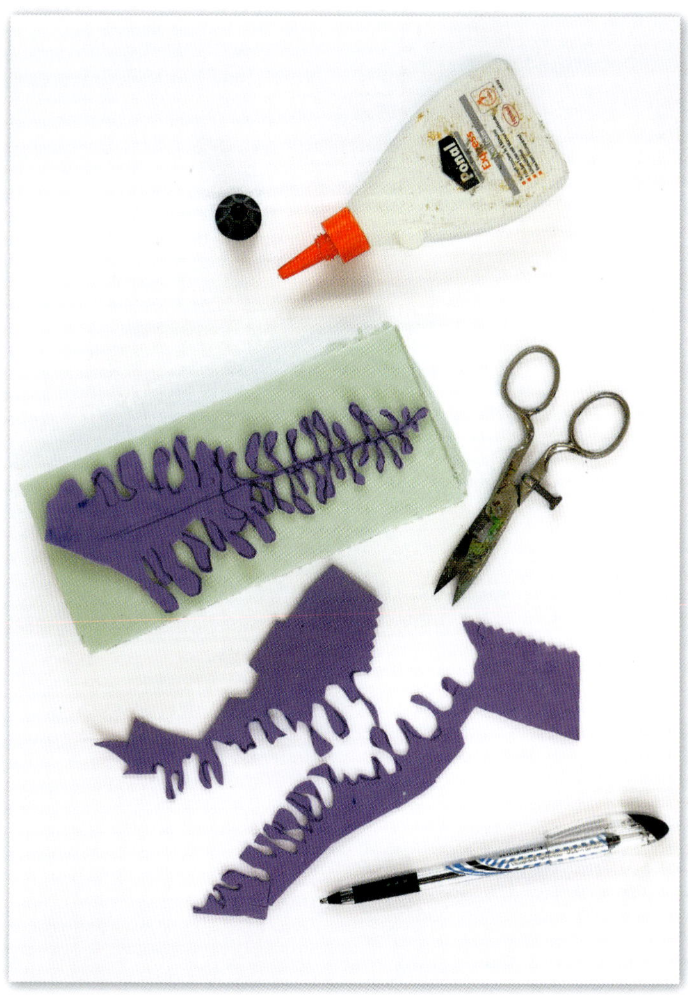

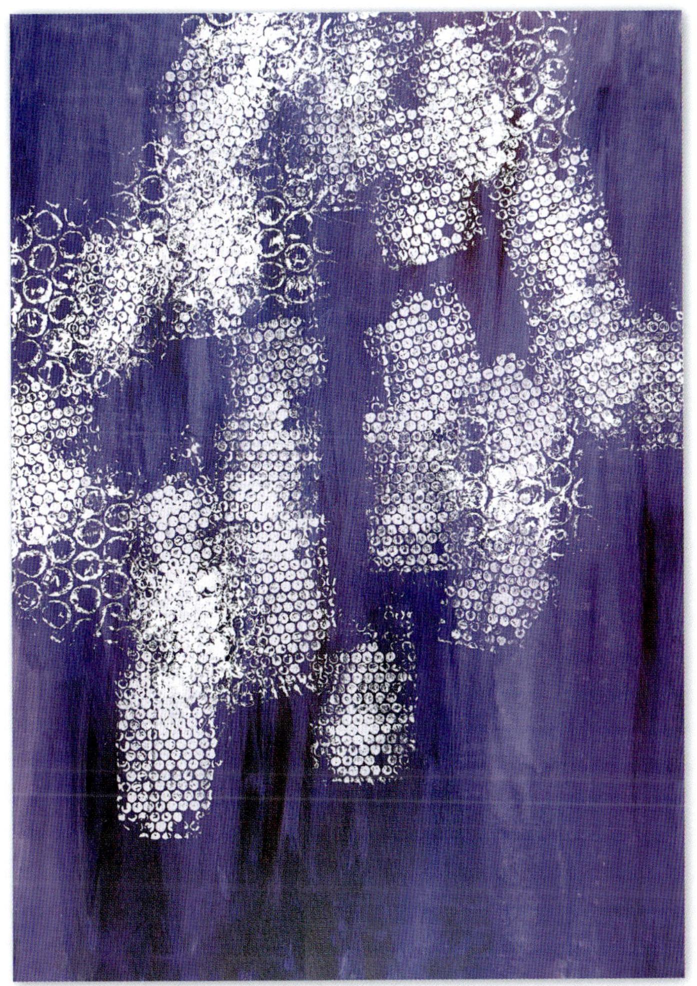

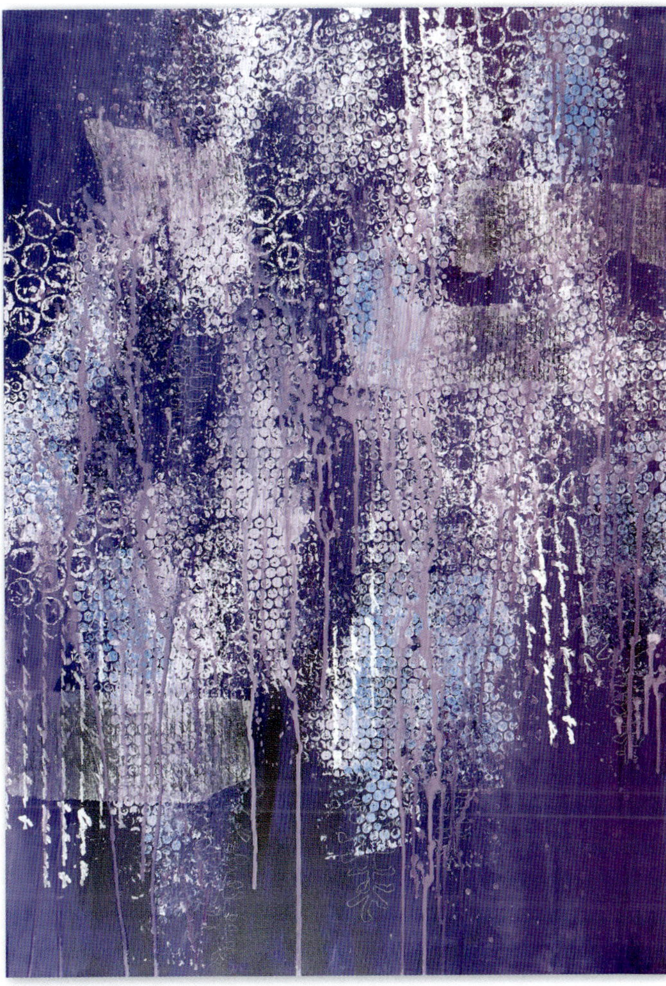

Step 2

Use a broad brush to give the canvas a base layer in dark violet and dark magenta. Move the brush only vertically to emphasize the hanging direction of the groups of flowers. Mix light violet from dark violet and titanium white and use the lino roller to roll it onto the palette. Cut long pieces of bubble wrap with small and large bubbles and press them into the paint on the palette. Now use the bubble wrap to print the shapes of the groups of flowers. For this step, mainly use the wrap with the small bubbles. Leave the lower area of the picture unprinted.

Step 3

Go over the groups of flowers with cerulean blue that has been lightened with titanium white. Print text on pieces of tissue paper and stick them in place with the binder. Ensure that the writing also runs vertically. Apply the text stencil in a few places between the flowers, using titanium white and a flat brush to do the stenciling. Spray on drops of dark violet and titanium white and then tilt the canvas so that the paint runs vertically. Allow to dry.

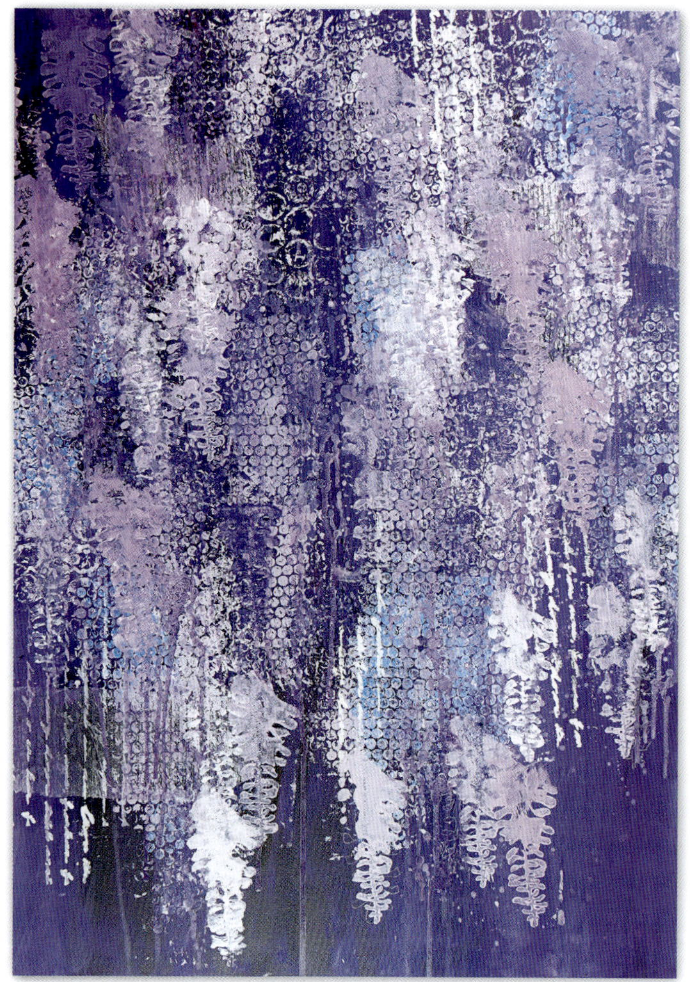

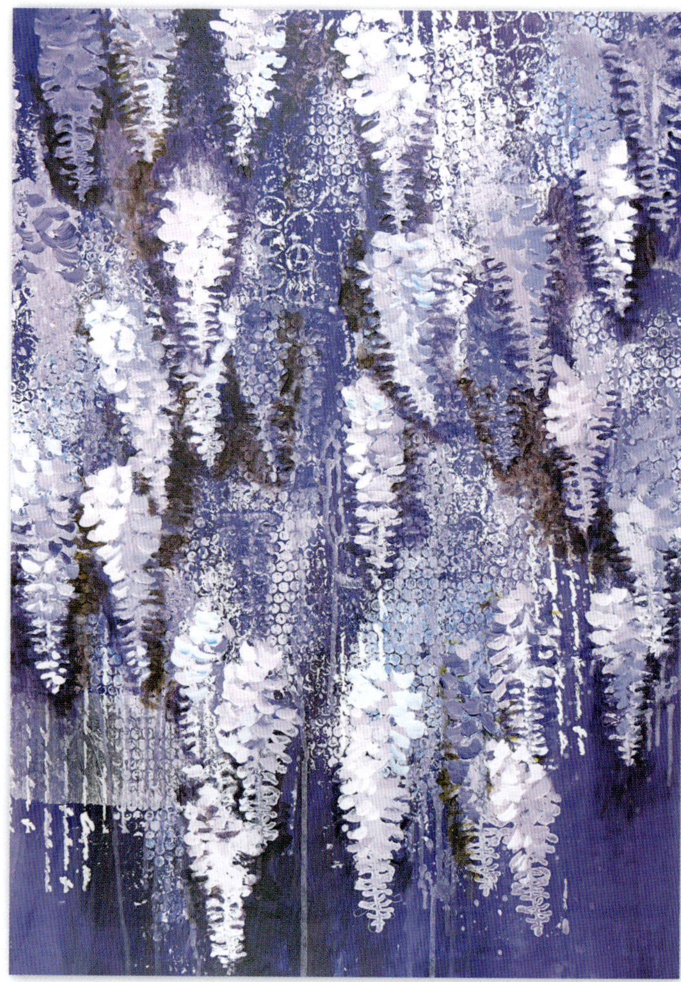

Step 4

Place a book of the same thickness as the stretcher frame under the places where you will print. The counterpressure is necessary so that the canvas does not sag and the imprint of stretcher frame does not show through. Roll a mixture of titanium white and dark violet directly on the foam stamp, using the lino roller. Add to the bubble wrap prints with the stamp. Mix various light-violet shades from dark violet and titanium white. Overlap some prints and ensure they are distributed randomly. Place a few prints on the unworked area, close to the lower edge.

Step 5

Mix dark violet and dark magenta and use it to highlight the printed tips by painting the surrounding area in these dark shades. Vary the color slightly. Use a brush to recreate individual flowers with light horizontal dabs. When doing so, place the lighter shades primarily on the left side of the groups of flowers. Mix many violet variations and occasionally work in blue shades.

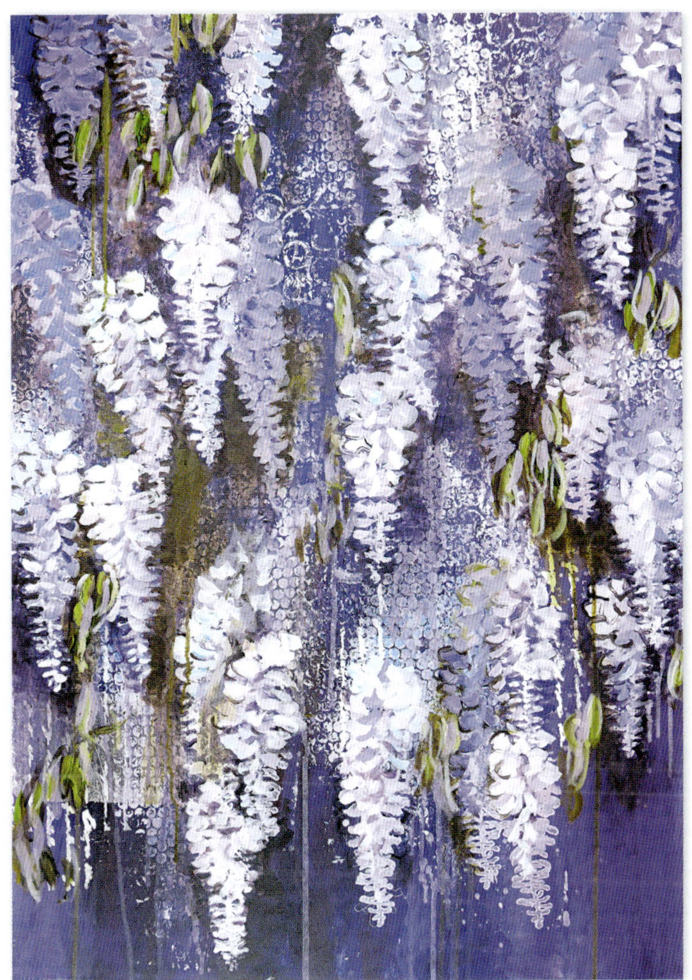

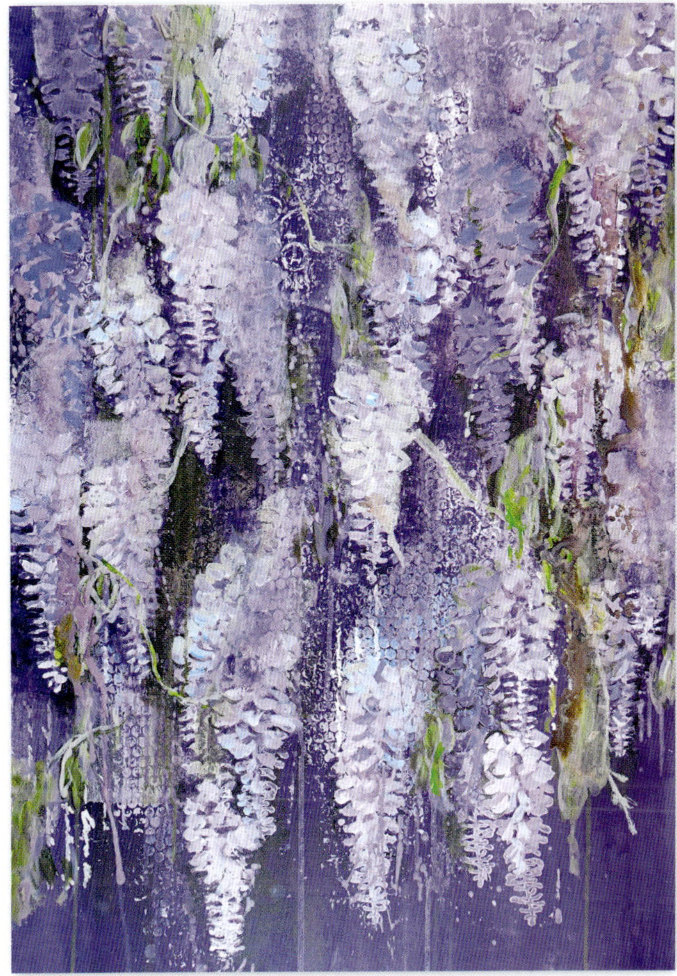

Step 6

Add leaves in shades of green, using a lot of mixed shades to which dark violet has been added. The leaves also hang vertically because they open only once the flowers have opened. Lightly go over the dark background shapes with shades of green. The dark shadow shapes form a stark contrast to the pale petals. Continue to work on the groups by dabbing flowers and occasionally adding outlines with a fine brush.

Step 7

Mix the dark green and dark violet on the palette with titanium white so that a pale brown is created. Use this mixture to work on a few groups close to the top edge, to show where the first flowers are wilting. Add a lot of water to this mix and use it as a glaze to cover the flowers and leaves so that the flowers painted under it still show through. Leave the tips of the groups of flowers as they are. In this way, a contrast is created between the clearly defined shapes and the blurred ones.

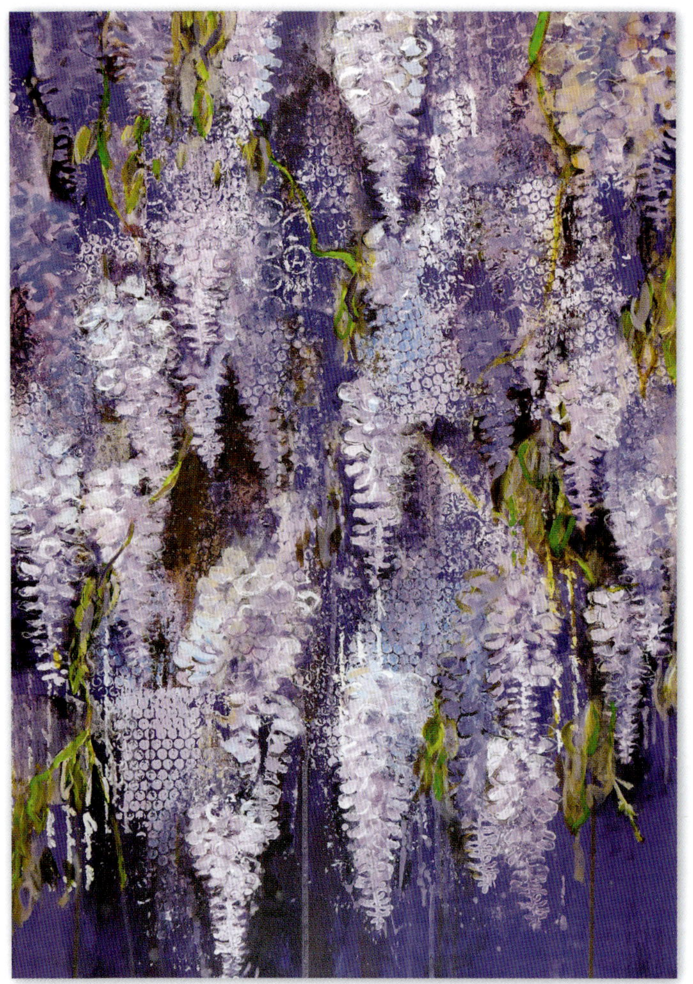

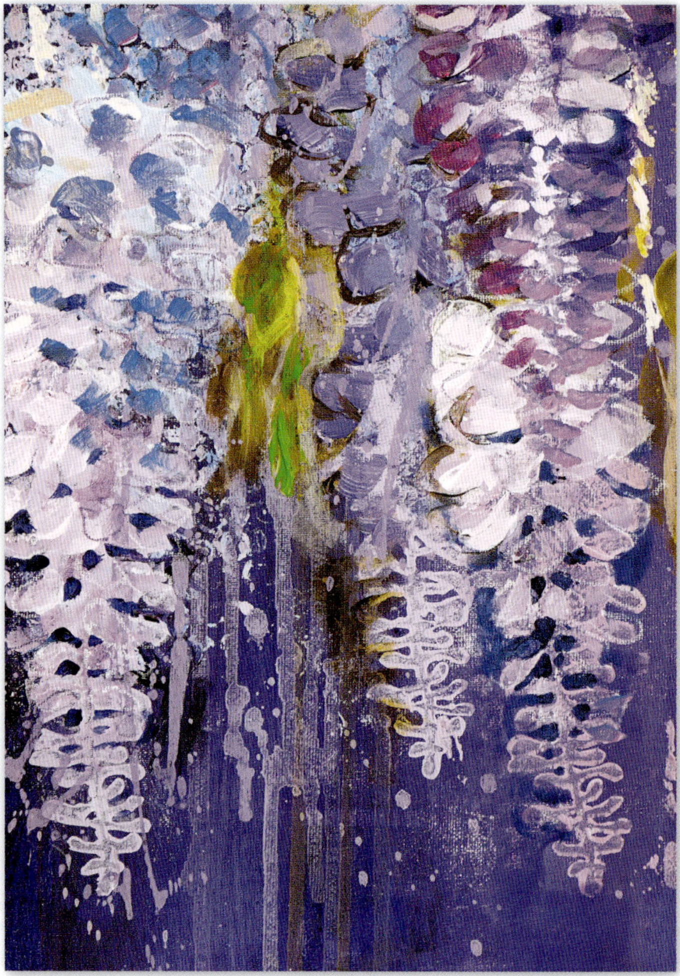

Step 8

Add some detail to the leaves and a few green branches in a random growth pattern. Draw these lines in different ways—some of them giving full color, and some of them as a glaze so that they are not too dominant. Use various green and mixed shades from the paint already on the palette. Roughly trace some outlines of the groups of flowers with white, violet, and blue watercolor pencils so that the outlines stand out from the dark background.

Close Up

The print from the foam stamp is integrated in the painting. The typical edges from the print are worked into the various outlines of the painting over them. The small random areas of shadow in the flowers disguise that the shape of the print repeats. The texts are embedded and can be seen only when the painting is inspected more closely.

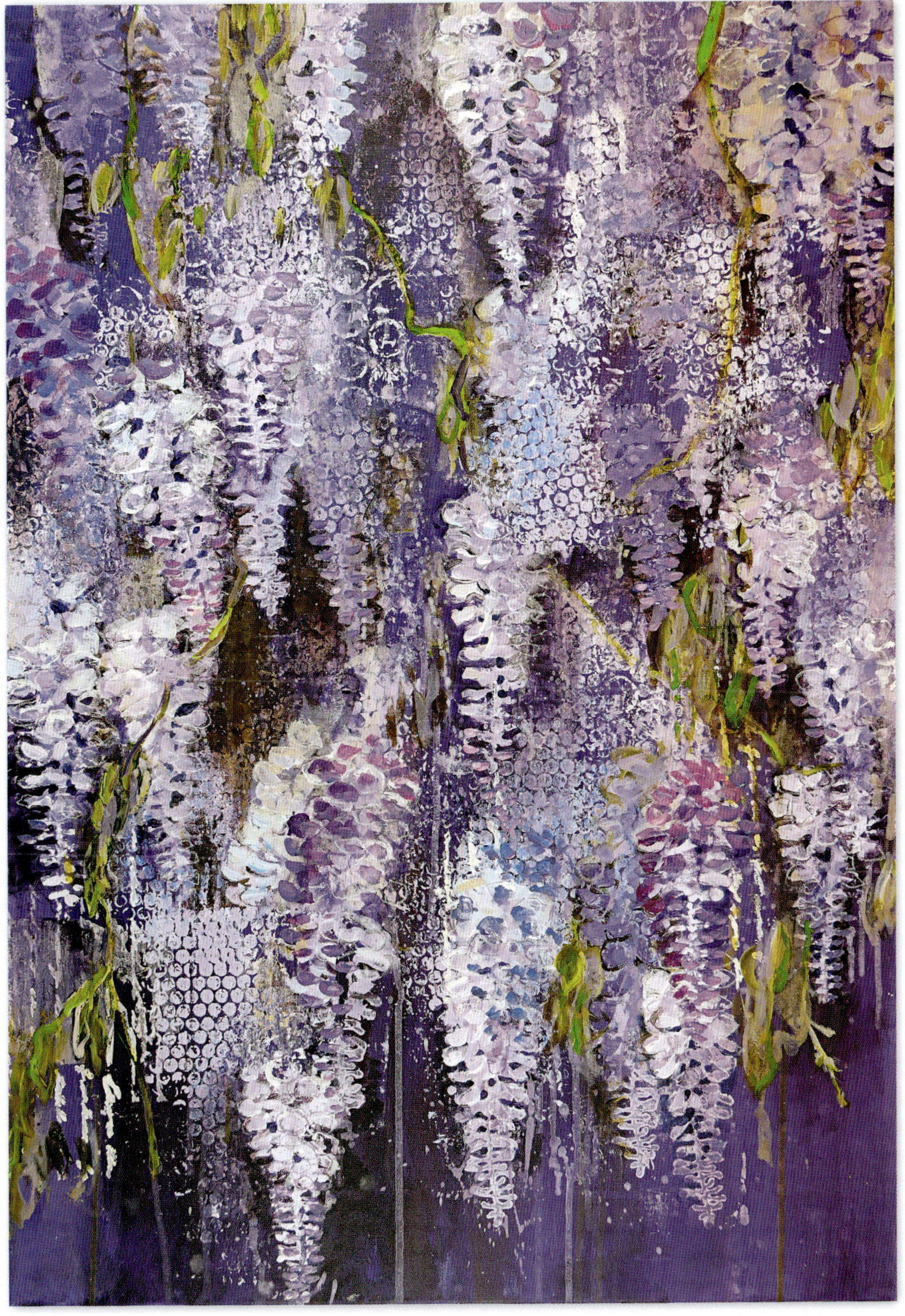

Finished Painting

Use a flat brush to add detail to the random shadow areas of the flowers. Use magenta, dark violet, and titanium white to mix new shades that have not yet been used. Use these shades to work on a few of the upper groups of flowers and add a slight curve resembling the way that wisteria really hangs. In a few places, do the same with cerulean blue. An attractive quantity contrast is created by the new colors, which have been only sparingly used.

Opened Tulips

Materials:

- Canvas, 36 x 56 in.
- Acrylic paints in titanium white, pastel yellow, rose, cadmium red, magenta, dark violet, cyan blue, cobalt blue, dark turquoise, indigo, and black
- Flat synthetic bristle brush, sizes 20 and 40
- Cat's-tongue brush, size 20
- Palette knife
- Foam roller, 2 in.
- Water spray bottle
- Rags
- Acrylic marker in dark blue
- Acrylic spray paint in yellow
- Painter's palette

Along with crocuses and snowdrops, tulips are the first signs of spring. There are several thousand types of tulips. Some of them open their petals all the way, enabling them to catch all the sunlight.
The composition of the painting—with gaps between the flowers' petals, the overlapping petals, and petals extending beyond the edge of the picture—gives the impression of a wealth of blooms. The vibrant style is created using a mixture of acrylic paint tools and techniques.

Section 1
The surfaces appear vivid as a result of using various tools and an inexact manner of work. Marks from the brushes and spatula overlap each other and are interspersed with scratches. Glazing and covering paints as well as shapes and outlines stand in contrast with each other.

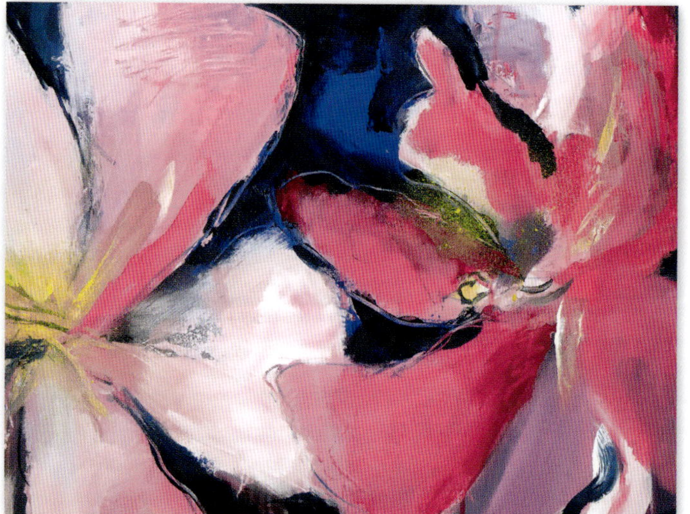

Section 2
Using wet paints to create running drips intensifies the character of a quick and imprecise manner of painting. The paint runs in different colors that overlap each other and create lines, harmoniously connecting with the outlines and the linear scratches.

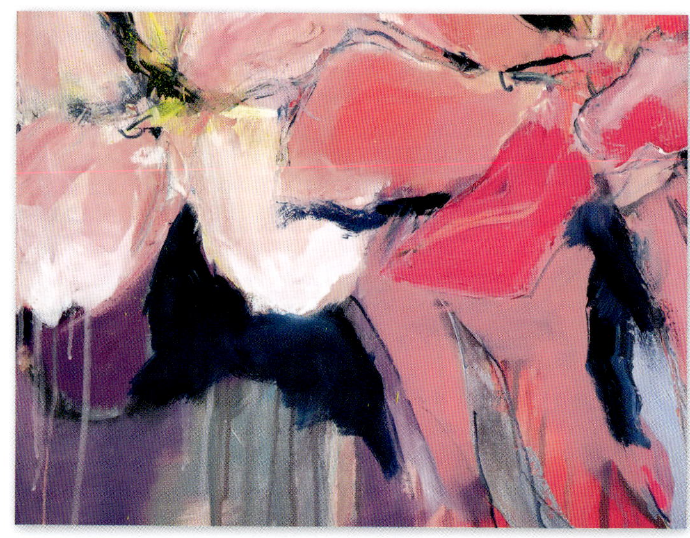

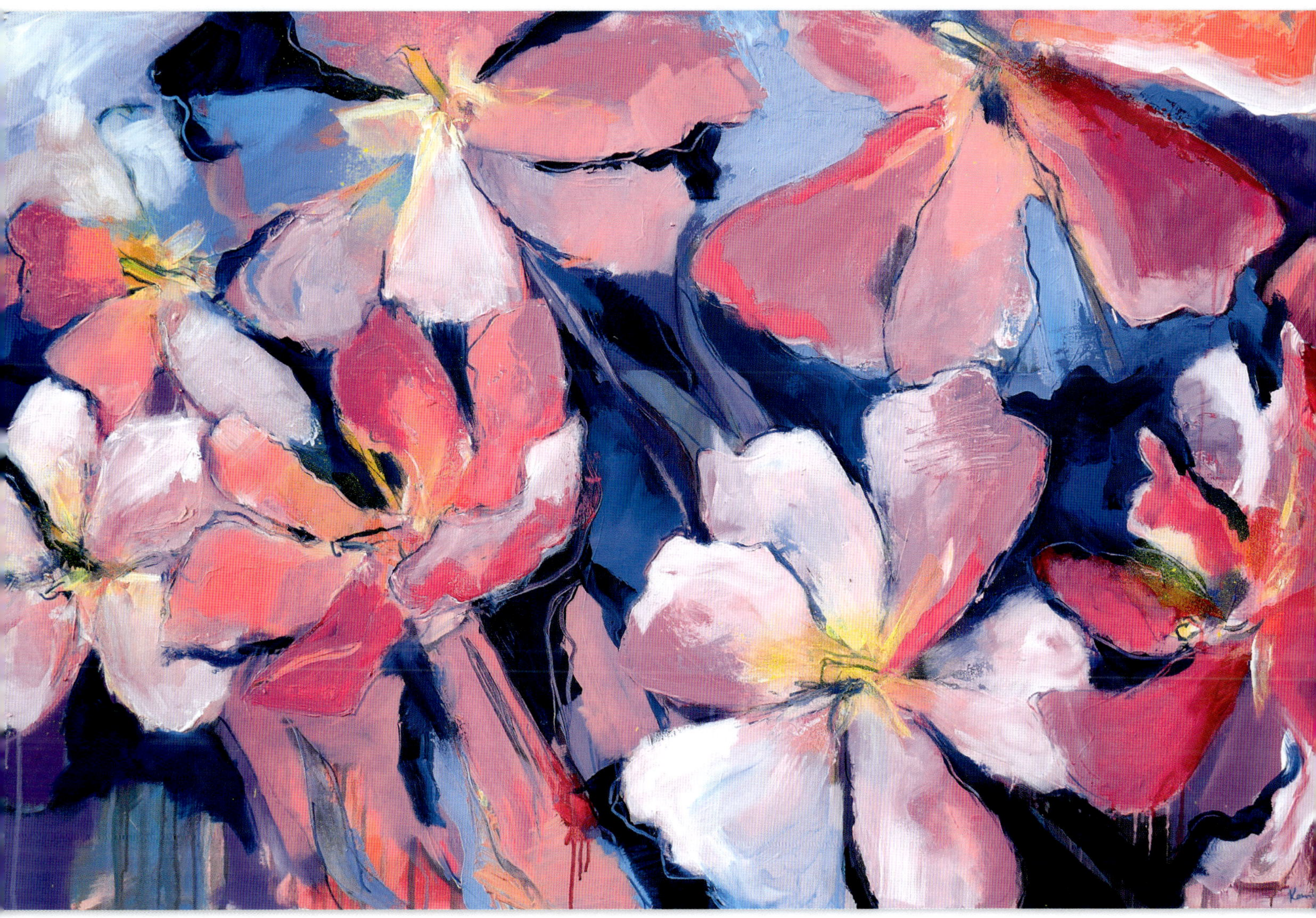

Instructions

Use a broad brush to spread various shades of rose and magenta on the canvas. Use the cat's-tongue brush to sketch the outlines in dark violet and cyan blue. Paint in the negative space. Work with wet paint, so that it runs. Paint over each petal with slight variations in shade. Work alternately with a palette knife and a brush, as well as adding scratches. Add accents to the edges of the petals. Wet small areas with a foam roller or a water spray bottle and wipe with a rag. Keep working over the picture. When doing so, pay attention to stark dark-light contrasts. Use a dark-blue acrylic marker to trace round a few outlines. Add the yellow acrylic spray paint to the centers of the flowers.

Chestnut Flowers

Materials:
- Canvas, 24 x 32 in.
- Acrylic paints in titanium white, cadmium yellow, rose, magenta, cyan blue, grass green, olive green, dark green, natural umber, and black
- Watercolor pencil in dark green, light blue, magenta, dark magenta, and dark violet
- Flat synthetic bristle brush, size 30
- Flat natural hair brush, size 12
- Round natural hair brush, size 1
- Drawing ink in white, red, and magenta
- Pipettes
- Binder and container
- Painter's palette

Materials for the chestnut leaves:
- Soft plastic wrap or gel-printing plate
- Lino roller
- Tissue paper
- Chestnut leaves
- Paper towels for cleaning

At the start of April, the chestnut flowers are in full bloom. The candelabras are illuminated in wonderful shades of pink that offer a magnificent contrast to the deep green. The leaves with their clearly visible veins are printed on tissue paper by using real chestnut leaves, while the clusters of flowers are painted. The combination of printing and painting creates an enthralling composition.

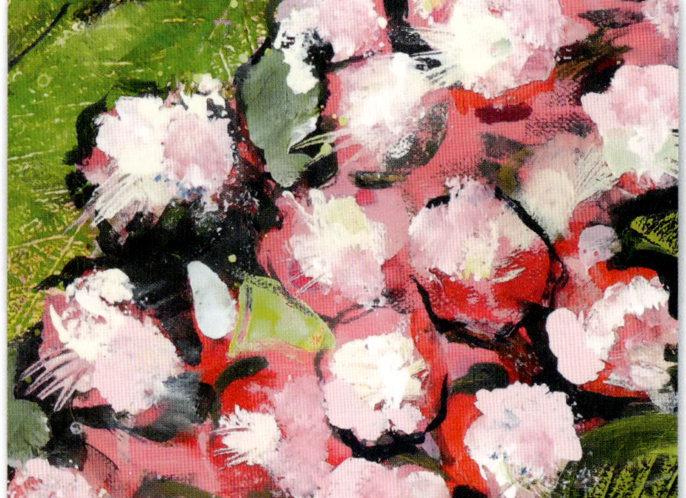

Section 1

The chestnut flower candelabras are partially painted, partially dabbed. The stamens are created by scratching into the paint with the back of a brush. In small areas of the background, the sky shows through with a light blue mixed from titanium white and a little cyan blue. Adding a few paint splatters in the already used shades loosens the composition.

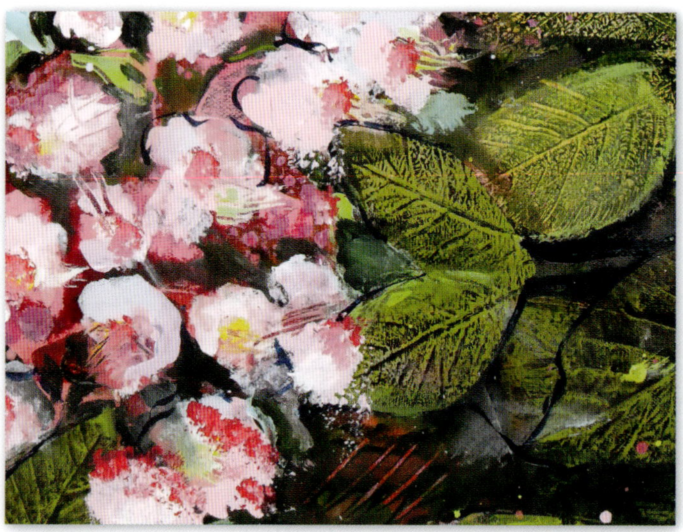

Section 2

The patchy layer of paint created by the printing technique is reflected in the dabbing painting technique used for the blossoms. By overlapping the shapes as well as adding small painted details in the leaves and overlaying splatters of paint, the two different techniques combine.

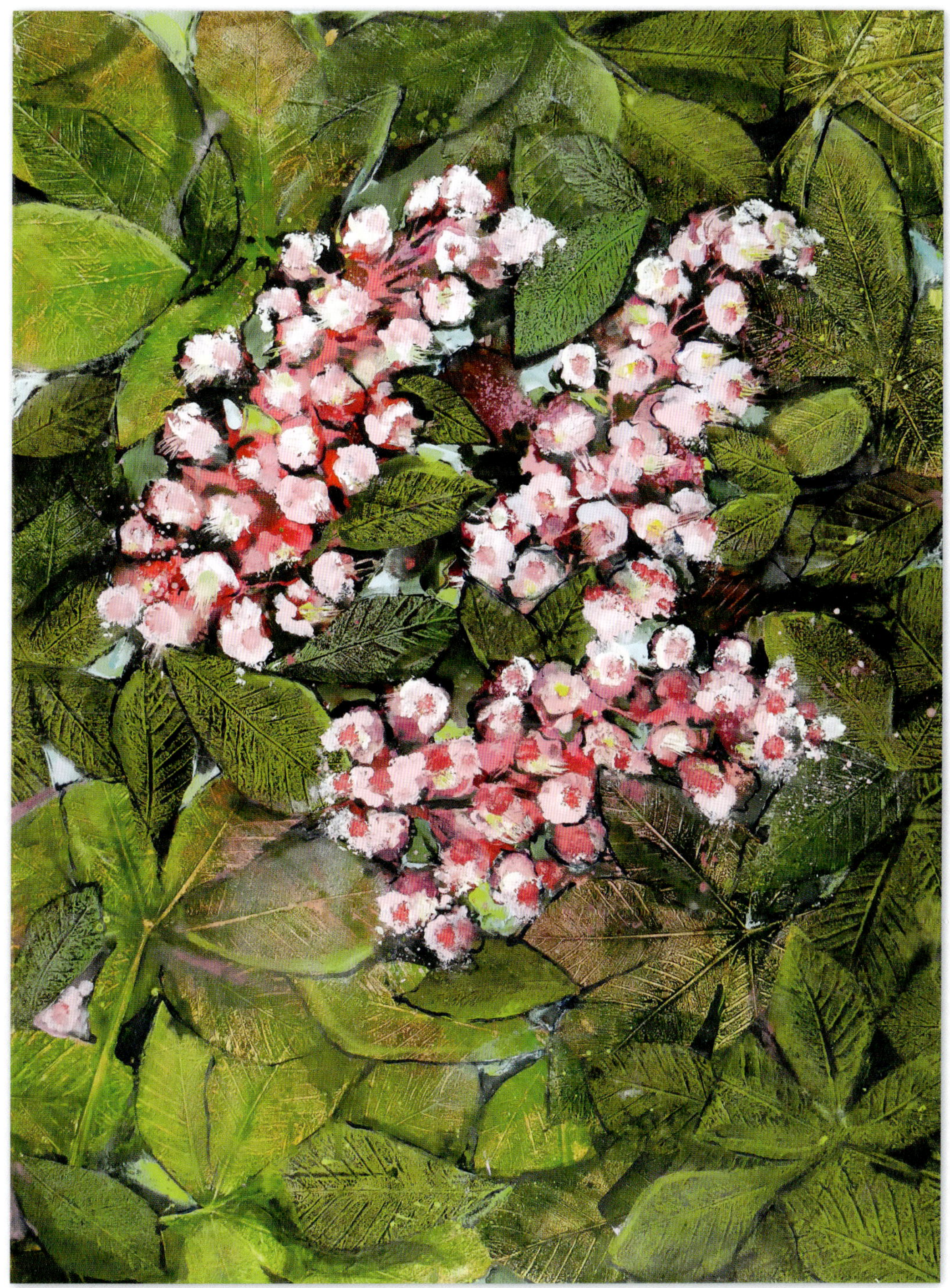

Instructions

Use a lino roller to spread various shades of green on a soft plastic wrap or gel-printing plate. Place the chestnut leaves on the paint, press them in, and remove. In the paint left on the wrap, the structure of the leaf should be clear. Print these leaf marks onto tissue paper. Let dry. Add a base layer in pink shades to the center of the canvas, and then a base of olive green where the leaves shall be. Use binder to stick on the tissue paper prints of the leaves. Sketch the clusters of flowers and fill the background with shades of brown mixed from natural umber and black. Add outlines to the blossoms with drawing ink, and spray with water. Rework with acrylic paint. Stick on further individual tissue leaves. Add dark tones in the background. Use a fine natural hair brush to give the leaves dark outlines and add splatters.

Irises

Materials:

- Canvas, 32 x 40 in.
- Acrylic paints in titanium white, pastel yellow, magenta, cyan blue, turquoise, dark turquoise, indigo, cerulean blue, light violet, dark violet, and natural sienna
- Flat synthetic bristle brush, size 30
- Angular brush, size 12
- Plastic Japanese spatula
- Watercolor pencil in white
- 2 thick sheets of plastic wrap
- Putty, fine
- Drawing ink in white, magenta, dark violet, and dark turquoise
- Pipettes, water spray bottle, terry towel, and painter's palette
- Fine sandpaper and thin cardboard

The Siberian blue lily is one of the few blue native flowers in Europe. The single-colored iris looks particularly beautiful when planted in large groups. Colors range from various shades of blue to deep violets.

The prominence of the veins in the petals is re-created using fine putty. Color pigment collects in the veins and in this way intensifies the structures. Add in drawing ink, which forms blooms when water is added, and a vivid composition is created that is full of controlled accidents.

Step 1

Place a piece of thin cardboard between the canvas and the stretch frame to prevent imprints from showing through after using the spatula. Squeeze all of the blue shades directly from the tubes onto the canvas, without layering them over each other. Spread uneven amounts of paint. Position the darker shades in the right section of the picture.

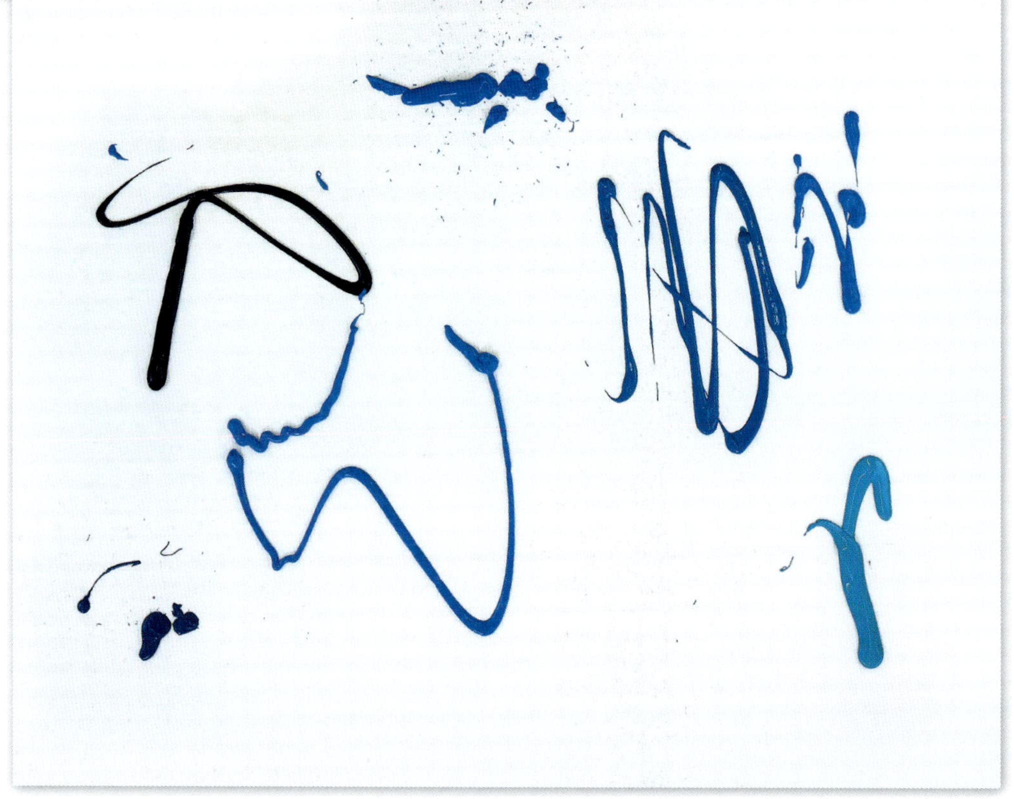

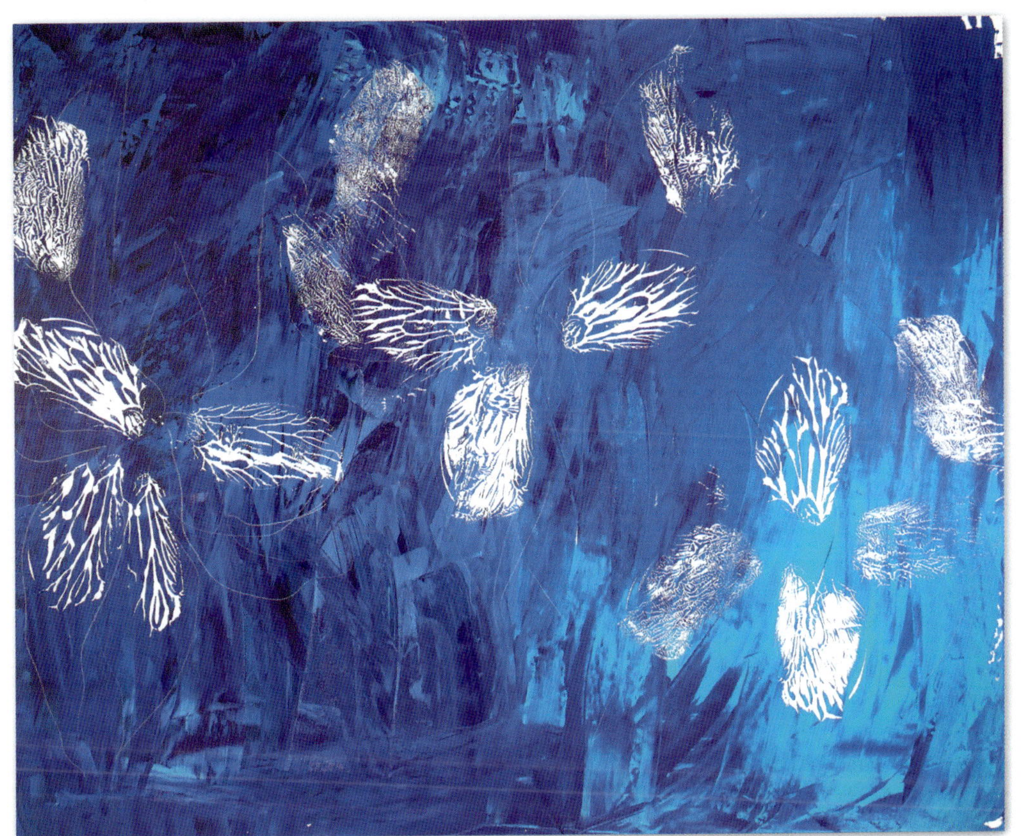

Step 2

Use the Japanese spatula to distribute the paint and mix it slightly. Let dry. Sketch the flowers with a white watercolor pencil. Press a large dollop of fine putty between two sheets of wrap and pull apart, which creates a vein pattern. Carefully press this vein pattern from the sheet onto the canvas. Carefully remove the sheet. For finer veins, use less putty and press harder. Let dry.

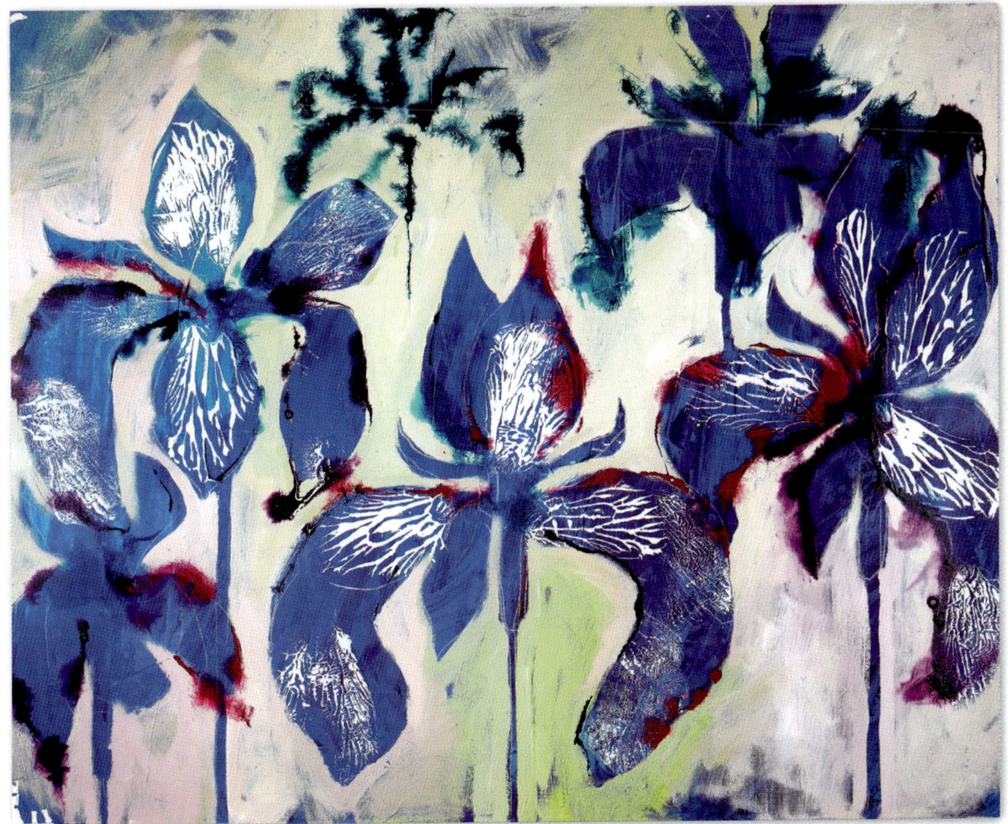

Step 3

Mix a few light background shades with titanium white as the base, with hints of pastel yellow, magenta, and natural sienna. Use a broad synthetic bristle brush to paint these background shades in the negative space to emphasize the flowers. In places, use the mixed paint as a glaze so that the underlying blue shades can show through. Use pipettes to apply spots of magenta, dark-violet, and dark-turquoise drawing ink and draw the outline of a flower in the background. Moisten the ink slightly with a water spray bottle. Let dry.

Step 4
Go over the background with acrylic paints again. In doing so, leave the lower layer of paint visible at the edges. Paint over any uncontrolled running from the drawing ink. Once again, outline the flowers with the pipette and the dark-violet drawing ink. Add some leaf outlines, which can also go over the petals so that the leaves are in the foreground. Add splats of white drawing ink, which combine with the wet paint. Let dry.

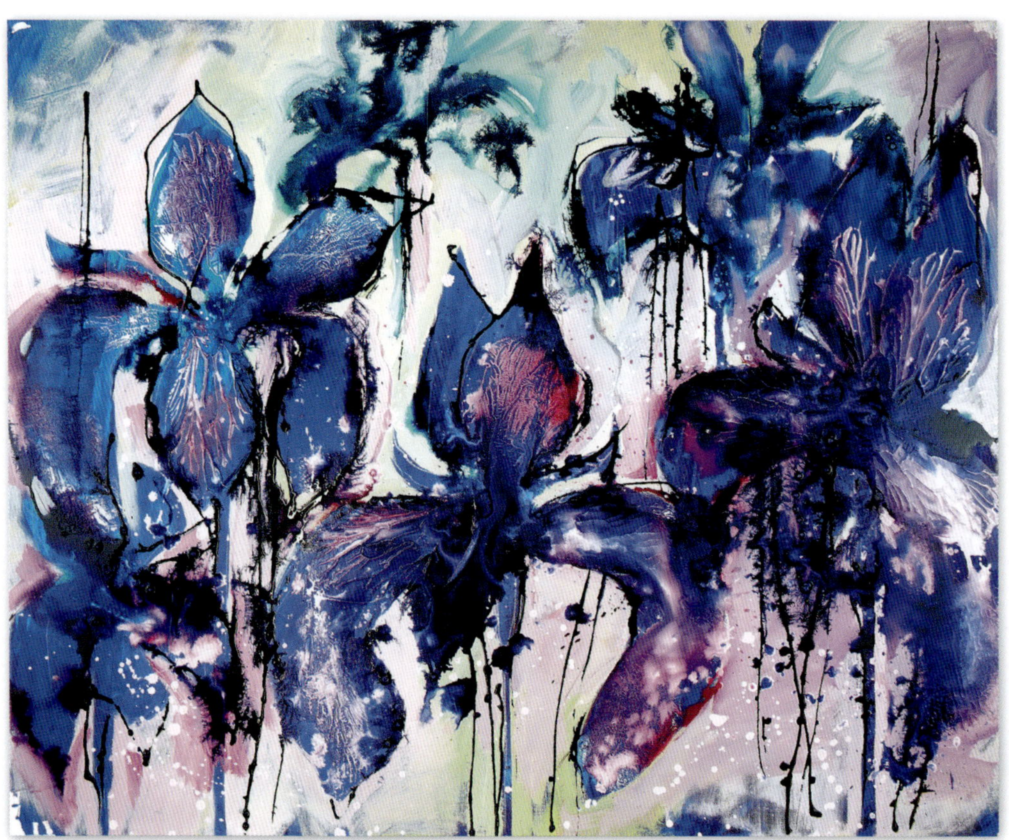

Step 5
Use the fine sandpaper to sand down the ridges of the putty veins. As a result, the veins once again appear white. Remove the sanding dust with a terry towel. Calm the background at the top of the picture by using light mixed shades to paint over drops, ink feathering, and any too-unsettled color effects. In the lower section of the picture, add light violet to the background.

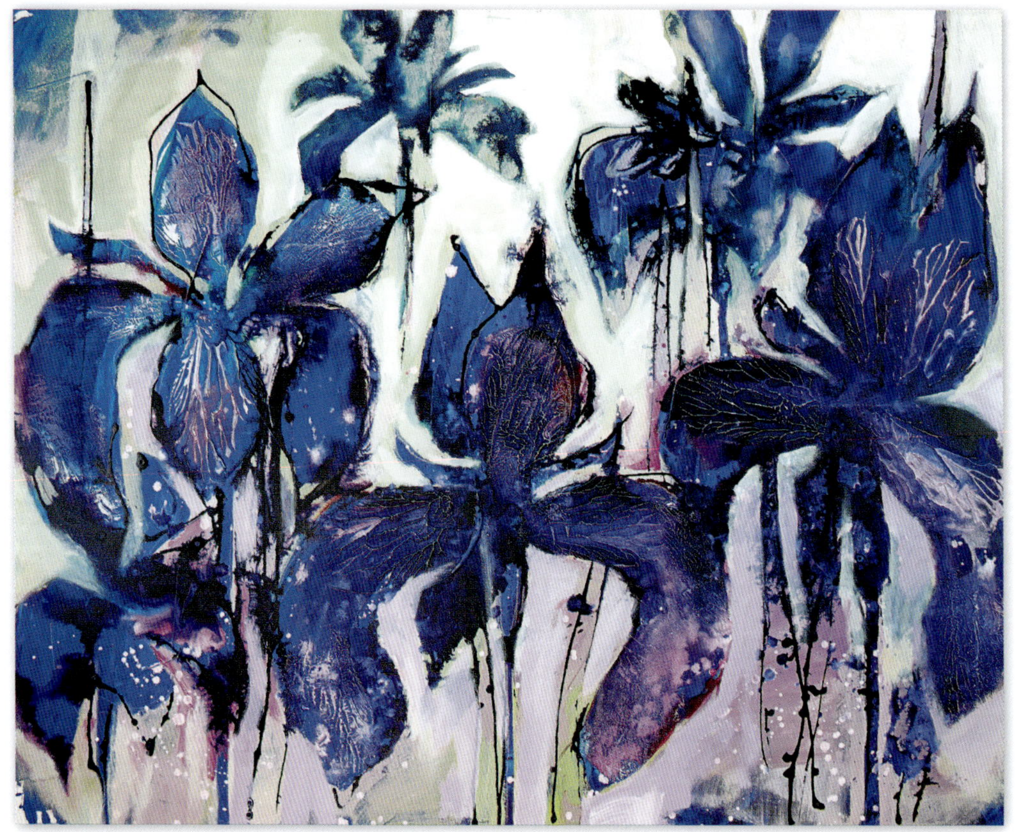

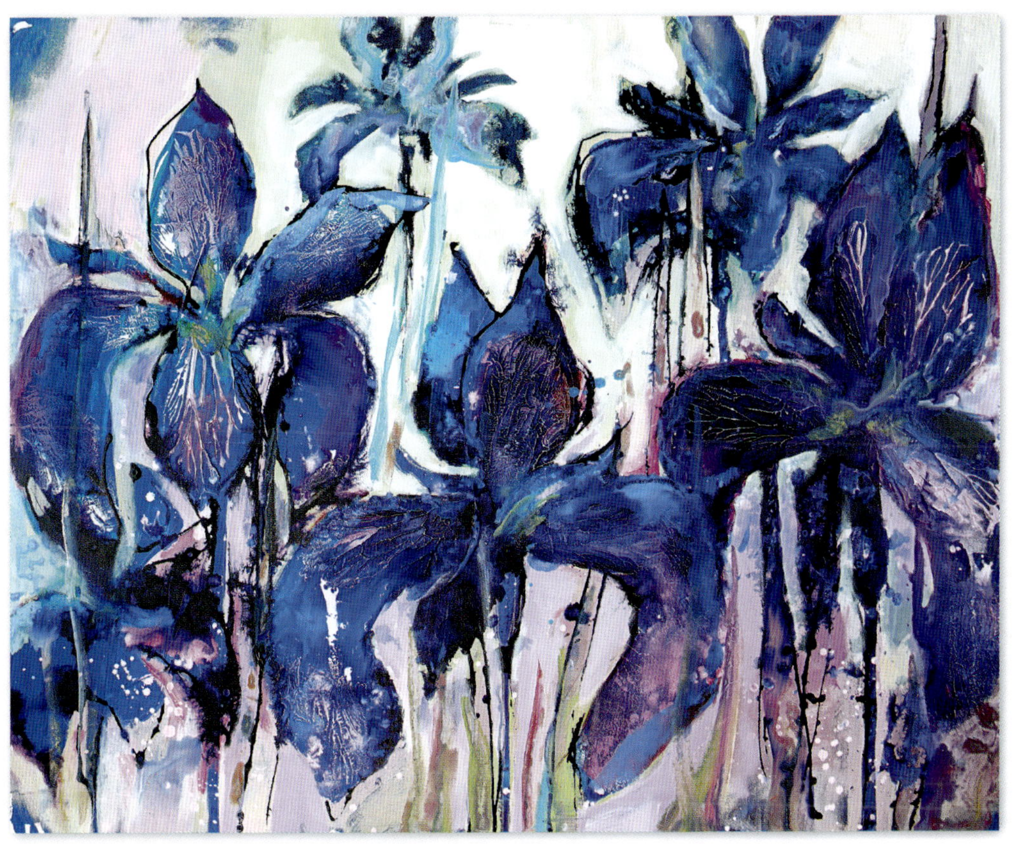

Step 6

Use light-green shades mixed from pastel yellow and cerulean blue to paint the pre-outlined vertical leave shapes. Add shades of blue lightened with titanium white to the petals. When doing so, give each flower its own color accent. Add a pastel-yellow glaze to the centers of the flowers. Reduce the dominance of the back flowers by lightening them with shades of blues mixed with a lot of titanium white, to create a perception of depth. In the background, the light pastel shades vary from pink to light blue, light violet, light yellow, and sand. They are mixed by adding a small amount of color to a lot of titanium white.

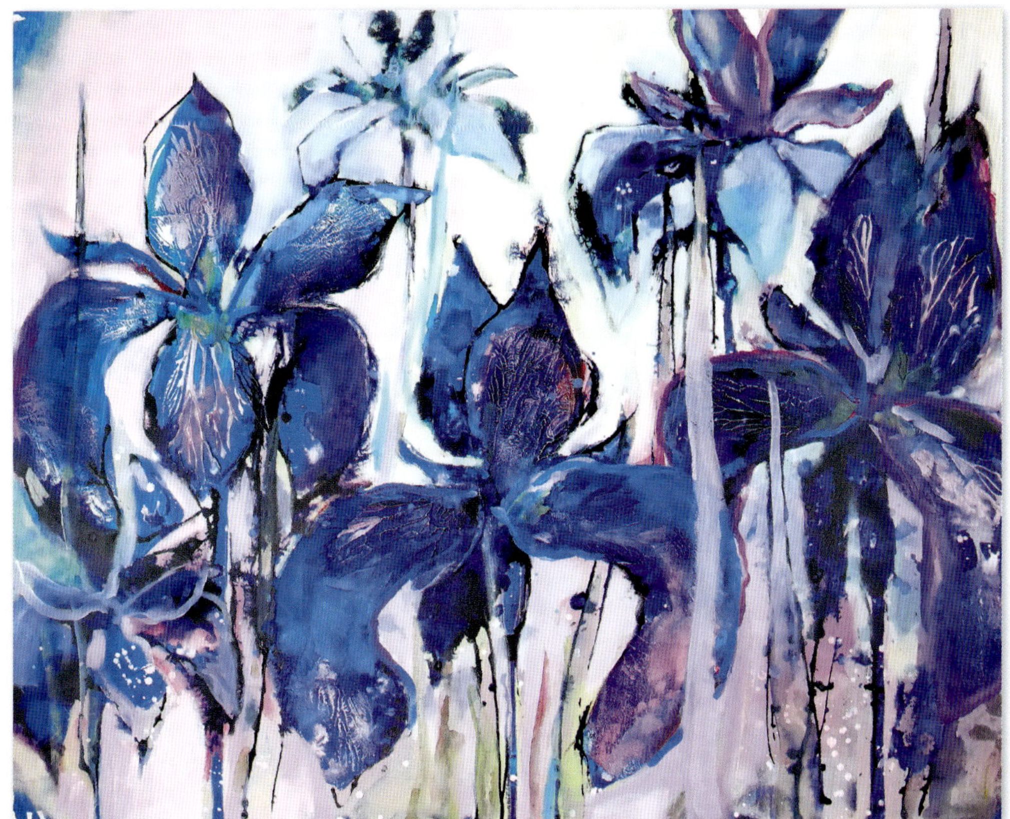

Step 7

Further lighten the flowers in the background. Use a broad natural hair brush to paint over a few splats in the upper section of the picture to create calm. Calm zones in the picture background create a pleasant contrast to the detailed and heavily structured flower heads. Use various shades that match the colors of the flowers to trace the outline and occasionally add new outlines that remain unfilled with color. Emphasize some of the vertical leaves with color.

Step 8

Use acrylic paint directly out of the tube to create outlines of the flowers on the canvas, using cyan blue for the center flower, dark violet for the right one, and turquoise for the left one. Add magenta drawing ink in a few places and spray with water so that it runs. In doing so, create a heavy emphasis on the lower-right section of the picture. Add a few splats of a mixture of titanium white with a little cyan blue and turquoise to the flower heads at the back. Also paint this mix as a glaze on a few petals. Allow to dry.

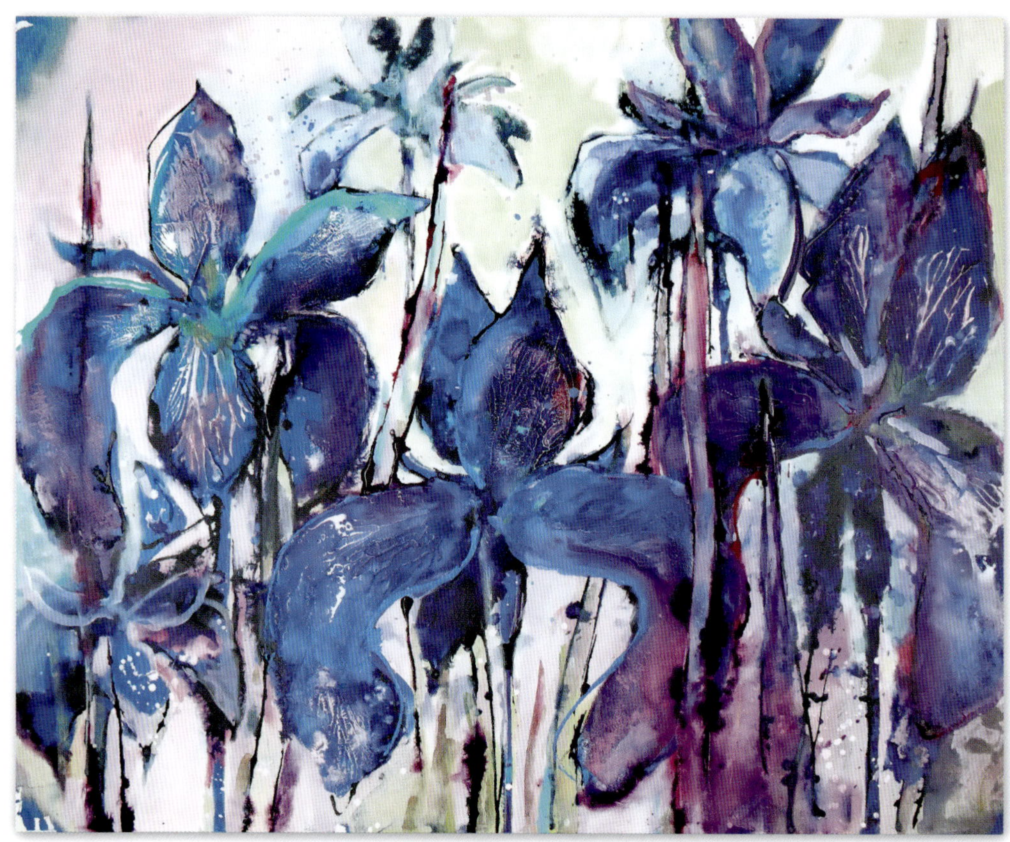

Close-Up

The runs from the drawing ink collect on the veins made of putty, which emphasizes the structures. The pigment of the acrylic glazes stands out clearly against the white putty. By sanding the thin ridges, the veins are particularly highlighted. Combined with the ink that blooms after being sprayed by water, these techniques form a game of coincidences, in which painting primarily fulfills calming and correcting functions.

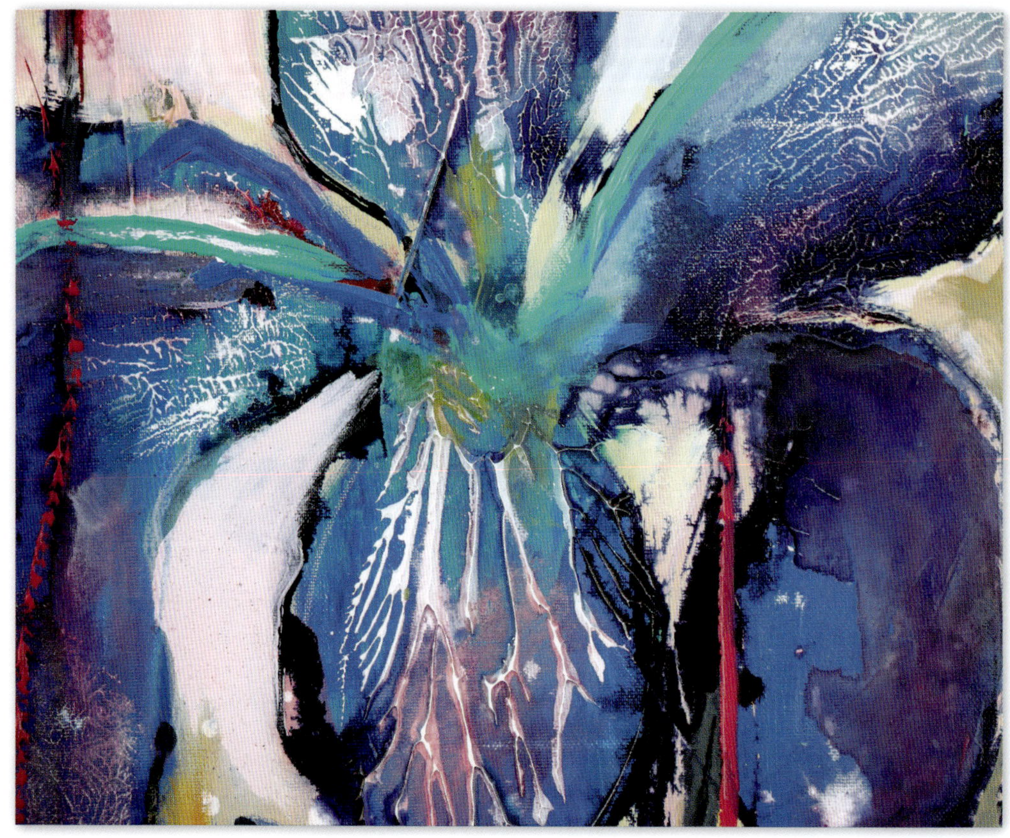

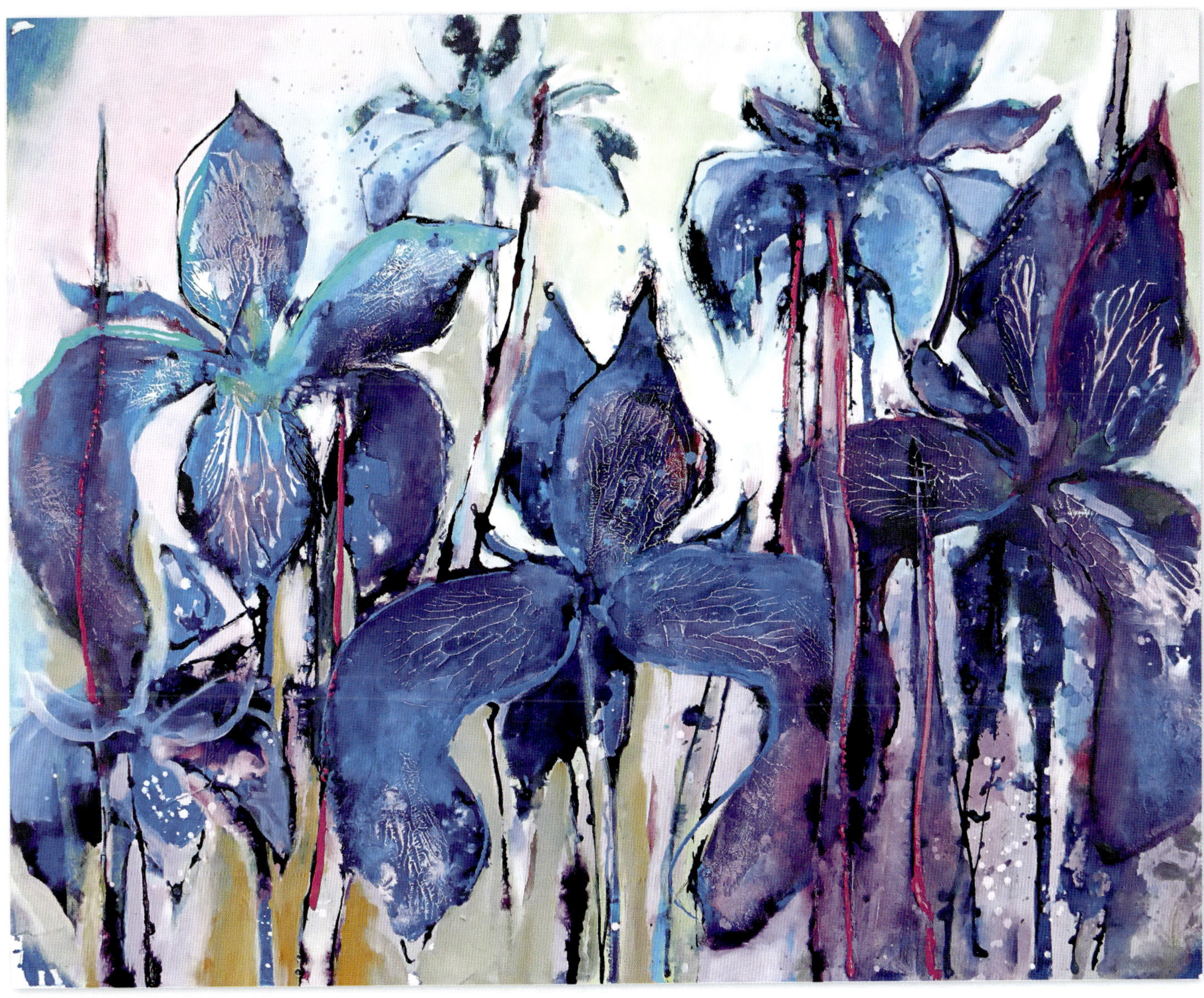

Finished Painting

Once again, use the sandpaper to sand the putty veins and remove the dust. In the lower-left section, add natural sienna and a somewhat fragmented green mixed with titanium white, natural sienna, and cyan blue. These two shades remain exclusively in the lower section of the picture and are not used elsewhere.

It creates a quantity contrast. Finally, draw thick magenta lines with paint directly from the tube along some leaves and one of the petals of the right-hand flower. Thanks to the emphasized overlapping of the vertical leaves over the central flower, the dominant central position is mitigated.

Foxgloves

Materials:

- Canvas, 24 x 28 in.
- Acrylic paints in titanium white, cadmium yellow, rose, orange, cadmium red, magenta, light blue, light green, dark violet, and Prussian blue
- Broad synthetic bristle brush, size 30
- Angular brush, size 10
- Watercolor pencils in carmine red, orange, magenta, dark magenta, dark blue, and dark violet
- Binder and container
- Oil pastels in white, pale yellow, skin, rose, magenta, dark red, and light violet
- Painter's palette

Foxgloves grow on the edges of the woodlands and look beautiful in a romantic cottage garden. With their upright stature and characteristic flowers, they are one of summer's classic blooms. Foxgloves flower in bold colors, such as lilac, red, and yellow, but also in delicate white and pinks.

The numerous individual flowers on the botryoid stem are created with acrylic paint combined with vibrant oil pastels. A small network of lines drawn in dissolved watercolor pencils gives the flowers more structure and emphasizes their delicate shapes.

Step 1

Use a broad brush to paint a base layer on the canvas with water-diluted acrylic paints in the various colors of the foxglove. To do so, move the brush in a vertical direction and let the colors flow into each other. In the upper section, lighten the shades with titanium white. In contrast to nature, painting allows the shades within a plant to change. As a result, interesting color gradients are created that loosen the picture.

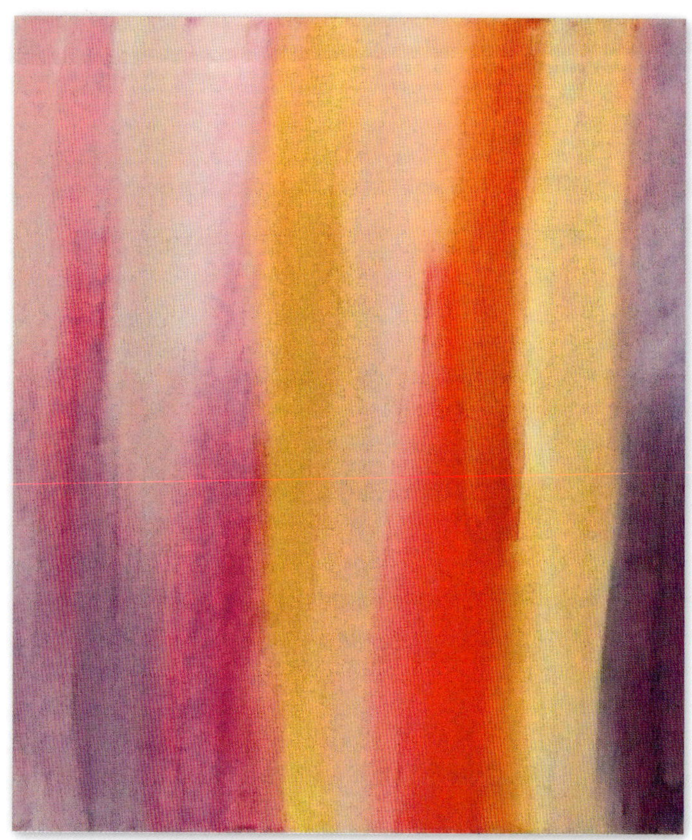

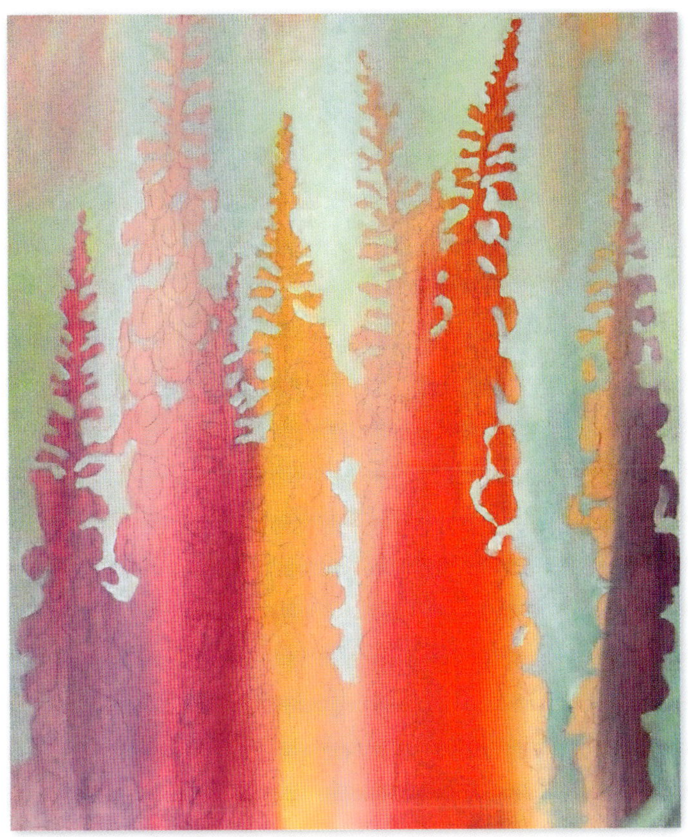

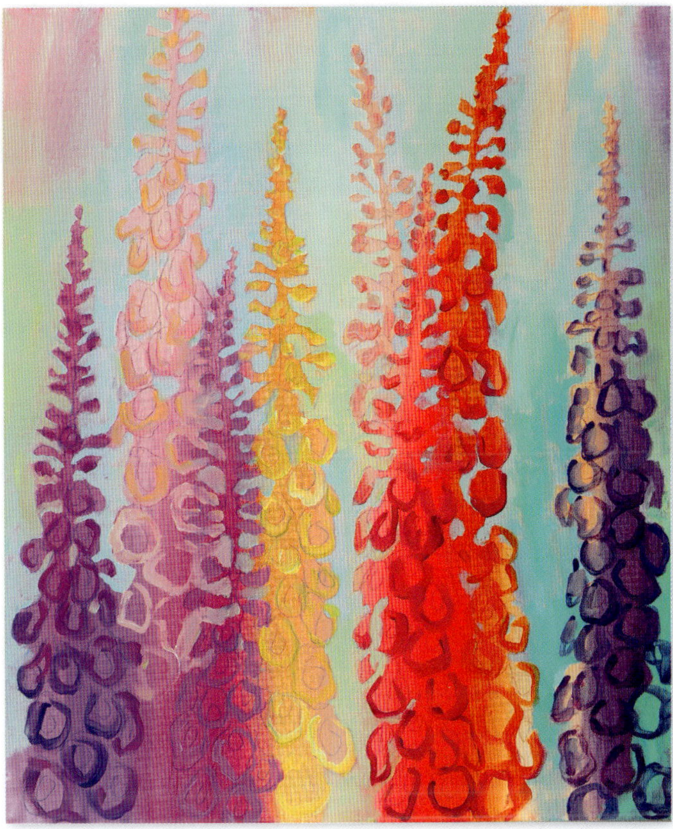

Step 2

Use the dark-magenta watercolor pencil to sketch the shapes. This step, in contrast to the following steps, should be carried out with precision. Ensure that the natural irregularities of the flower shapes remain clearly visible. Use the angular brush to paint the background in variations of light blue and light green. Paint around the flowers again, so that the flowers stand out. Leave some areas along the top edge of the picture unpainted.

Step 3

Use the acrylic paints to mix a color variation according to each plant and add outlines to the edges of the flowers. Work loosely. Show only a few flowers as a closed circle and predominantly draw open "U" forms. Dab paint on the closed upper flowers. Create flowing color changes within some plants.

Tip: The base colors run into each other, meaning that this technique sometimes creates plants that have a color gradient consisting of two shades. Although it isn't realistic, it's very picturesque.

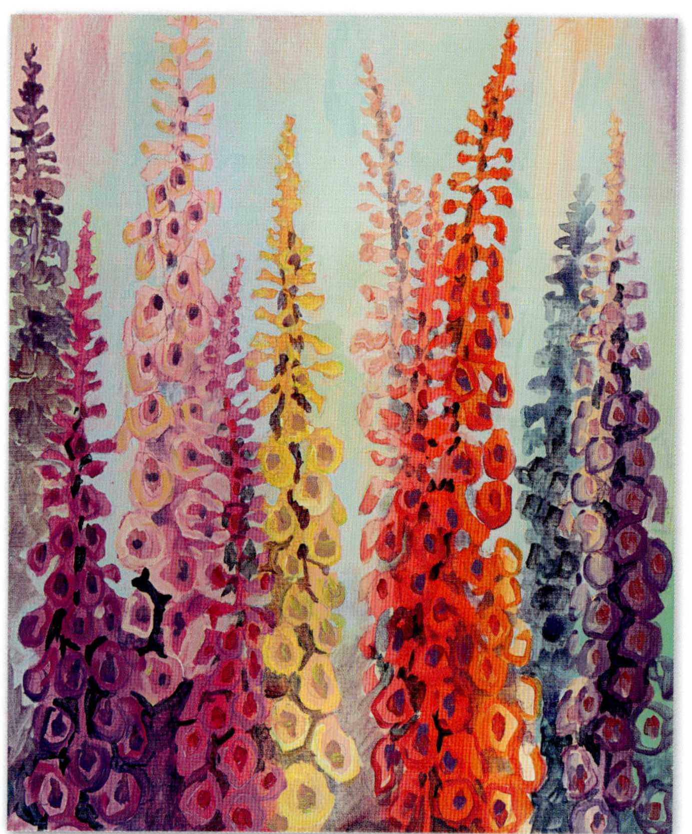

Step 4

Add dark loose circles to the centers of the flowers. Use different shades so that each plant is truly individual. The color choices do not have to correspond to nature. Add some darkness in Prussian blue to the lower section of the picture and intensify the center of each plant along the stalk. Add two further foxgloves as dark silhouettes in the background.

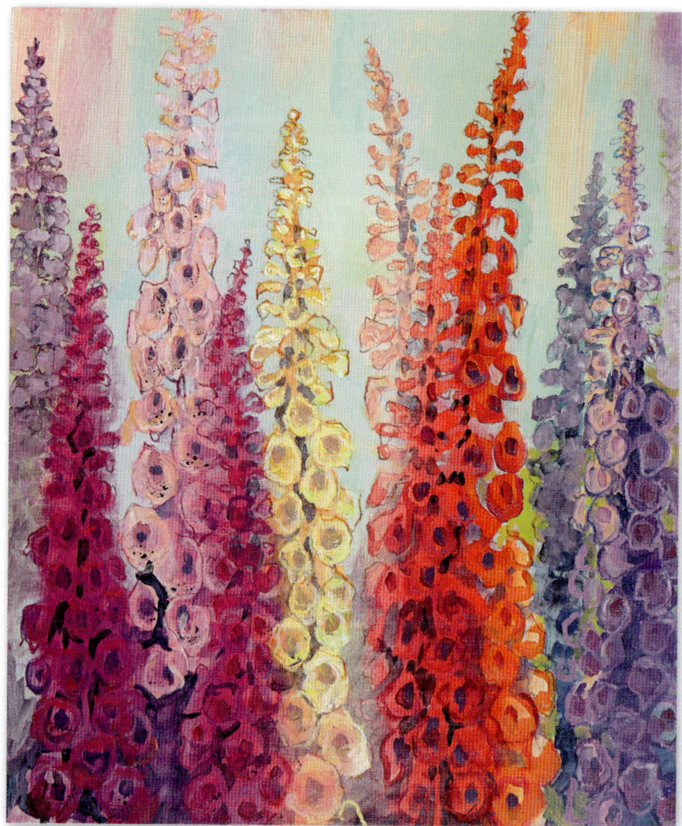

Step 5

Select oil pastels according to the flower color and loosely go around the outlines of the flowers. In places, overlay the colors and mix them. Add a few daps to the lower petals on a few flowers. Select watercolor pencils according to the petal colors, and dip in water-diluted binder and use to go over the outlines. Work loosely and add empty shapes. Add a small amount of light green to the background.

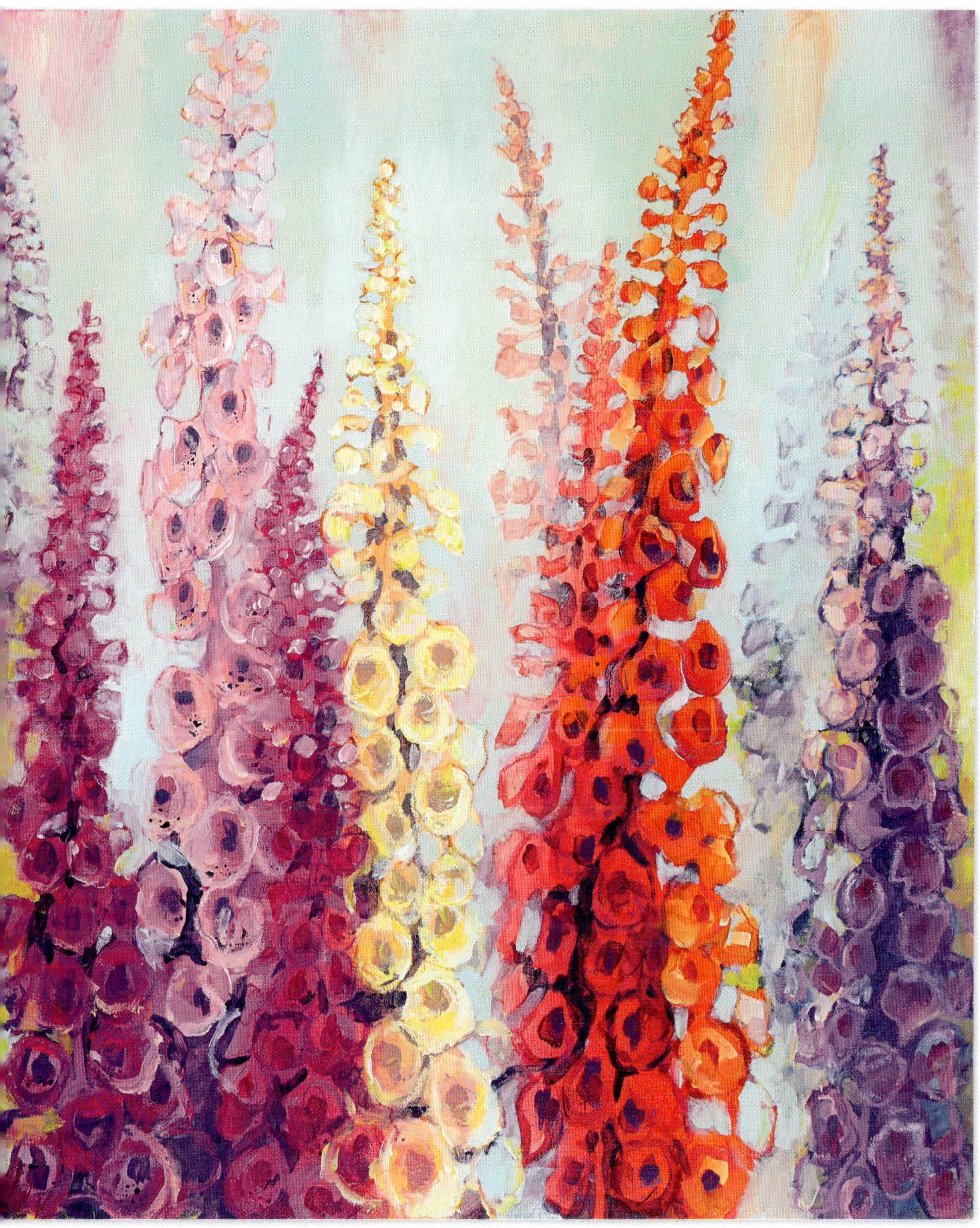

Finished Painting

Paint over the most recently added foxgloves. Because the background colors run within them, they appear misty, which allows a depth effect to be created. Continue to connect the background and foreground by using some of the light blue of the background in a few places in the lower section of the picture. Paint light green mixed with cadmium yellow on the left and right edges of the painting. Slightly lighten the tips of the foxgloves with titanium white and make them lighter than the opened flowers. Keep lightly working over all sections so that the individual layers of the various media show through each other.

Dandelion Flowers and Seeds

Materials:

- Stretch frame, 22 x 36 in.
- Jute sack
- Acrylic paints in titanium white, cadmium yellow, Indian yellow, orange, light green, olive green, dark violet, Prussian blue, light umber, and burnt umber
- Broad synthetic bristle brush, size 30
- Round natural hair brush, size 2
- Watercolor pencil in white
- Fine putty
- Binder
- Palette knife with thin, long blade
- Rags
- Painter's palette

Material for stretching the jute sack:

- Stapler and staples
- Hammer
- Tongs
- Scissors

Dandelions grow nearly everywhere and are one of the most healthy and versatile edible wild herbs ever. I allow them to grow and bloom freely in a few places in my garden because I believe them to be beautiful and important. For their picture, they get a special canvas: self-stretched jute on a stretch frame. The rough jute material underlines the dandelions' natural strength. The paints are bold and intense and the composition spreads beyond the frame, just like the dandelions themselves.

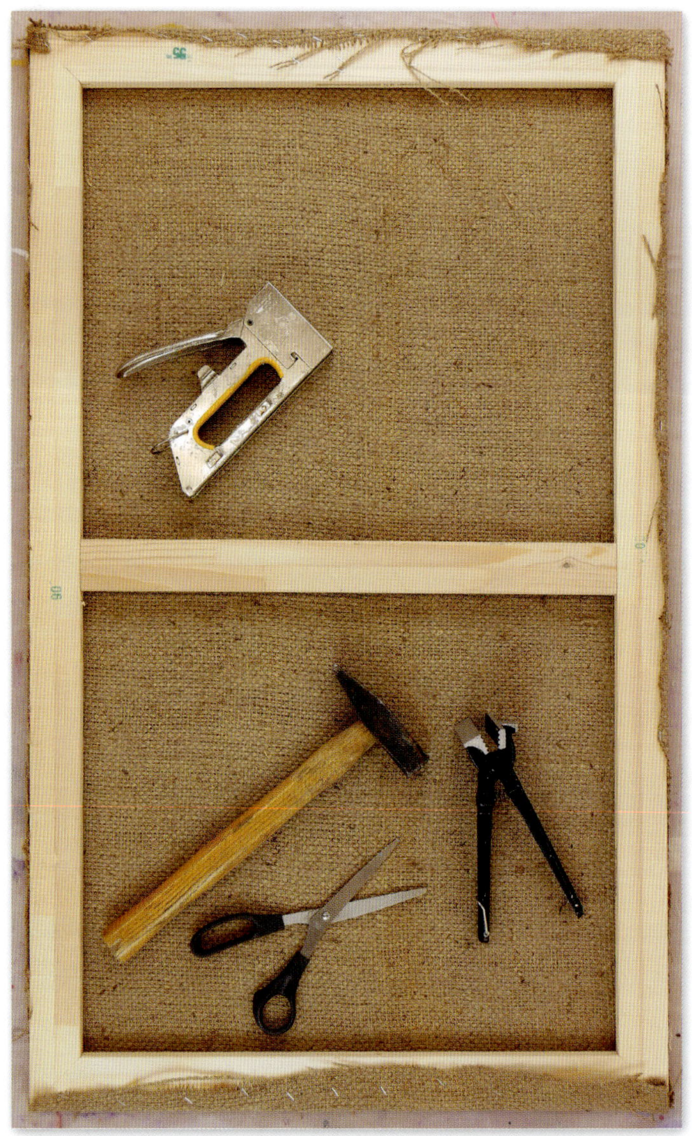

Step 1

For the stretch frame, buy four batons of wood that match the size of the jute sack. The material must be 2.5 to 3 inches larger than the frame on all sides. Use a hammer to knock together the miter corners and check the right angle. From the center of a long baton, use a stapler to secure the jute with a few staples. Use tongs to pull the material to the center of the opposite baton, and staple in place. Staple the jute to the centers of the short batons in the same way. Finally, stretch the fabric diagonally and staple up to the corners.

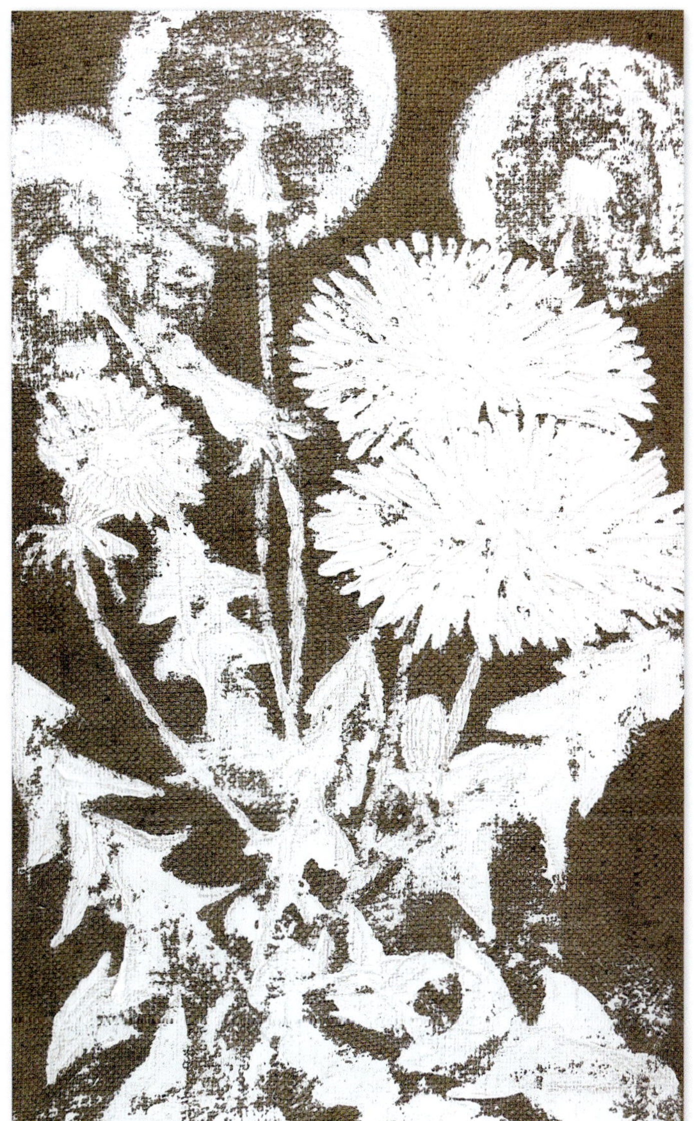

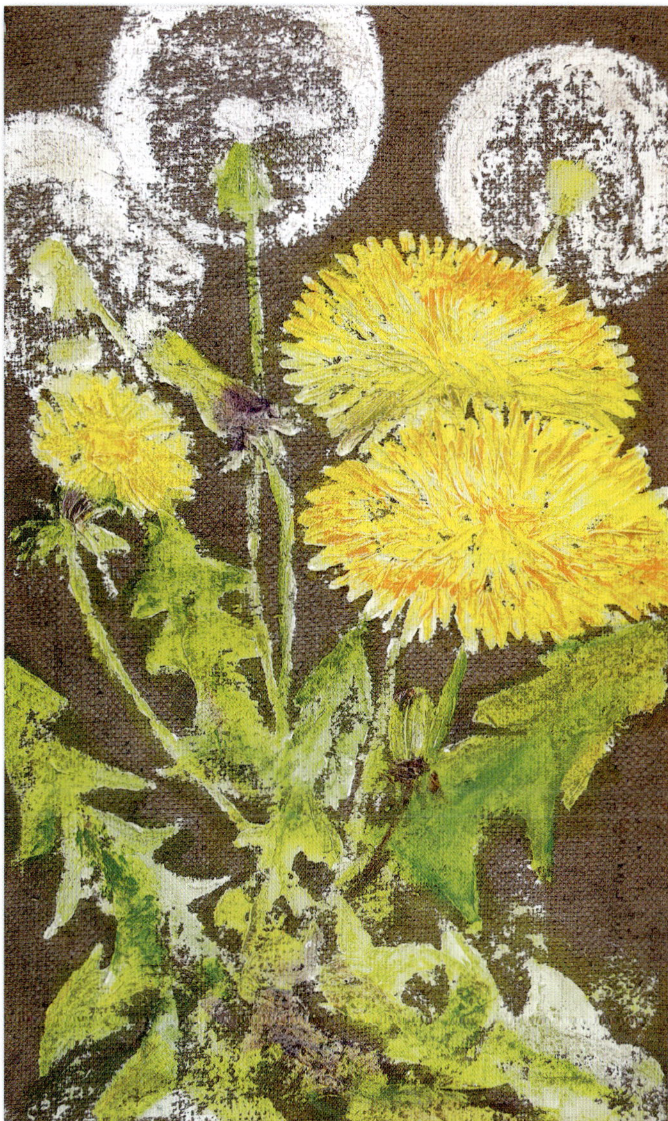

Step 2

Use a broad brush to add a base coat of binder so that you can paint on the material later, without it absorbing the paint. Let dry. Use a white watercolor pencil to sketch the shape of the plants. Use a palette knife to fill the shapes with a fine putty. For the flowers, work the petals from the edges toward the centers. Cover the seeds fully on the edges. Do not add a putty base coat to the full surface of the leaves, but leave some free space.

Step 3

Mix cadmium yellow with a little water and apply to the flowers with a broad brush. When doing so, wipe the brush on the ridges so that as much paint as possible collects in the dells. Work with different shades of yellow. Give the petals at the back a slight shadow. Occasionally use a rag to wipe some paint from the leaves so that it looks patchy. The paint may run over the putty onto the jute. Add some accents in dark violet.

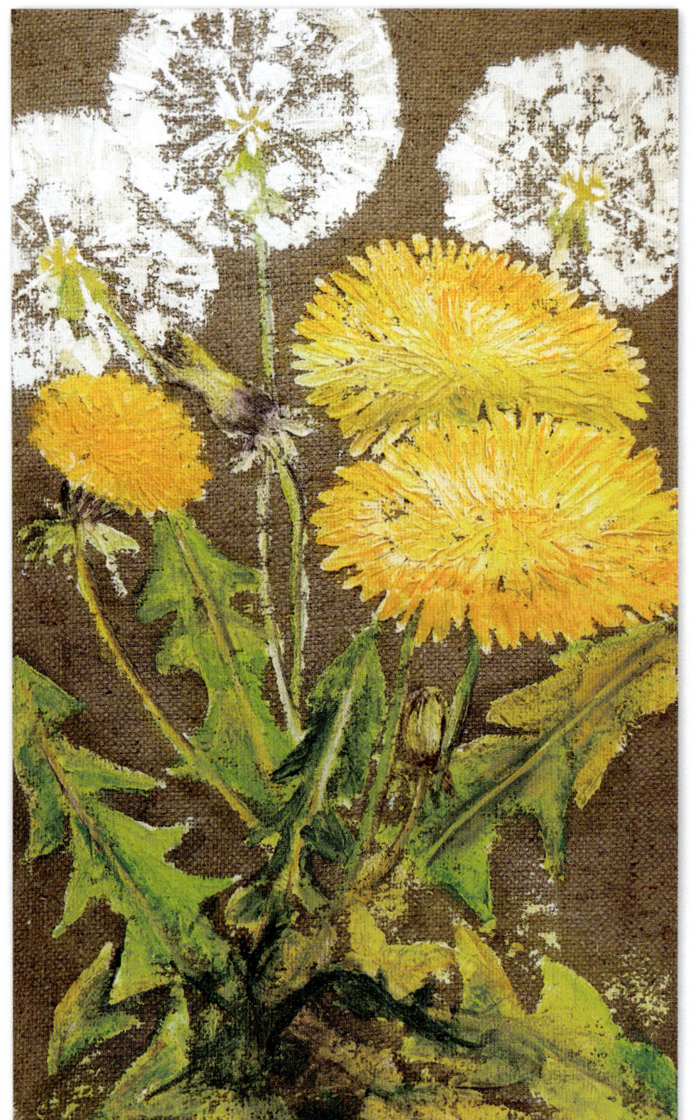

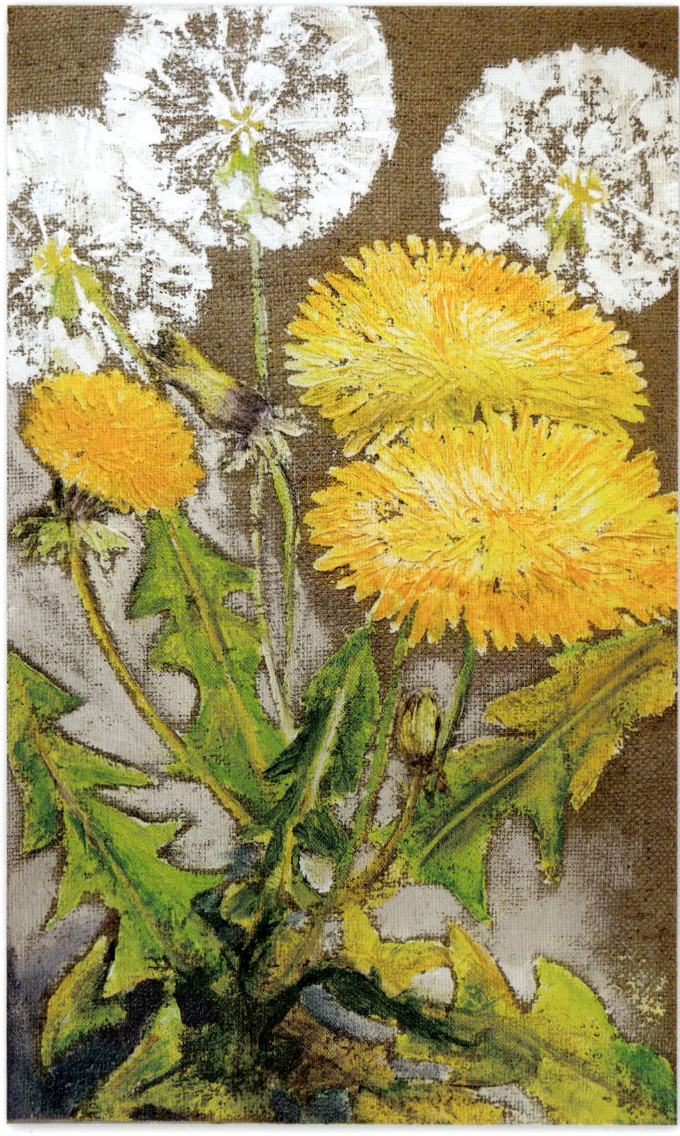

Step 4

Use a fine brush to paint on the central leaf vein. Cover the shaded areas with burnt umber and olive green. Add details to the flowers with a dark yellow made of cadmium yellow and a little burnt umber, so that they appear more sculpted. Go over the seeds with a glaze of titanium white and burnt umber. Dab them with white paint and add some lines of putty radiating from the centers, using the edge of the palette knife.

Step 5

Add light umber to the left section of the background and run it diagonally through the picture. When the paint is dry, rub the edge to create a smoother transition to the brown of the jute sack. Leave a gap between the background and the plant shape so that the brown color of the jute sack forms a border. Concentrate Prussian blue and dark violet in the bottom left corner.

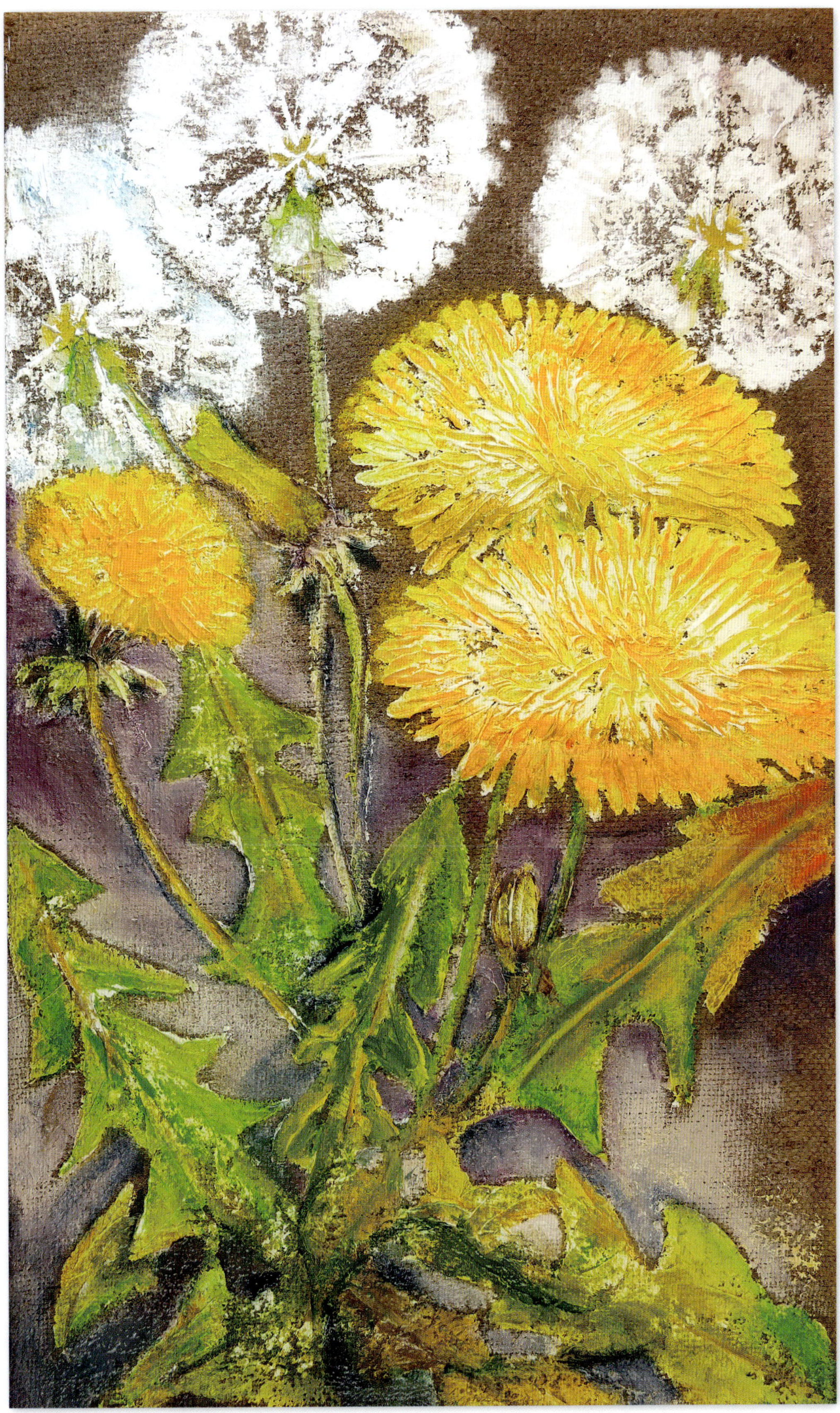

Finished Painting

Add dark violet below the flowers so that a complementary contrast is created. Add a light glaze of Prussian blue to the left seed pod. Add a few accents in Prussian blue along the stems and the leaves. Add Prussian blue and burnt umber to a few spots. Finally, add orange and some burnt umber to the top of a dandelion leaf. Adding these small amounts of new shades in the picture is called quantity contrast. It's best not to position these colors in the center of the picture, but rather on the edge. A quantity contrast enlivens the painting.

Tip: As soon as you've learned the art of stretching, it is a good idea to use nonstandard picture sizes. It creates the attraction of the unusual. In addition to jute and linen, with their various structures, printed cotton fabric can also be used. However, pay attention that the fabric is taut and will not stretch further.

Buddleia

Materials:

- Canvas, 28 x 40 in.
- Acrylic paints in titanium white, cadmium yellow, madder red, magenta, Prussian blue, dark violet, and black
- Flat synthetic bristle brush, size 30
- Angular brush, sizes 10 and 12
- Round natural hair brush, size 1
- Watercolor pencil in white
- Nepalese Lokta paper with flower pattern
- Cleaning sponge
- Binder
- Painter's palette

Butterflies, bumblebees, and honeybees hover around the magnificent clusters of flowers on the buddleia bush. The long panicles on the ends of the branches are studded with hundreds of tiny flowers.
However, only a few clusters are needed to show this abundance of flowers in this painting. Nepalese Lokta paper with a pattern of small flowers is added to the majority of clusters. This change in the surface creates a tension that enlivens the picture.

Section 1
Only some of the small flowers in the clusters need to be explicitly illustrated. Some small areas can remain unfinished. In this way, it allows the observer's imagination to add to these areas itself. The Nepalese Lokta paper is integrated using glazes and outlines.

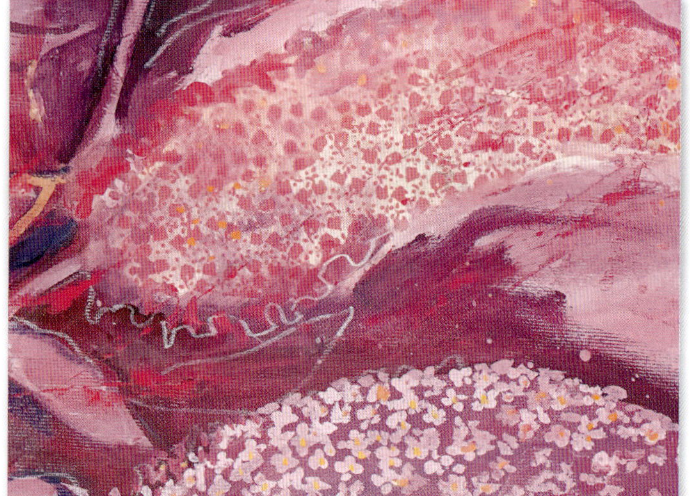

Section 2
The foliage is painted in the colors of the flowers in order to create the harmony of a limited color palette. The leaves are sometimes shown as outlines or sketchy shapes. They overlap and poke through each other to form a vibrant sea of leaves.

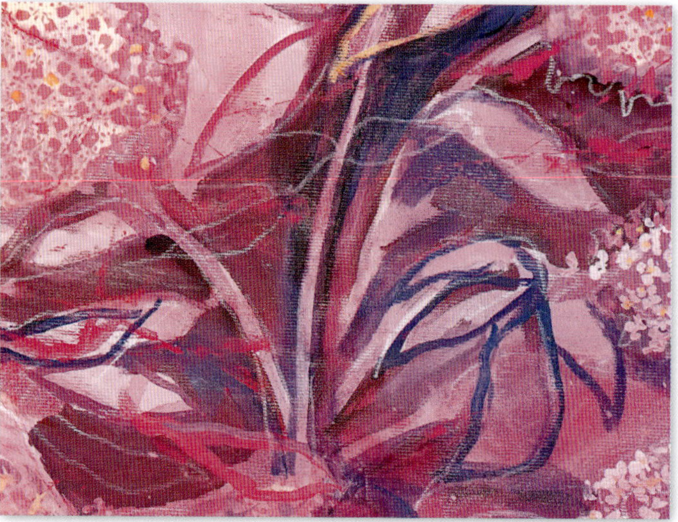

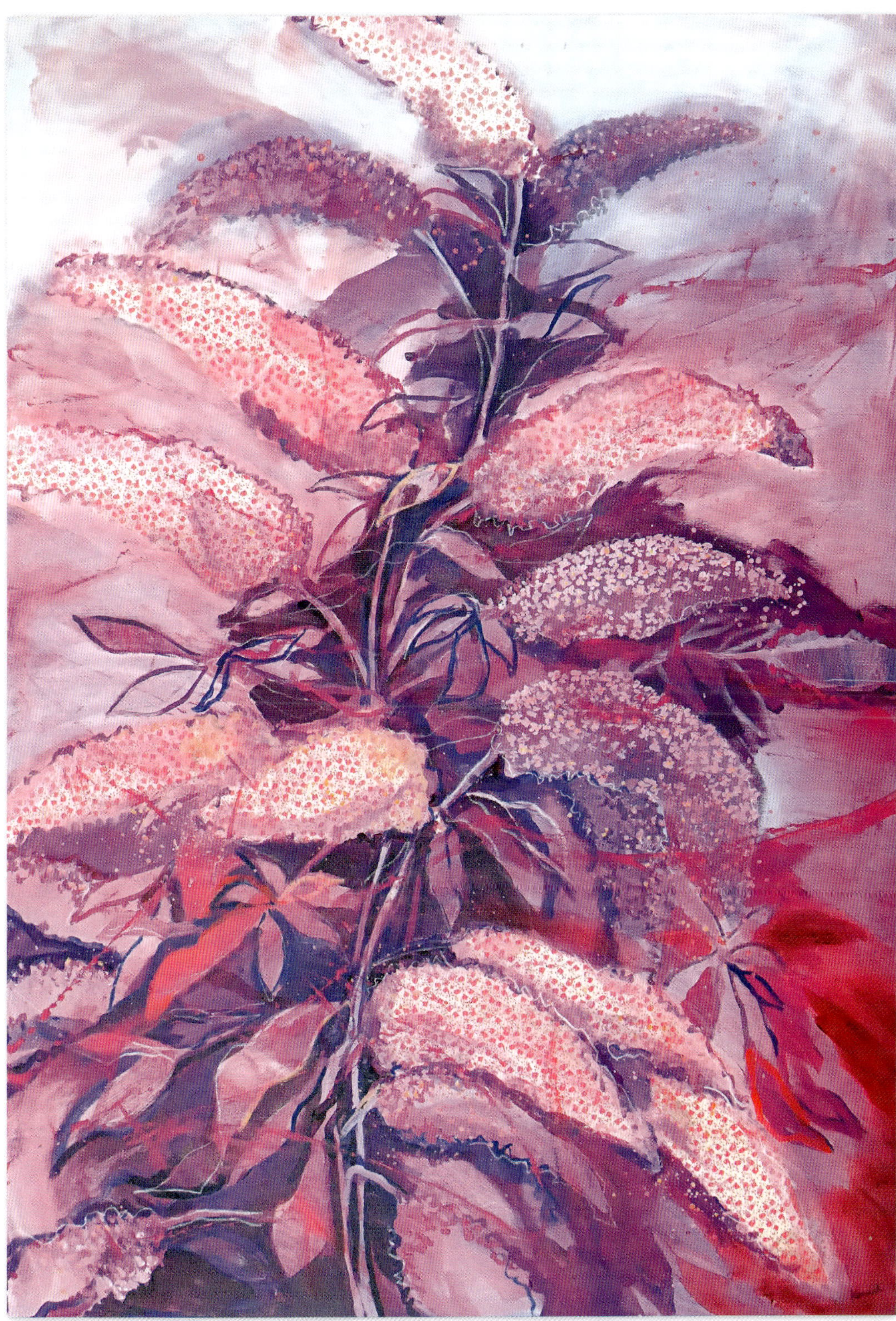

Instructions

Use a piece of cleaning sponge to apply a base coat of magenta and madder red. Sketch out the shapes with a white watercolor pencil. Roughly rip the Nepalese Lokta paper into the cone shapes of the flower clusters and use a broad brush and binder to glue them in place. Paint the background with dark violet that has been lightened up with titanium white, and add dark violet to the center of the shrub. For a few flower clusters, use a fine natural hair brush to add a slight color gradient in order to create a vivid image. Paint a glaze over the shaded areas. Add detail to the leaf outlines in different shades of blue and violet. Use a white watercolor pencil to trace the outlines. Add splats of paint and smudge in places. Add a strong madder red to the right section of the picture.

Lemon Blossom

Materials:

- Canvas, 32 x 32 in.
- Acrylic paints in titanium white, lemon yellow, cadmium yellow, magenta, sap green, olive green, dark violet, light umber, light gray, and black
- Watercolor pencil in dark green
- Angular brush, sizes 10 and 12
- Finishing spatula, 6 in.
- Charcoal pencil
- Thin cardboard
- Rags
- Painter's palette

When the lemon trees flower in Spain, the fruits and blossom decorate the tree at the same time. The bold yellow of the lemons and the exotic, irregular growth of the branches form a contrast to the delicate pink flowers.
The shadow areas are painted in shades of violet as a complementary contrast that makes the yellow of the lemons glow more intensely. Finally, the subject is covered in a glaze, using dynamic brushstrokes, and then dappled with vibrant yellow spatters, which are reminiscent of the shimmering heat of southern Europe.

Step 1

Place the cardboard under the stretch frame of the canvas so that the wooden cross does not leave marks when using the spatula. Squirt lemon yellow, cadmium yellow, and sap green directly from the tubes onto the canvas. Use the spatula to distribute them in all directions. If any ridges are made, just leave them. Concentrate the green in the lower section. Make some scratches with the spatula. Let dry.

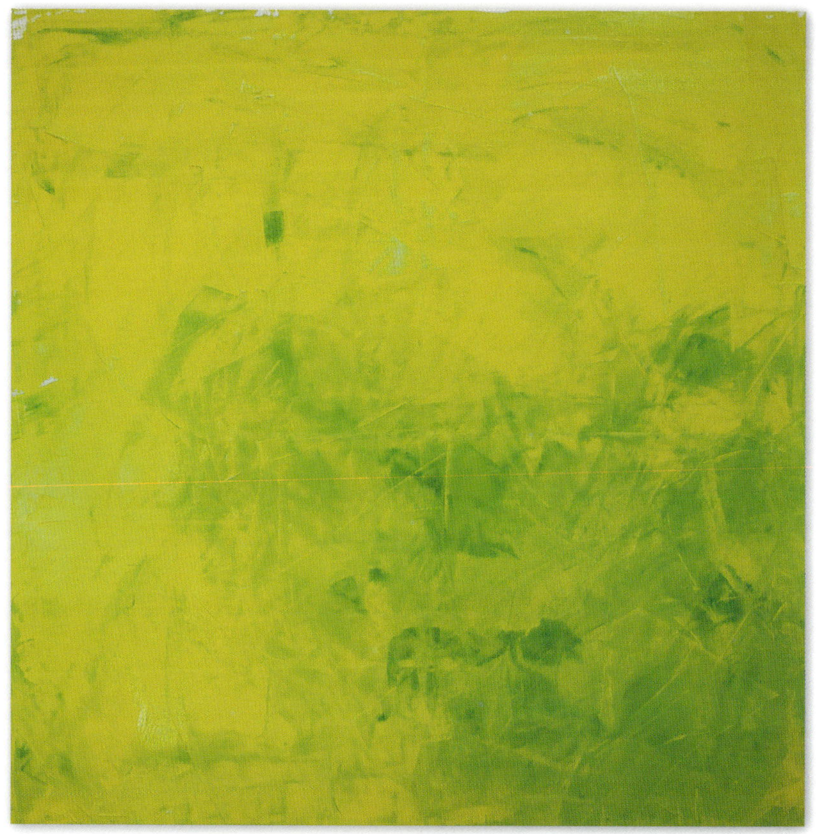

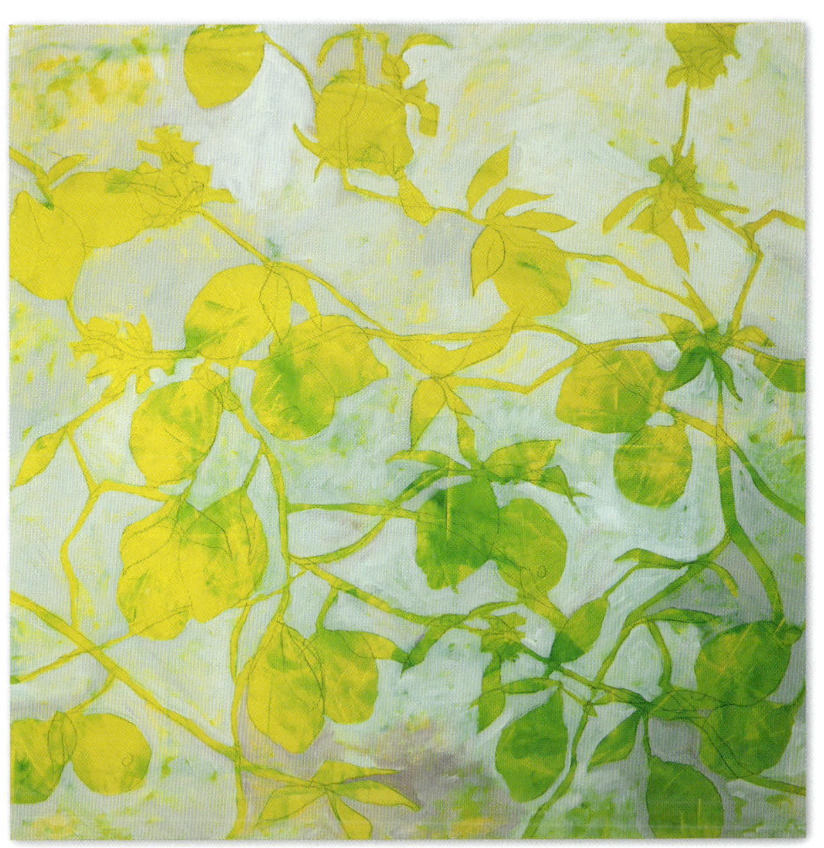

Step 2

Use a dark-green watercolor pencil to sketch out the lemons, the branches, and foliage. Mix titanium white with some lemon yellow, light gray, and light umber and use it to paint the background with an angular brush. The angular bush is well suited to exactly filling the small corners and fine edges of the negative space. Create slight color variations so that mixed shades are used and some sections are painted lighter and some darker. The yellow of the branches and the leaves appears particularly picturesque.

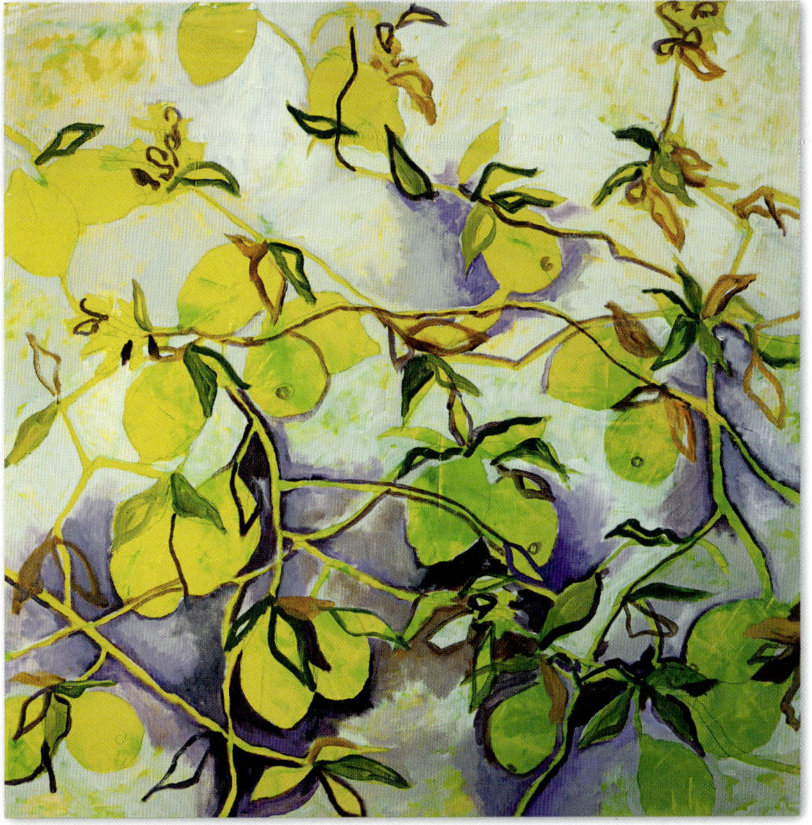

Step 3

Mix a glaze of dark violet and black and use the tip of the angular brush to draw outlines. Position some branches in front of the lemons, so that the fruits appear to be in the background. Work loosely. Shade the glaze with magenta as you work, so that different shades of brown are created. Add further outlines in a dark green mixed from olive green and black. Fill out some leaf shapes. Add some open leaf shapes that remain empty. In the lower section of the picture, add background areas, using a mixture of dark violet and titanium white. Leave the upper section of the picture light.

Step 4

Paint blossoms and buds, using titanium white and magenta. Use titanium white for the open flowers and bold magenta shades for the buds. Add mixed shades. Add exact detail to only a few flowers; loosely dab them in the other areas. This contrast between precision and looseness creates more tension than precisely defining all details. Also, painting empty leaf outlines is a helpful trick to create looseness. Add some shadows to the lemons and the leaves in a light brown mixed from lemon yellow, magenta, and a little black.

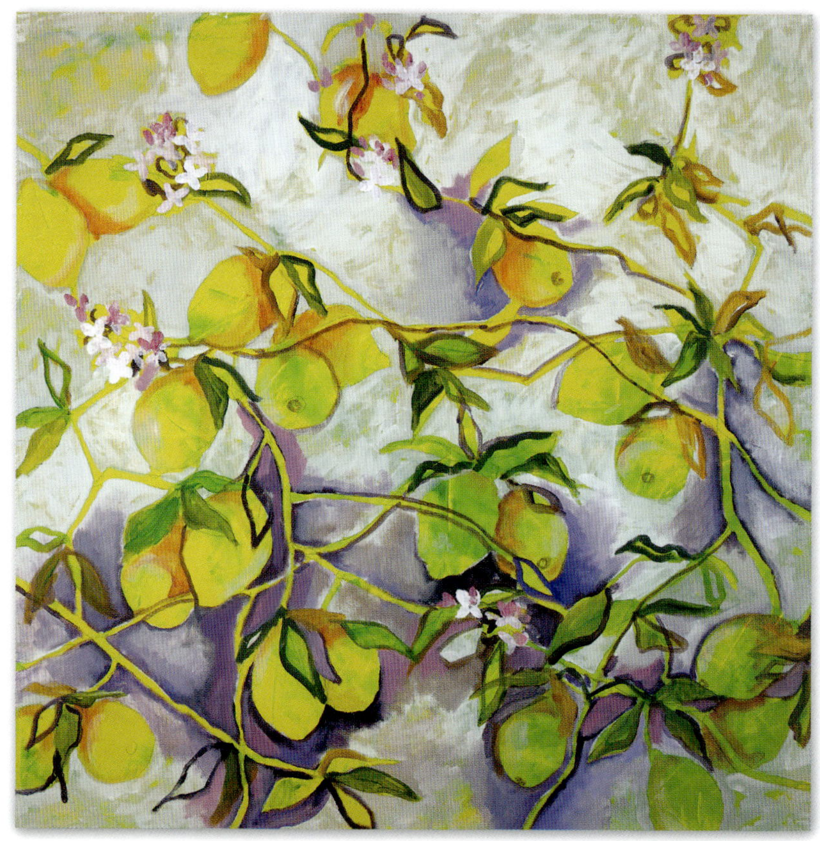

Step 5

Use the charcoal pencil to trace outlines and add new branches, flowers, and leaves. Also allow them to be overlapped so that they appear as a second level behind the first. The new leaves and branches keep the shade of the background, which is clearly lighter compared to the previous layer of paint. As a result, the second level appears farther away and creates the appearance of depth. These colors are slightly different from the natural colors of a lemon tree, which creates a painterly tension.

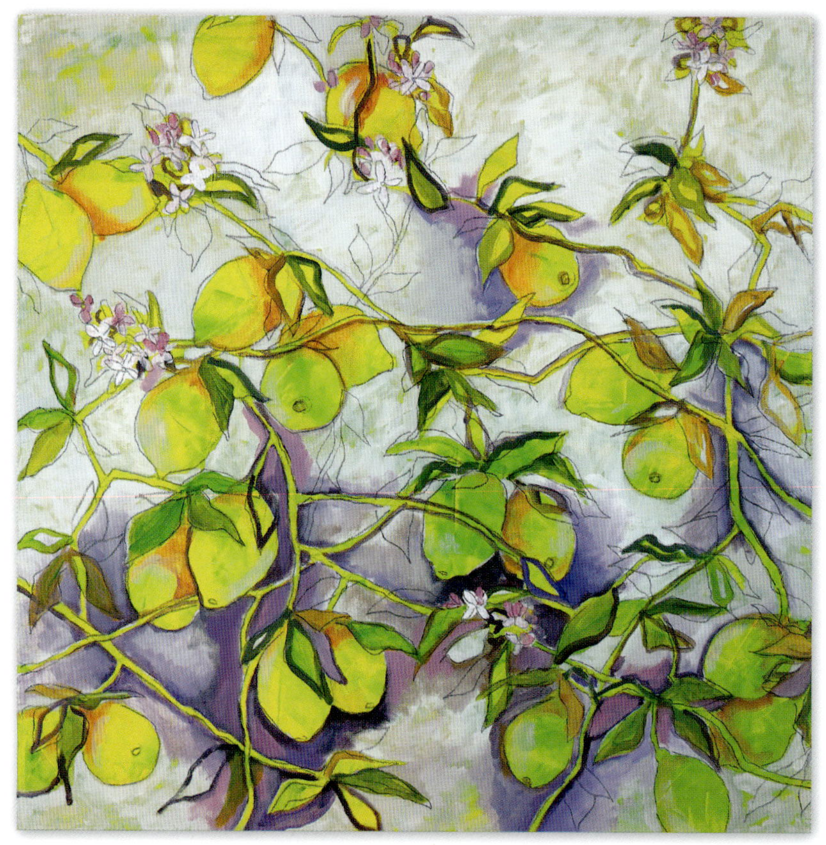

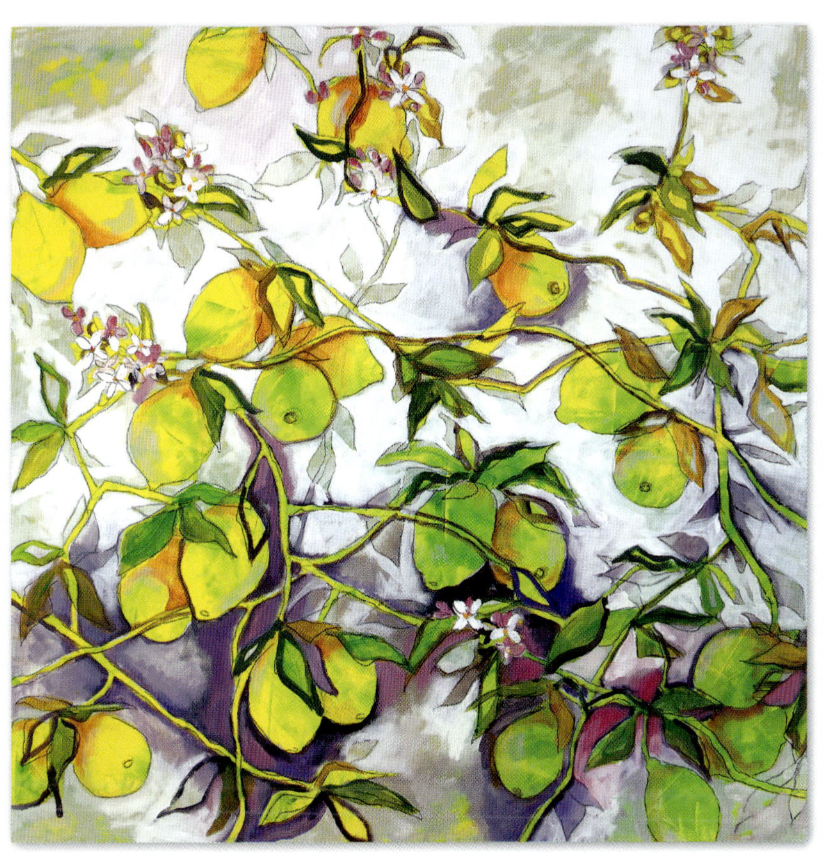

Step 6

Go over the background again with titanium white, light gray, and light umber. Mix the shades to be a little lighter than the previous layer, so that the shapes that were subsequently drawn will be visible. Work on the flowers, using cadmium yellow in the centers. Go over the background again. Leave some of the underlying colors untouched or only partially add new shades so that lively and diverse nuances come about. The combination of painting and sketch elements allows the loose character of sketch to be incorporated in the picture.

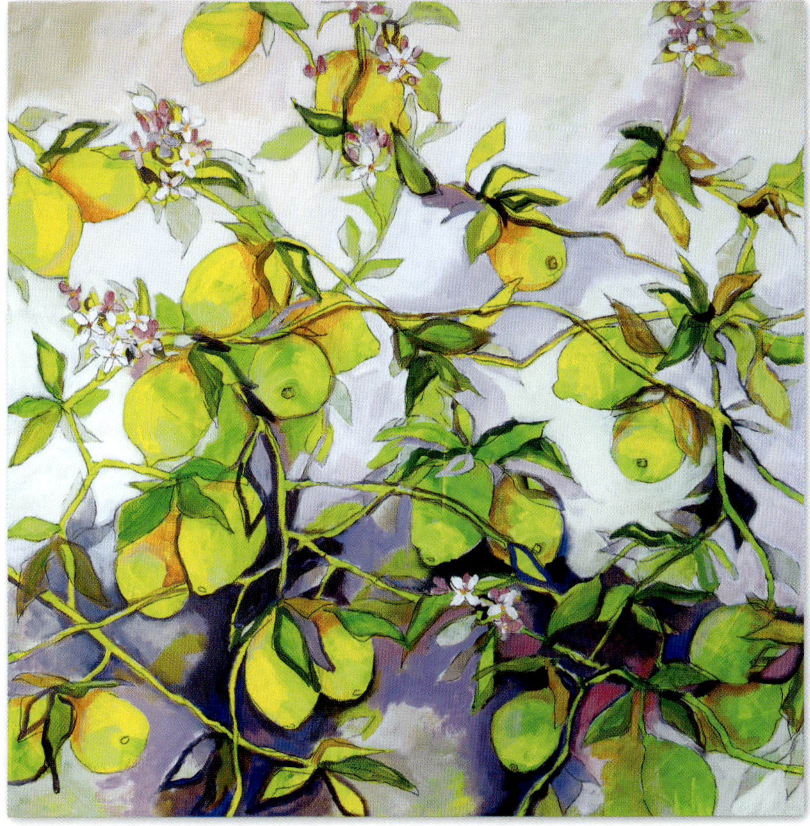

Step 7

Work on the lemons again, painting highlights in lemon yellow. Use a brush to add cadmium yellow so that it is opaque and so that it follows the round contours of the lemons to make the shape clear. Add a delicate lilac mixed from titanium white with a little dark violet to the background diagonally across the motif, up to the top edge of the picture. Paint a glaze in a shade mixed from sap green and lemon yellow on the leaves of the second level. Work loosely and do not completely fill many leaves. Intensify the dark violet in the lower section of the picture.

Step 8

Mix the paints on the palette with water to create thin glazes so that there are various mixed shades created from titanium white, sap green, dark violet, and citron yellow. Add loose, irregular strokes in a glaze of dark violet that has been lightened with titanium white around the violet shades. The paint underneath should show through. Areas where the paint has run may remain, so long as they do not create distracting puddles. Otherwise wipe them up with a rag. Often, once they have dried, the puddles create interesting patterns. Add the light-green and brown shades to the background along the branches. Some sections of the background remain untouched by the glazes.

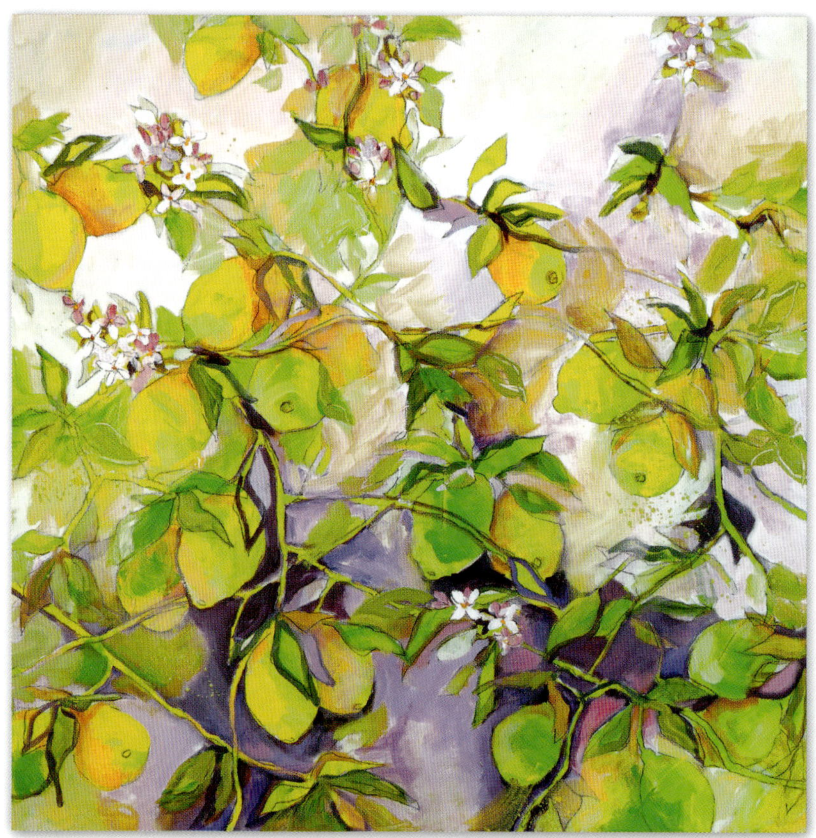

Close-Up

Dynamic acrylic painting leaves are loosely represented to let the viewer use their imagination. Leaf contours are scratched into the wet green paint of the other leaves. They sit alongside pencil outlines that have been partially edged with acrylic paint and partially left open. The paint is used as both covering and glazing. New shades—for example, a violet—break through the predominantly green leaves. The different media and techniques are laid over each other and show through each other, creating a vibrant juxtaposition of color and shape.

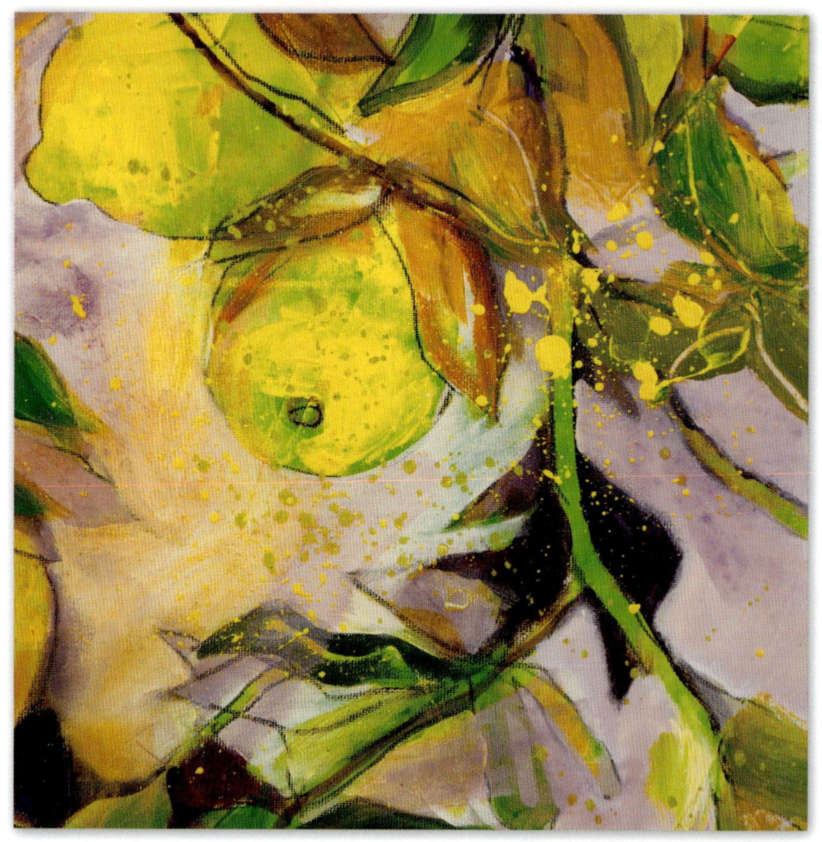

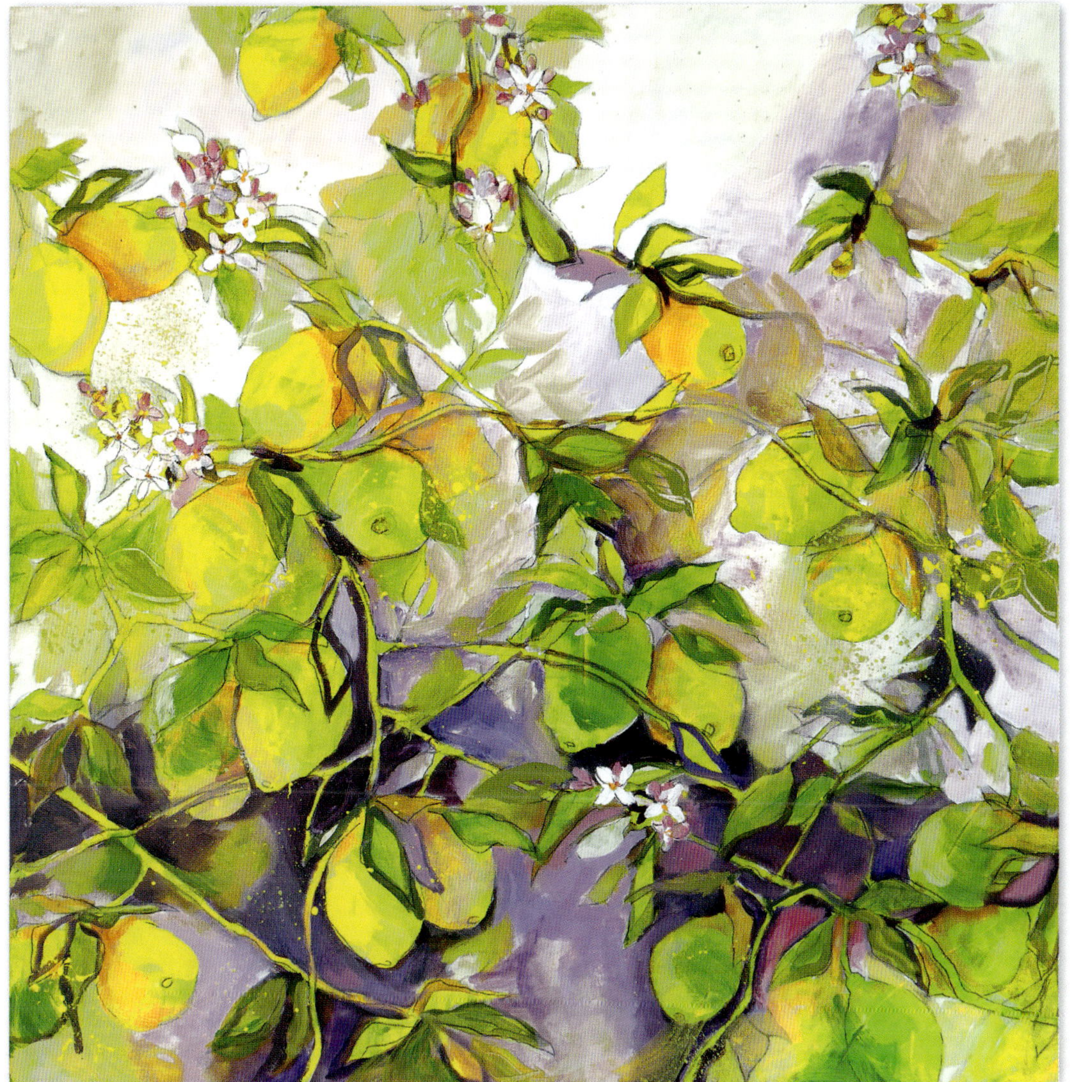

Finished Painting

Finally, add a few splats of cadmium yellow. Usually, splats are created with water-diluted paint. As a result, they lose their vibrance, which is particularly true for yellows. So that the yellow splats keep their intensity, use the paint without diluting it. To do so, turn an almost empty tube of cadmium yellow on its head and use force to expel the air. A tube with a pointed nozzle is particularly suitable for this technique. The splats will not have a uniform size, will have a few runs, and are very opaque.

Tip: The liveliness of a painting can be increased by the style on its own. When glazed and covered sections alternate, when some areas are painted by brush and in other areas the spatula is used, and when precisely defined details are found next to blurred, loosely drawn elements, a diverse and dynamic surface is created. Quick brushstrokes add to this character.

Pink Delphiniums

Materials:

- Canvas, 24 x 28 in.
- Acrylic paints in titanium white, rose, cadmium yellow, cadmium red, madder red, magenta, cyan blue, olive green, dark violet, sand, and light gray
- Flat synthetic bristle brush, size 30
- Angular brush, sizes 10 and 12
- Watercolor pencils: in dark red and dark violet
- Wallpaper seam roller
- Binder and container
- Palette knife with a small blade
- Painter's palette

Delphiniums are royalty among summer flowers and are truly magnificent perennials. They enrich any summer garden with their striking clusters of flowers. Delphiniums not only bloom in bright blues but can also flower in an unusual pink.
To create a vivid contrast, a light-blue stem of flowers is positioned among its pink companions. Using a wallpaper seam roller from the hardware store to apply acrylic paints leaves slightly haptic structures, which imitates the subtlety of the delicate petals by painting over and scratching it.

Step 1

Use a broad, flat brush to paint a base layer on the canvas in titanium white, cadmium red, madder red, and magenta. Move the brush in a vertical manner. In the upper section of the picture, use more titanium white. Sketch the flowers with the dark-red watercolor pencil. To better distinguish the flowers, cover the outlines and a part of the background with a sand-colored glaze. Use the wallpaper seam roller to paint the petal shapes with undiluted acrylic paint, which allows a texture to be created.

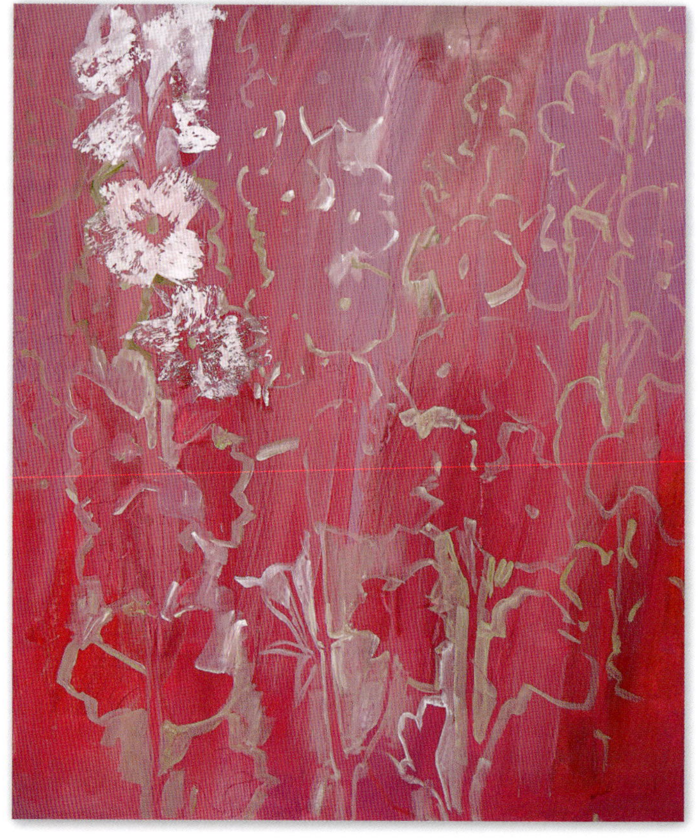

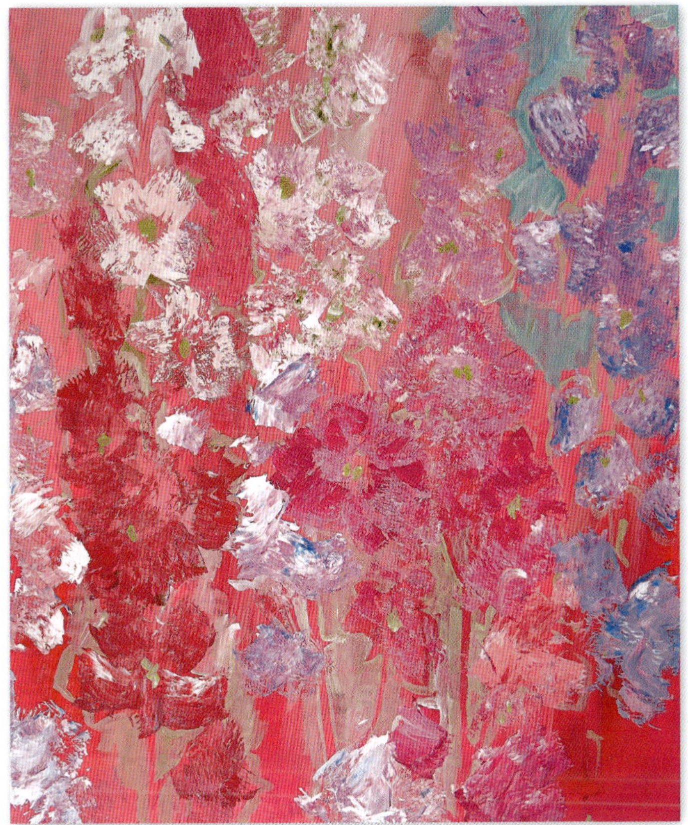

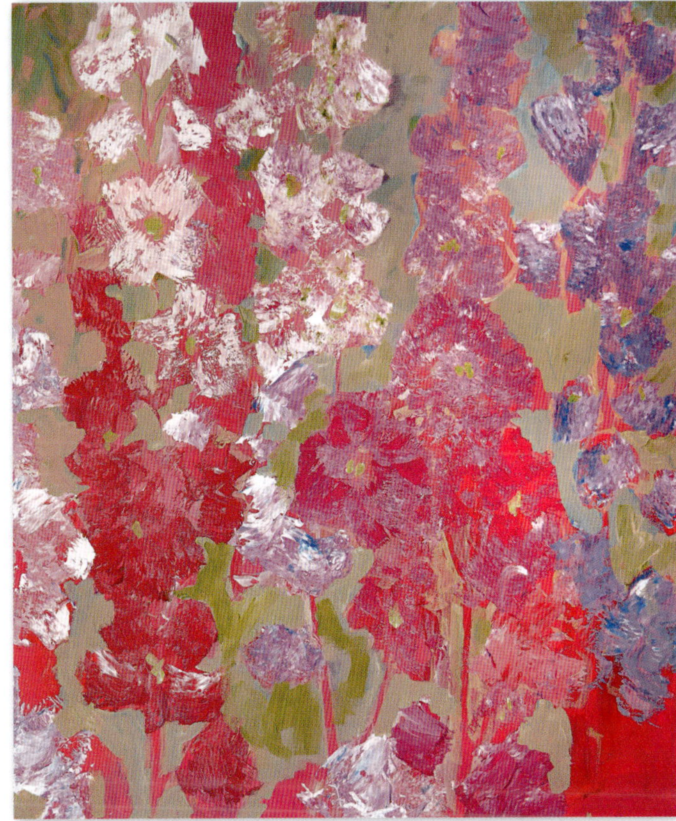

Step 2

Give each plant its own color nuance. Work with several colors so that the wallpaper seam roller gives each flower at least two color nuances. You can apply two colors at the same time by dipping the roller into several shades at once on the palette. By nature, painting with the roller is inexact, which is conducive to the loose style. Add cadmium yellow and sand to the center of the flowers.

Step 3

Paint the background after applying the first layer for the flowers. If required, sketch the flowers again, since the roller will have partially painted over the first sketch. The background areas are based on the newly created shapes. Paint the background with a small gap to the flowers, so that a part of the first layer of paint remains visible. In contrast to the red and pink shades, use green-gray shades mixed from titanium white, cyan blue, and olive green in various gradations for the background. Leave the lower-right corner of the picture unpainted.

Tip: The main color becomes more vibrant if other shades are added in a reduced or fragmented fashion. In this picture, the pink and magenta shades of the flowers are complemented by a small amount of blue. The background colors consist of fragmented green and sand shades.

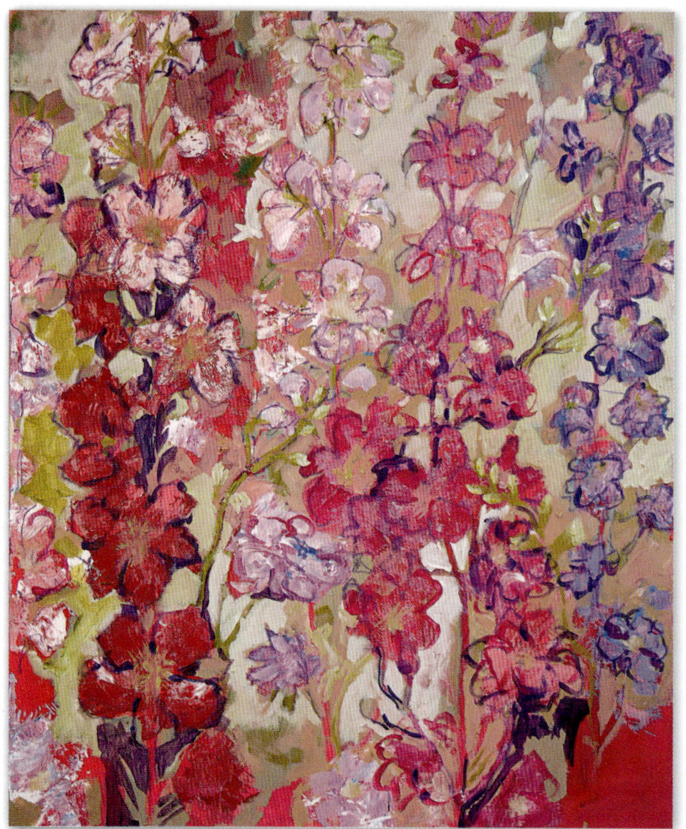

Step 4

Use an angular brush to trace around a few broad and thin outlines of the flowers, some in dark violet, others in madder red, cyan blue, or magenta, depending on the color of the flower in question. By changing the width of the stroke, the outlines look more vivid. Add a few young shoots with buds. Add olive green to the left section of the picture. Pick out the plant forms and add a few silhouettes to the negative space in the background, using light-beige shades mixed from titanium white and sand.

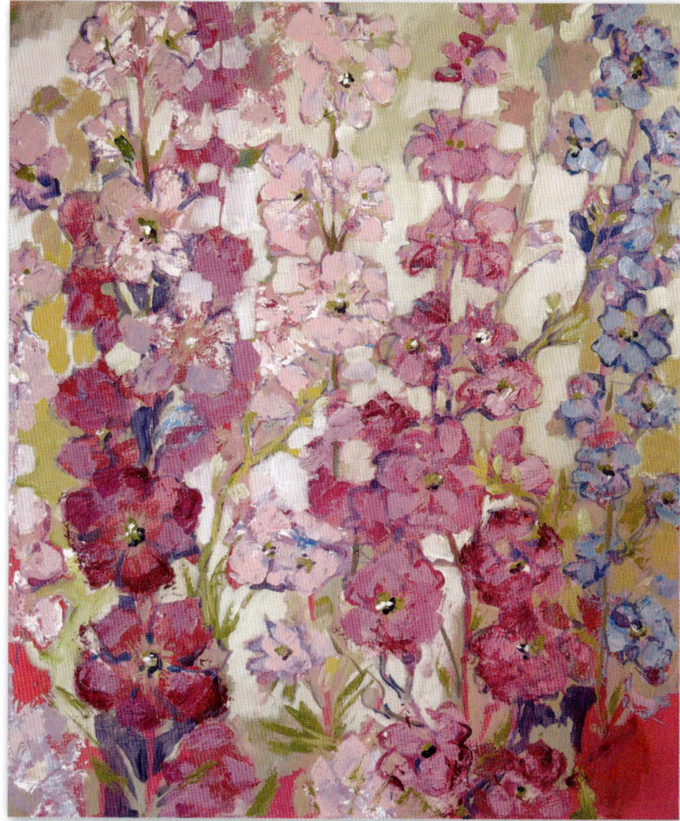

Step 5

Add a few details by using a dark-violet watercolor pencil, so that the individual petals are more clearly visible. Add lightness to the edges of the petals. Accentuate the flower centers with olive green, white, and dark violet. Further lighten the background areas. Leave the base colors visible at the edges. Add olive-green leaves structures to the lower edge of the picture.

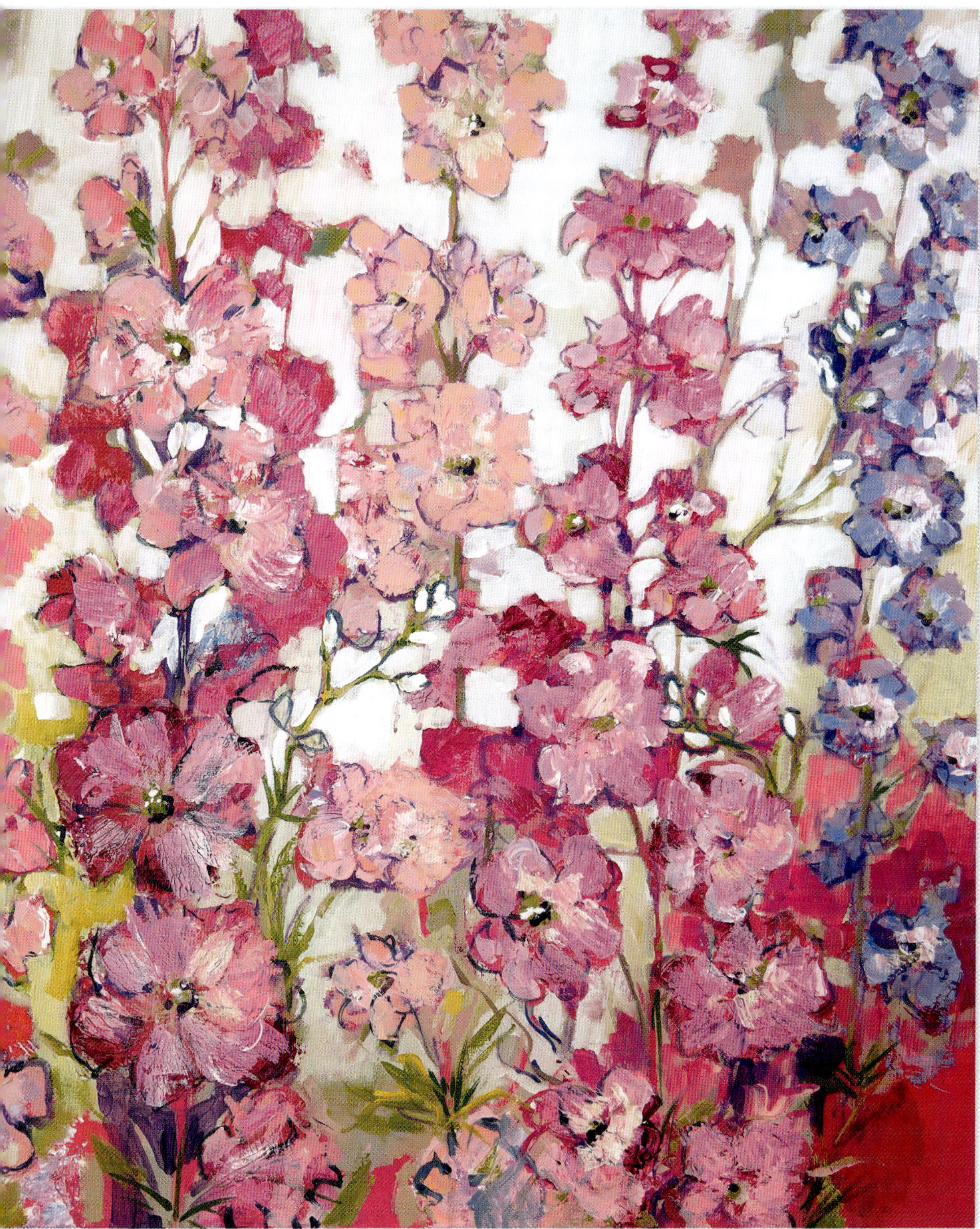

Finished Painting

For the large flowers, use a palette knife with a small blade to apply paint in the shade of the flower that has been lightened with titanium white. Then scratch it hard with the flat end of the blade. As a result, the underlying structures created by the wallpaper seam roller become visible as delicate veins. Use this technique in only a few places. It creates an interesting tension when certain techniques are only sparingly used. Then use titanium white to increase the light in the upper section of the picture. Finally, brighten the buds with titanium white and give them dark accents, using cyan blue and olive green.

Saffron Thistle

Materials:

- Canvas, 24 x 32 in.
- Acrylic paints in titanium white, lemon yellow, Indian yellow, orange, cadmium red, madder red, light blue, grass green, light umber, and burnt umber
- Angular brush, size 12
- Watercolor pencil in dark gray
- Finishing spatula, 6 in.
- Charcoal pencil
- Painter's palette

The saffron thistle is also known as the safflower and is often used in place of the extremely expensive saffron. Dyes are made from its bright-orange blossoms. The ribbonlike flowers are created with wild scratches in thick paint, making them look as if they are exploding. The delicate hues of light green and light blue in the background allow the red-orange extravaganza of color to unfold. Some flower heads appear to extend beyond the frame and increase the intensity of the colorful composition.

Step 1

Squeeze cadmium red, Indian yellow, and orange directly from the tubes onto the canvas. Use the finishing spatula to distribute the paint in all directions. Don't completely cover everywhere at the edge of the picture, so that small parts of the white canvas remain visible. These small gaps allow the painting style to appear looser. Let dry.

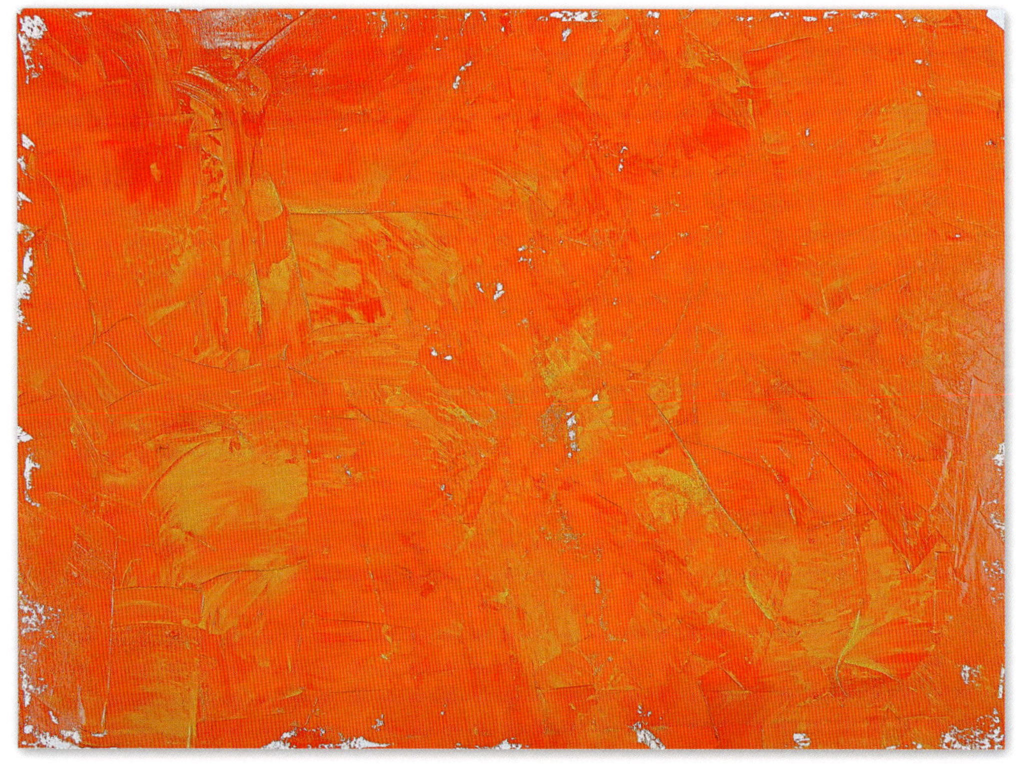

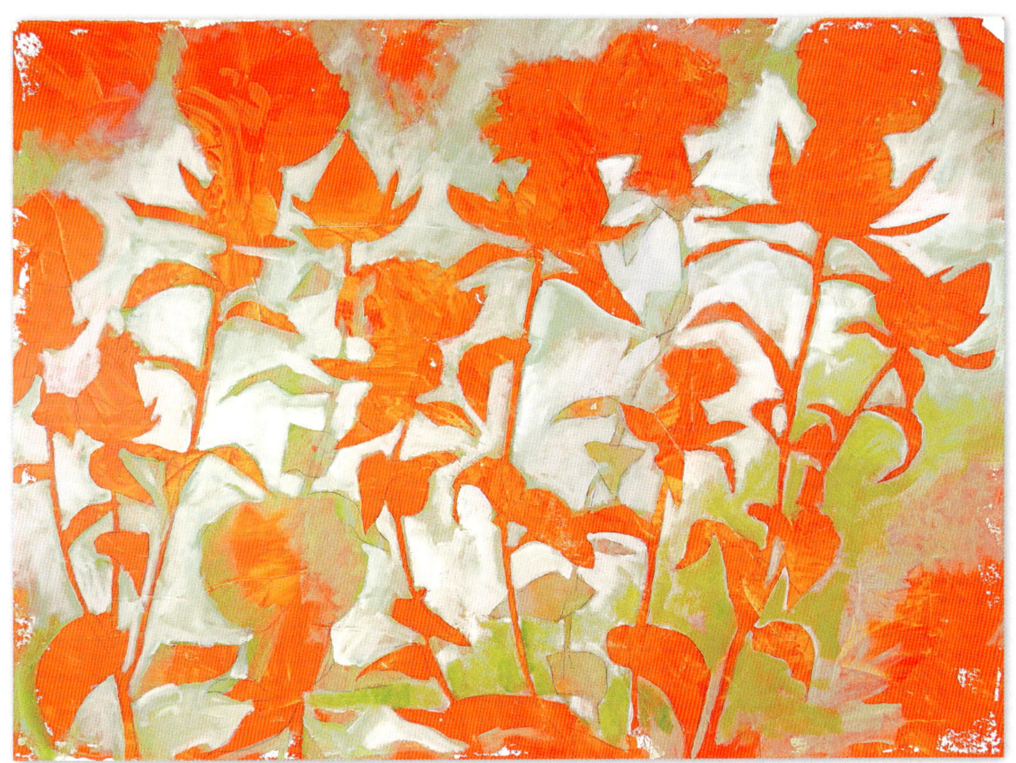

Step 2
Use the dark-gray watercolor pencil to sketch the thistles. Paint the background in a mixture of lemon yellow, light umber, Indian yellow, and grass green, making the upper area lighter and the lower areas greener. Leave some spaces on the edge of the picture unpainted. Once again, use the watercolor pencil to sketch more plants and surround them with lighter shades. For this second application of paint, use a light blue. This second level makes it appear as if these plants are in the background.

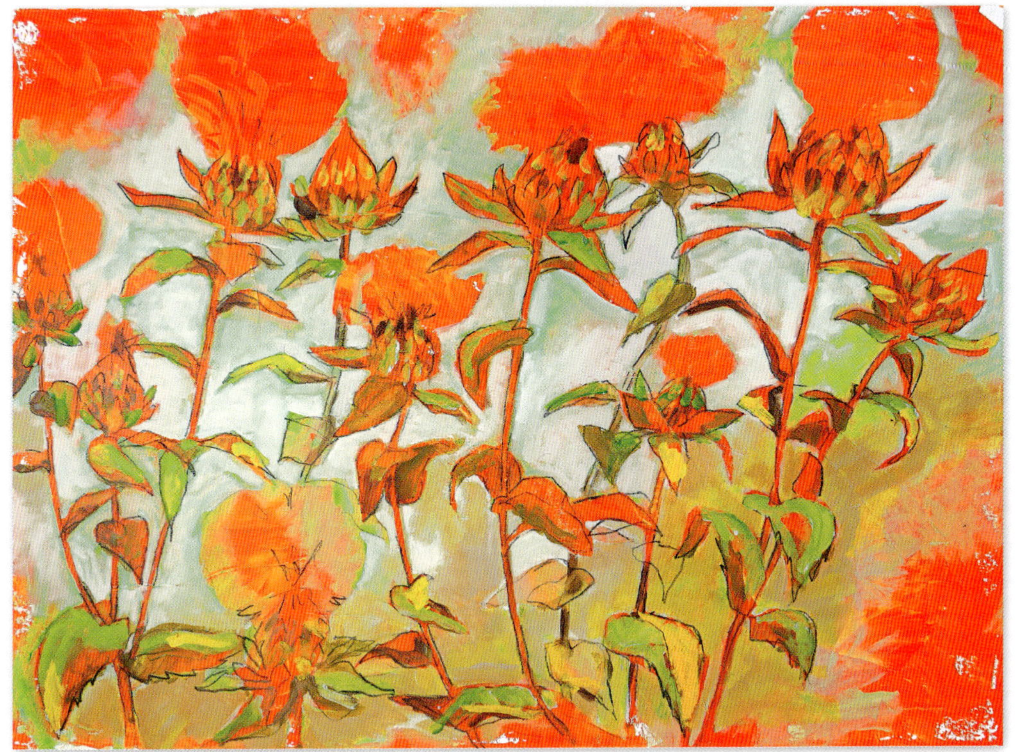

Step 3
Use a charcoal pencil to loosely trace around the outlines. Use burnt umber, light green, and Indian yellow to fill the leaves with color. Deliberately work loosely so that the orange shows through in many places. Leave some leaves and stalks unworked, so that they remain in the orange of the base layer. Also leave some outlines of the sketch unfilled.

Step 4

Use burnt and light umber to add to the dark areas. Primarily paint in the lower section of the picture and add just a few accents in the upper section. Surround some of the lower leaves and emphasize the serrated edges to illustrate the thorny leaves, a characteristic of the saffron thistle. The stalks remain primarily in the original orange shades. This painterly technique connects the flowers, stalks, and leaves with each other because the orange shows through everywhere.

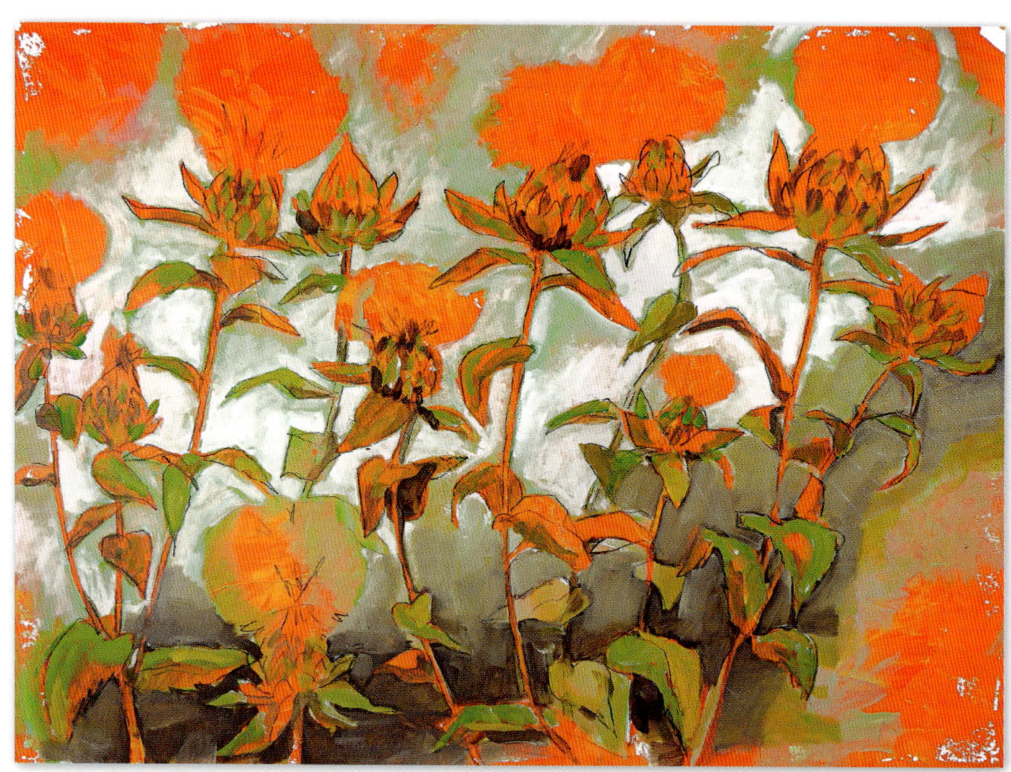

Step 5

In the center of each flower head, add a dollop of cadmium red directly from the tube. Add Indian yellow directly from the tube over it in a semicircle. Using the back of a brush, scratch lines in the paint from the center outward. When scratched, the two colors combine into multicolored lines. Use the same technique, but with burnt umber and madder for the wilted flowers. Also add some dark shades, using burnt umber to the lower areas of the large blooms. Let dry.

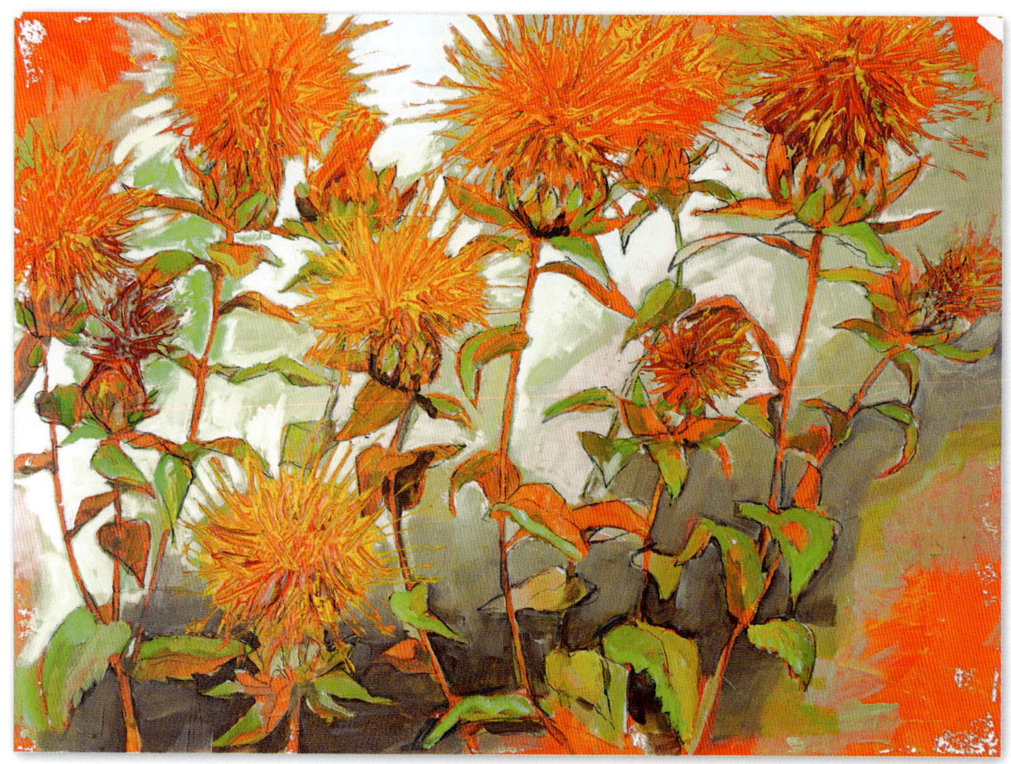

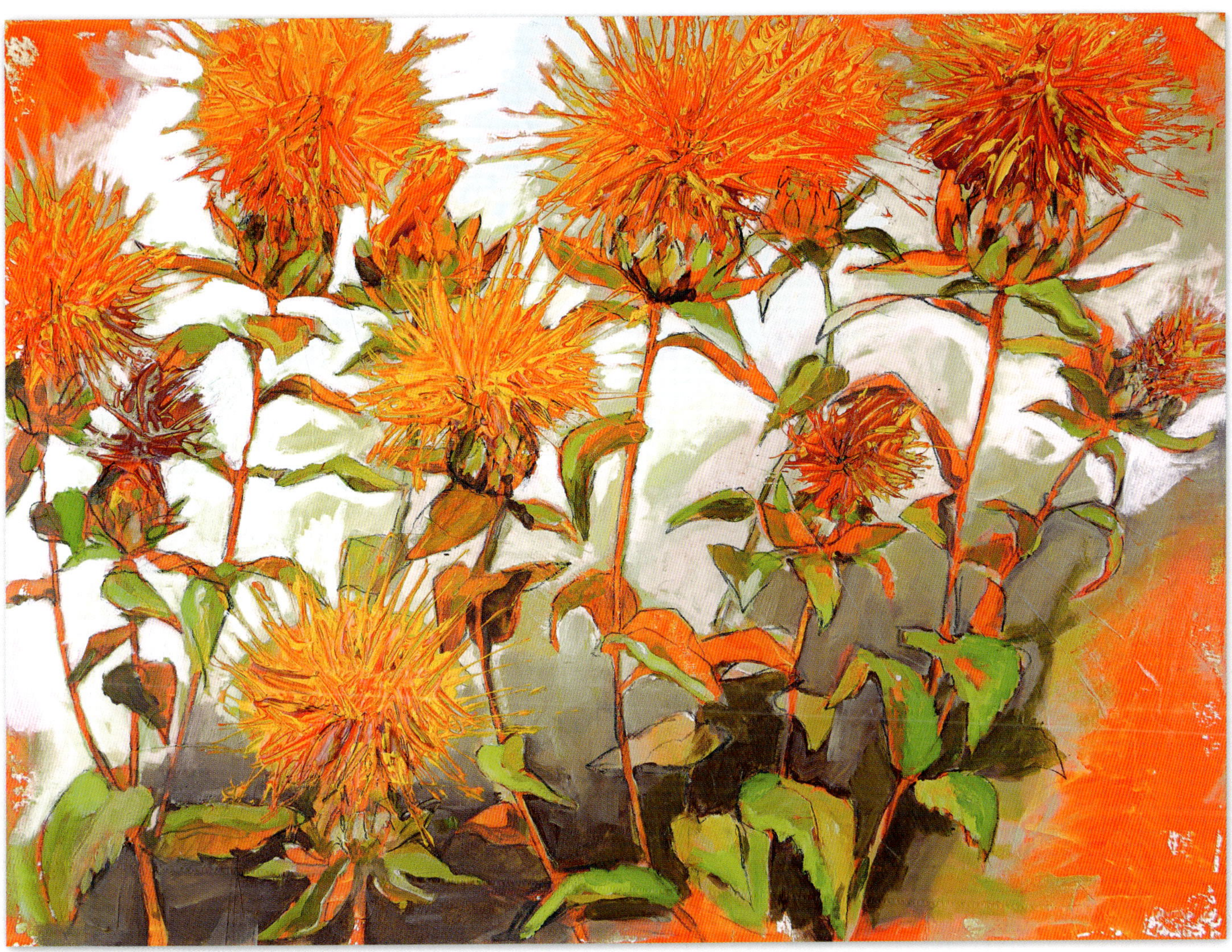

Finished Painting

Use a brush to add accents of grass green mixed with lemon yellow to the leaves. At the top edge of the picture, add light blue to the background but do not fully cover the underlying layers of paint, so that they remain visible like a frame around the petals. In the lower section of the picture, concentrate a bold grass green. Keep the grass green in this section and do not use it elsewhere, so that a quantity contrast is created. Finally, add dark areas with the charcoal pencil.

Tip: Different flower sizes, irregular distribution of the flowers, plants overlapping each other, and plants extending beyond the edge of the canvas are important elements in creating an organic and natural effect in the composition of floral subjects.

Hollyhocks

Materials

- Canvas, 24 x 32 in.
- Acrylic paints in titanium white, cadmium yellow, rose, cadmium red, magenta, dark violet, indigo, and light umber
- Flat synthetic bristle brush, size 30
- Angular brush, size 12
- Round natural hair brush, size 1
- Watercolor pencil in dark magenta
- Tissue paper
- Binder and container
- Drawing ink in magenta, dark blue, and dark violet
- Pipettes, water spray bottle
- Paper towels
- Painter's palette

Hollyhocks can turn any garden into a flower paradise. Acrylic paint and drawing ink combine with tissue paper to create delicate structures that are similar to the fine petals of the hollyhocks. The watery glazes are absorbed differently due to the folds in the paper, so that a varied surface with delicate veins is created.

Section 1

The tiny pigments of the drawing ink collect in the folds of the tissue paper. The stark contrast between the light flowers and dark drawing ink allows the folds to show clearly. The delicate, uncontrolled ink feathering must be covered in some places by painting over it.

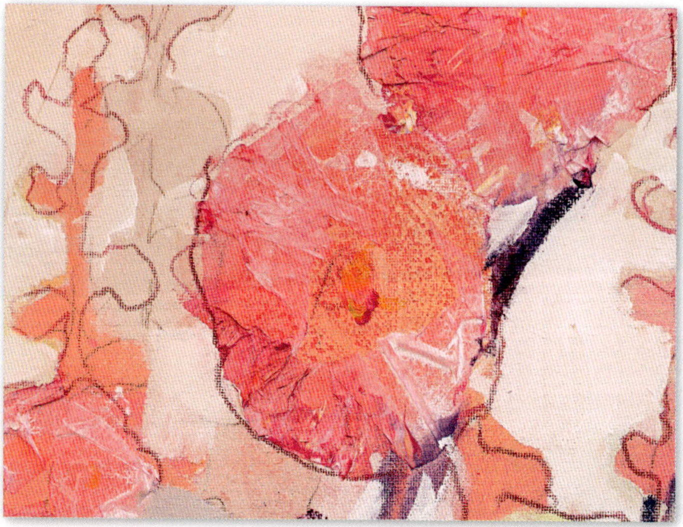

Section 2

The different colors of the individual hollyhocks should be clearly separated from each other; however, the flowers should also contain shades from the neighboring plants, so that in contrast to nature, each flower has areas of color matching other flowers. As a result, there is a visual connection between them.

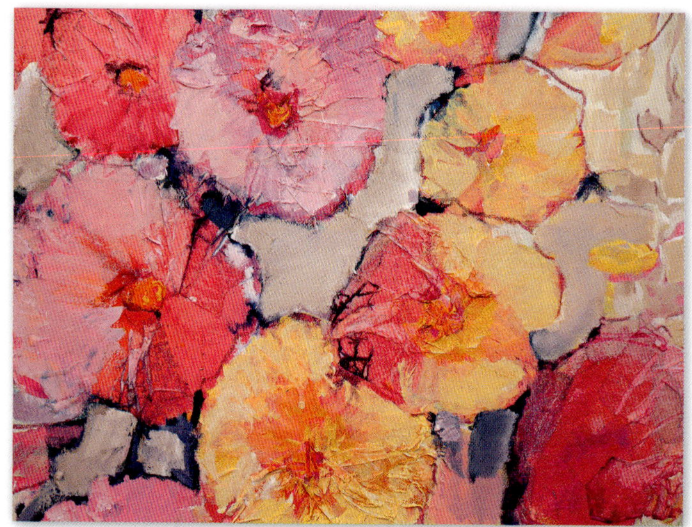

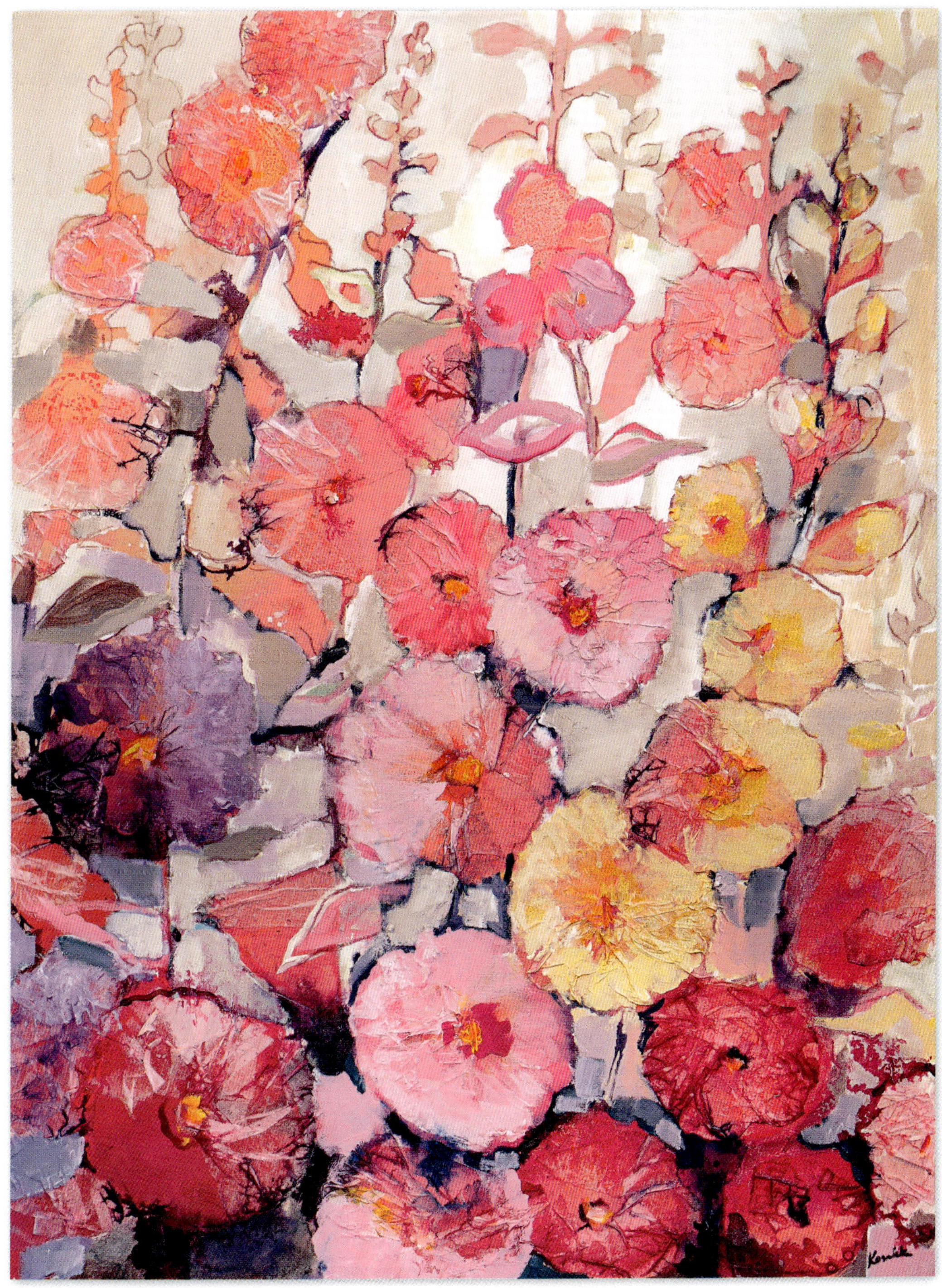

Instructions

Use the dark-magenta watercolor pencil to sketch the flowers on the canvas over a base layer in the colors of the flowers. Draw flower shapes on tissue paper with a fine natural hair brush dipped in water, and pull the flower shapes free from the paper. Use water-diluted binder to glue them to the canvas. Allow to dry. Fill the background with titanium white mixed with light umber. Go over the flowers with acrylic paints. Use a pipette to trace some of the outlines with drawing ink in magenta, dark blue, and dark violet. Spray on water with the spray bottle. Work on the background again and add light umber. Add a few leaf outlines, filling some with acrylic paint and leaving others empty.

Sunflowers

Materials:

- Stretch frame, 32 x 40 in.
- Acrylic paints in titanium white, lemon yellow, cadmium yellow, Indian yellow, cadmium red, cyan blue, Prussian blue, light green, olive green, phthalo green, dark green, and light gray
- Watercolor pencil in red brown
- Oil pastels in lemon yellow, cadmium yellow, orange, light green, red brown, and dark brown
- Flat synthetic bristle brush, sizes 10 and 30
- Wallpaper seam roller
- Palette knife with long pointed blade
- Drawing ink in black
- Drawing ink pen
- Water spray bottle
- Gold metal leaf
- Painter's palette

Summer, sun, and the abundance of light and life become particularly clear in the bold yellow shades of the radiant sunflowers, which are an absolute must for any summer garden.

The shimmering light of the summer is emphasized by the vibrant colors and the loose style of painting. Gold metal leaf bolsters the intensity of the bright yellow petals.

Step 1

Squeeze lemon yellow, cadmium yellow, and Indian yellow directly from the tubes onto the top half of the canvas. Add light green, olive green, dark green, and black to the lower section. Use a wallpaper seam roller to distribute the paint in different directions to create an irregularly textured surface. In the upper section of the picture, lay seven pieces of gold metal leaf directly in the wet paint. Use the roller and paint to work in the straight edges of the metal leaf. Let dry.

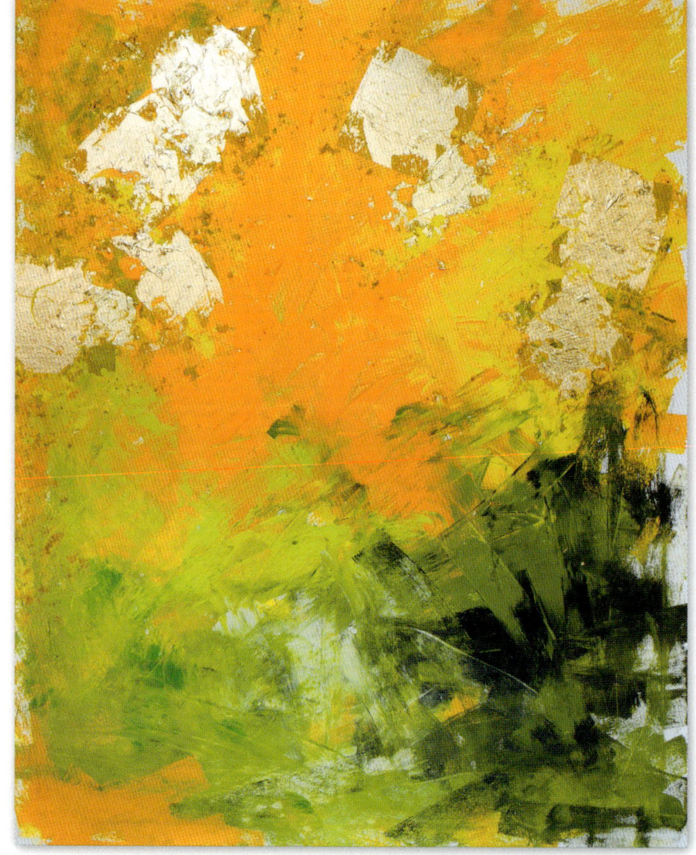

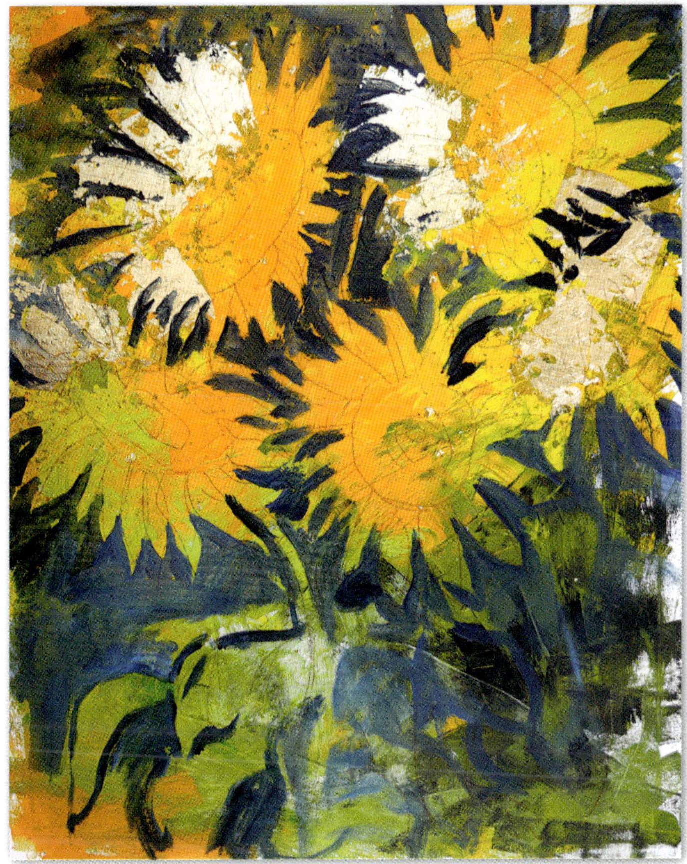

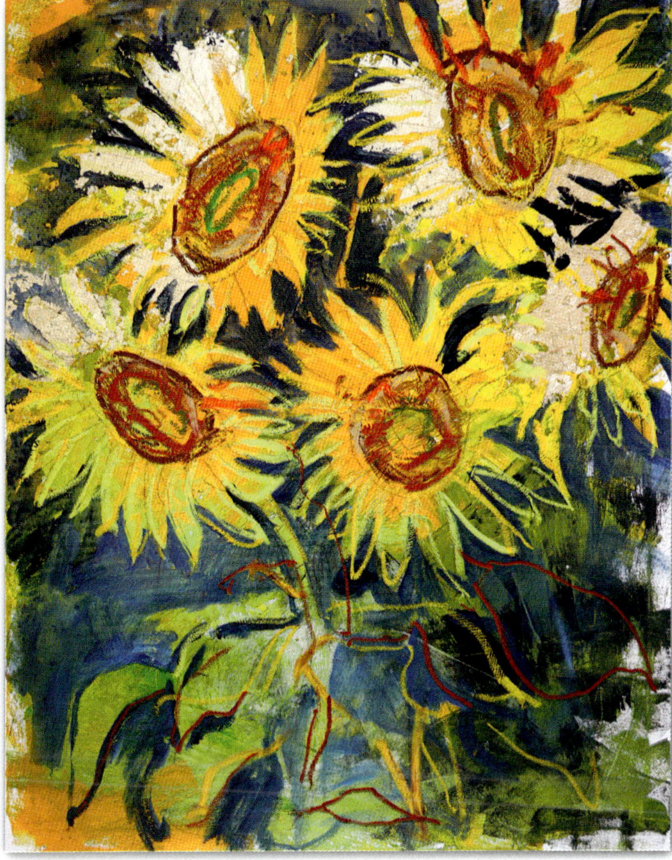

Step 2

Sketch the flower heads, using a watercolor pencil. Use a broad synthetic brush and water-diluted Prussian blue to loosely fill the background. You want to have inaccuracies; therefore, the wide synthetic bristle brush is well suited for this step because it doesn't allow any exact detail. Use undiluted Prussian blue over the gold foil; otherwise, it would run off the surface. Don't fully cover the edges and the corners, so that the base layer can still be seen.

Step 3

Trace outlines with oil pastels. In many places, the outline should not touch the colored area but should be somewhat aside it. Position some outlines of leaves and petals on the dark background, without filling them. For the centers of the flower heads, loosely draw the shapes of the central ovals with oil pastels in red brown and dark brown. Add a couple of light-green and orange accents.

Tip: In acrylic painting, using a variety of tools already creates an exciting statement. However, if other painting media are deployed, then a multilayered and vivid picture is developed.

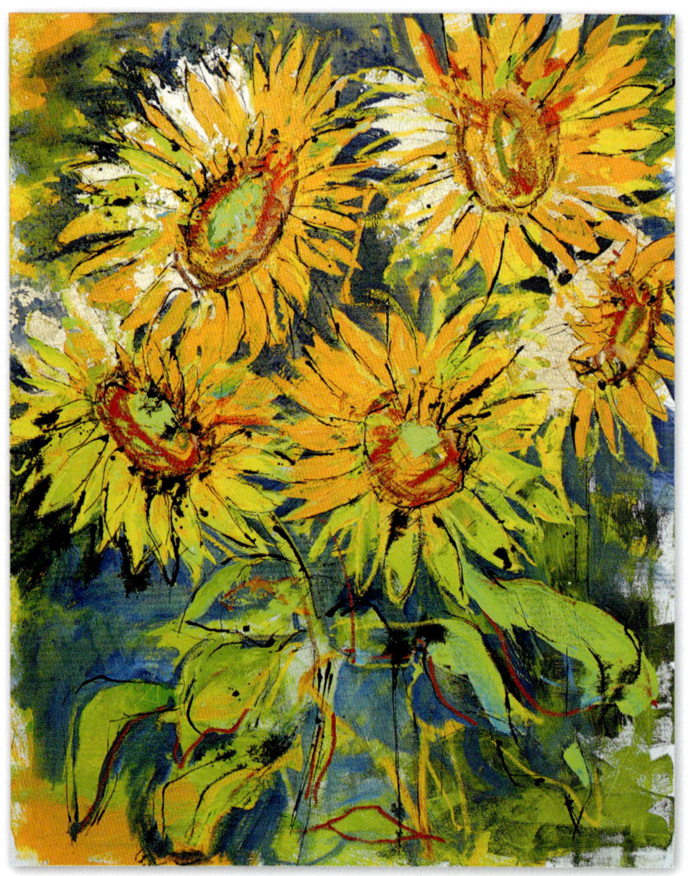

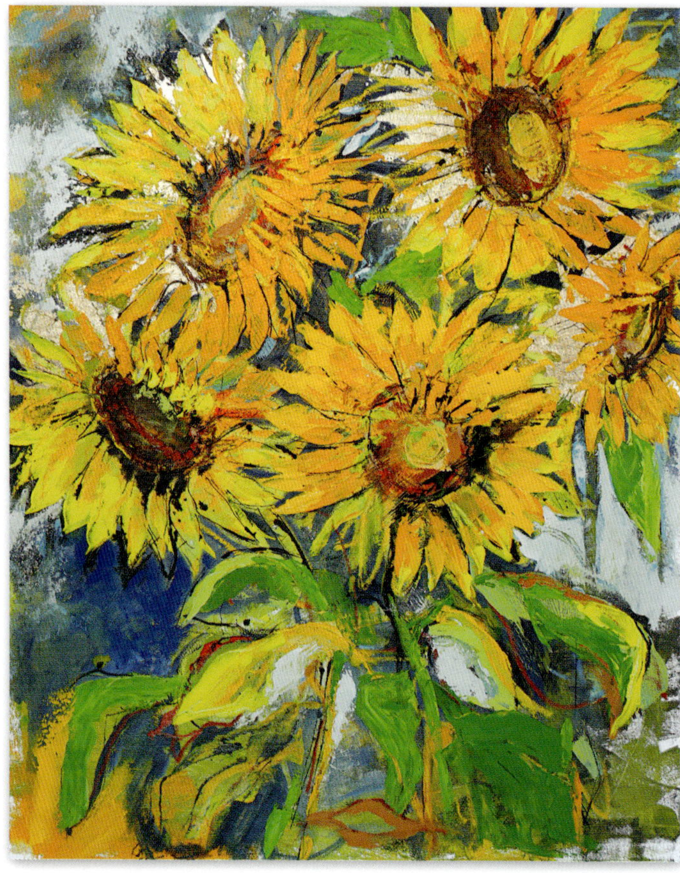

Step 4

Use a long, pointed palette knife to apply undiluted acrylic paint in lemon yellow, cadmium yellow, and Indian yellow to the petals, positioning the tip of the knife at the top of the petals. Add a few small petals to the inner edge of the flower head. Let dry. Trace loose outlines in black, using the drawing ink and the drawing pen, and partially spray with water so that pretty runs are formed. Allow any accidental blots to remain.

Step 5

Use the palette knife to work on the petals or add extra petals so that the dominance of the black drawing ink subsides. Use a small brush to go over the background of the upper section of the picture with light-blue acrylic paint, which is a mixture of titanium white and cyan blue. To do so, pick up a small amount of paint and rub the brush on the canvas (dry brush technique), so that broken surfaces are created and the base color shows through. Add light gray to the background. In the lower section of the picture, add a calming zone in Prussian blue.

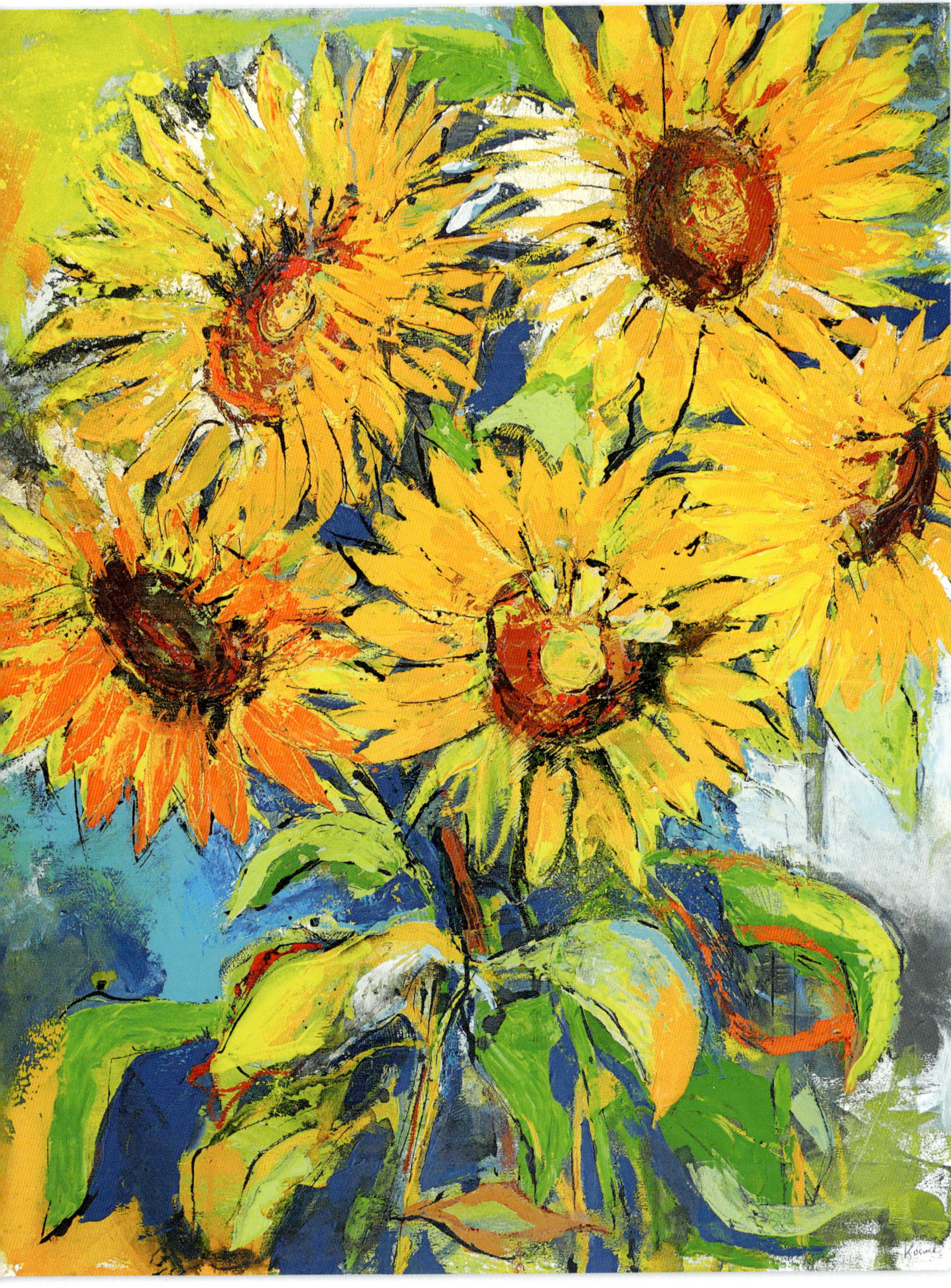

Finished Painting

Go over the leaves and stalks with green shades mixed with Indian yellow. For this step, use undiluted acrylic paint and a palette knife. When working, pay attention that the shapes and outlines are not exactly lined up but are often offset to each other. Also leave some leaf outlines without filling them in. Add a few green shades as an indication of more leaves in the upper section of the picture. Add detail to one of the flowers with a mixture of cadmium yellow and cadmium red to give it a contrast to the other flowers. Add accents in cyan blue that has been lightened with titanium white, and add other accents in cadmium red.

Snapdragons

Materials:

- Stretch frame, 24 x 32 in.
- Acrylic paints in titanium white, pastel yellow, cadmium yellow, orange, cadmium red, magenta, violet, dark violet, sand, and light gray
- Flat synthetic bristle brush, size 30
- Angular brush, sizes 10 and 12
- Watercolor pencil in dark violet and orange
- Binder and container
- Cardboard, thin
- Painter's palette

It'snot just their fairytale-like name but also the multifaceted shades and dainty shapes of the snapdragons that enchant every garden. They're rewarding, long-flowering, and robust despite their delicate appearance.
The abundance of shades, their rapid growth, and their playful vividness is captured in this composition, using depth effect, a limited palette, and a loose style of painting.

Step 1
If there is a supporting baton in the stretch frame, place a thin piece of cardboard between it and the canvas to prevent an imprint of it showing through. Use a broad, flat brush to paint the different flower colors in vertical strips, creating transitions between the colors that form mixed shades. Lighten the upper edge of the picture, using titanium white.

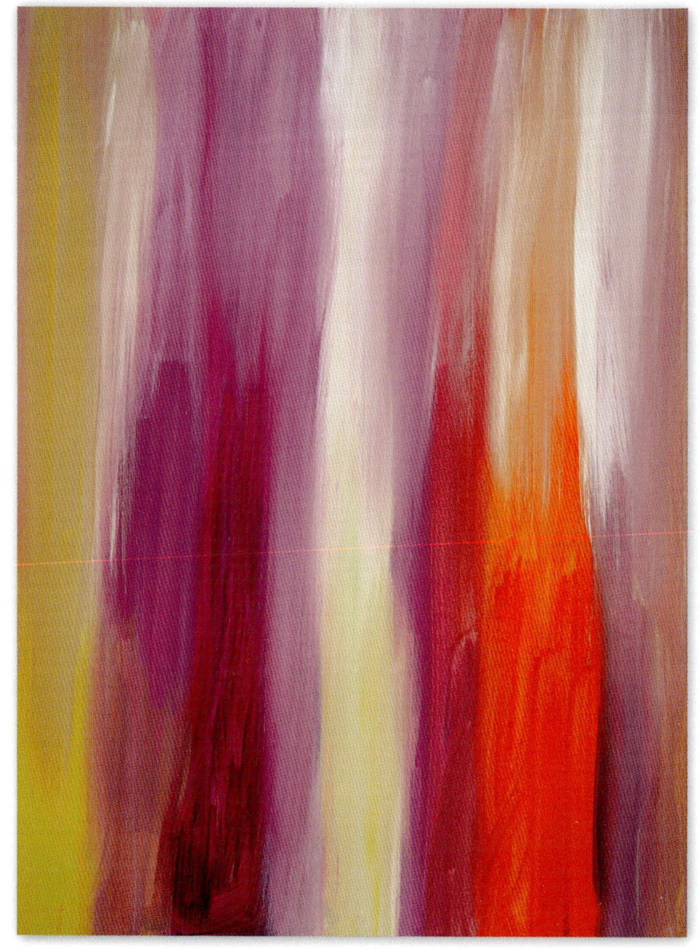

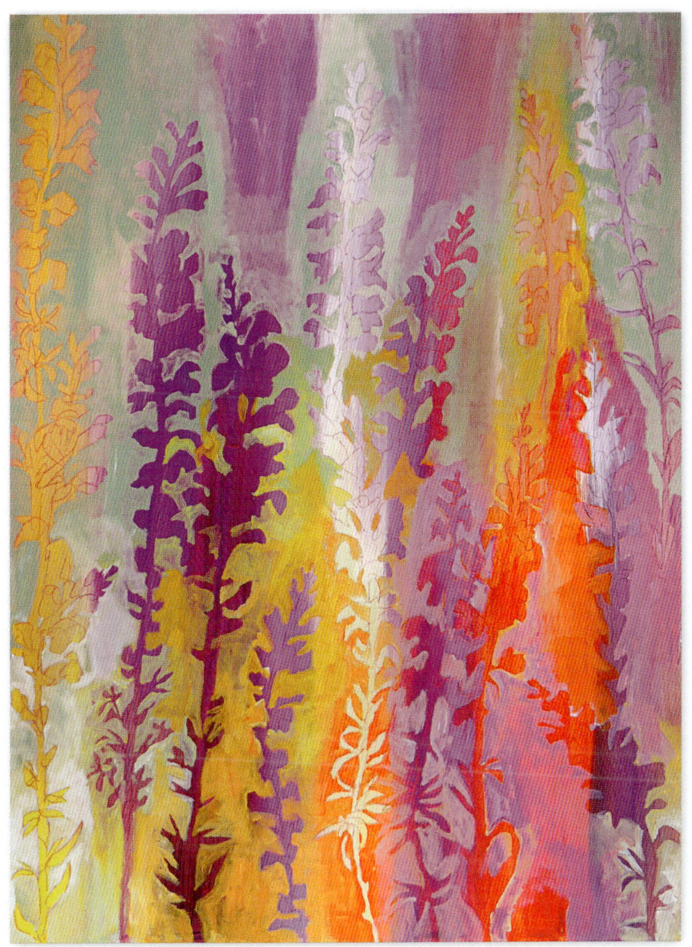

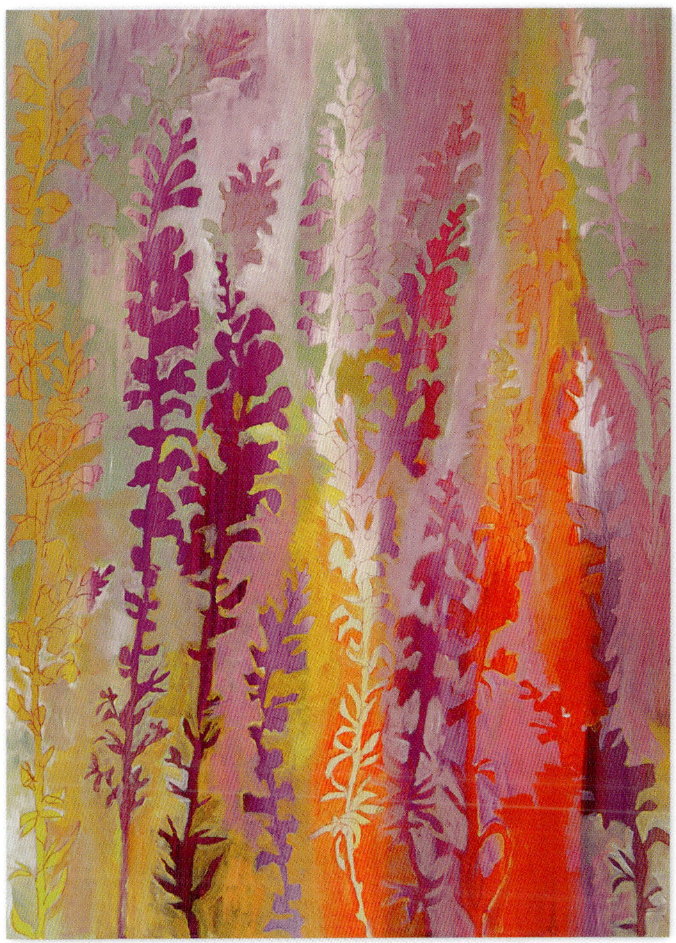

Step 2

Use a dark-violet watercolor pencil to sketch out the outlines of the individual snapdragons. Some plants touch or extend beyond the edges of the canvas, indicating a lush abundance of plants. Use an angular brush to paint the background in various shades, interspersed with light gray to create a contrast to the colors underneath it and create soft transitions between colors. Leave some areas untouched in the upper area of the picture.

Step 3

Use the watercolor pencil to add further outlines of snapdragons on the second layer of paint on the background. Create a few overlaps so that the new plants appear behind the ones already painted. Pay attention to the characteristic undulation of the plants. Once again, paint the background, because the fragmented and light shades as well as the composition create depth.

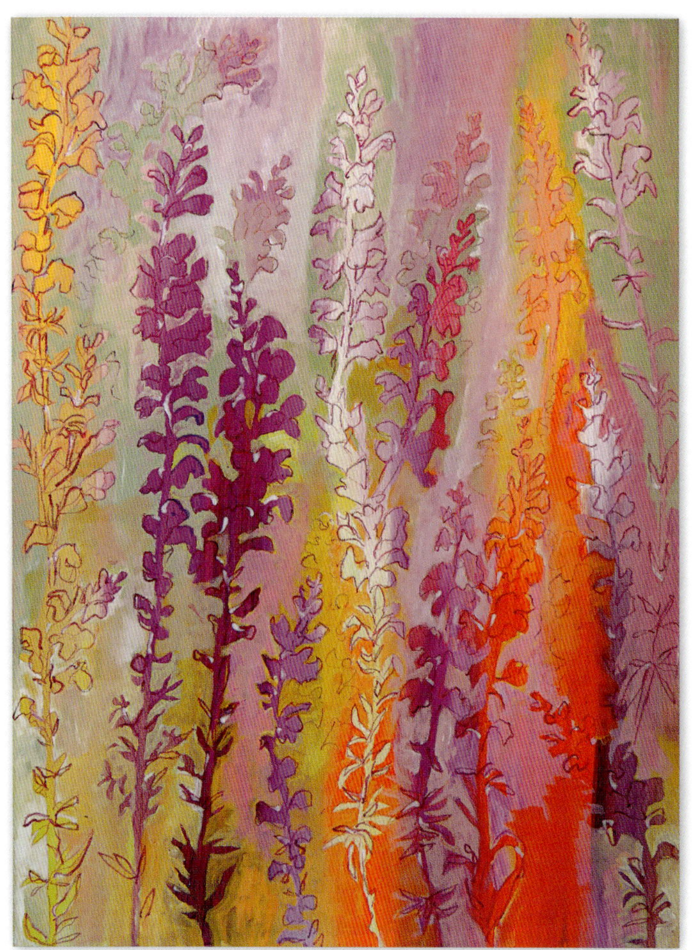

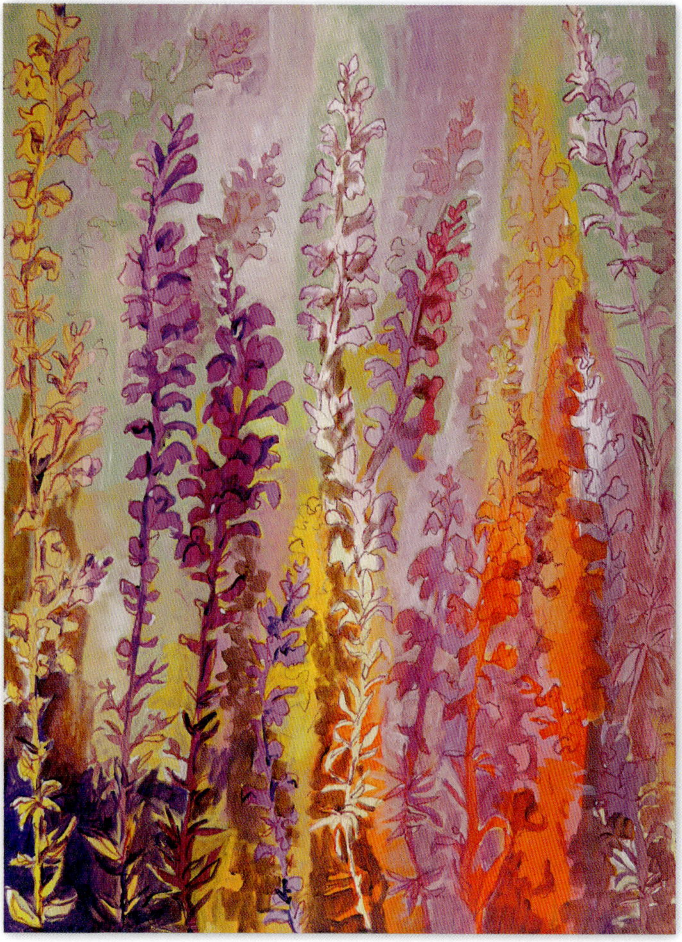

Step 4

Dip a dark-violet watercolor pencil into the binder and trace around the outlines. The binder dissolves the watercolor pencil, which allows the lines to be bolder and, at the same time, fixes the pigment. Work deliberately loosely. Change the width of the lines and break the outlines in places. The outlines do not have to exactly go over the shape but can sit slightly aside of them. Add a delicate outline to the plants at the back.

Step 5

Use shades mixed from dark violet and orange to add dark areas in the lower section of the picture that appear like the shadows creeping up the snapdragons. Use dark violet to add further shadows to the individual flowers. Fully fill the background area in the lower-left corner to create a central darkness there. Lighten the dark mixed shade with magenta and add further dark accents in the upper section of the picture. On the right edge, add a plant as a silhouette.

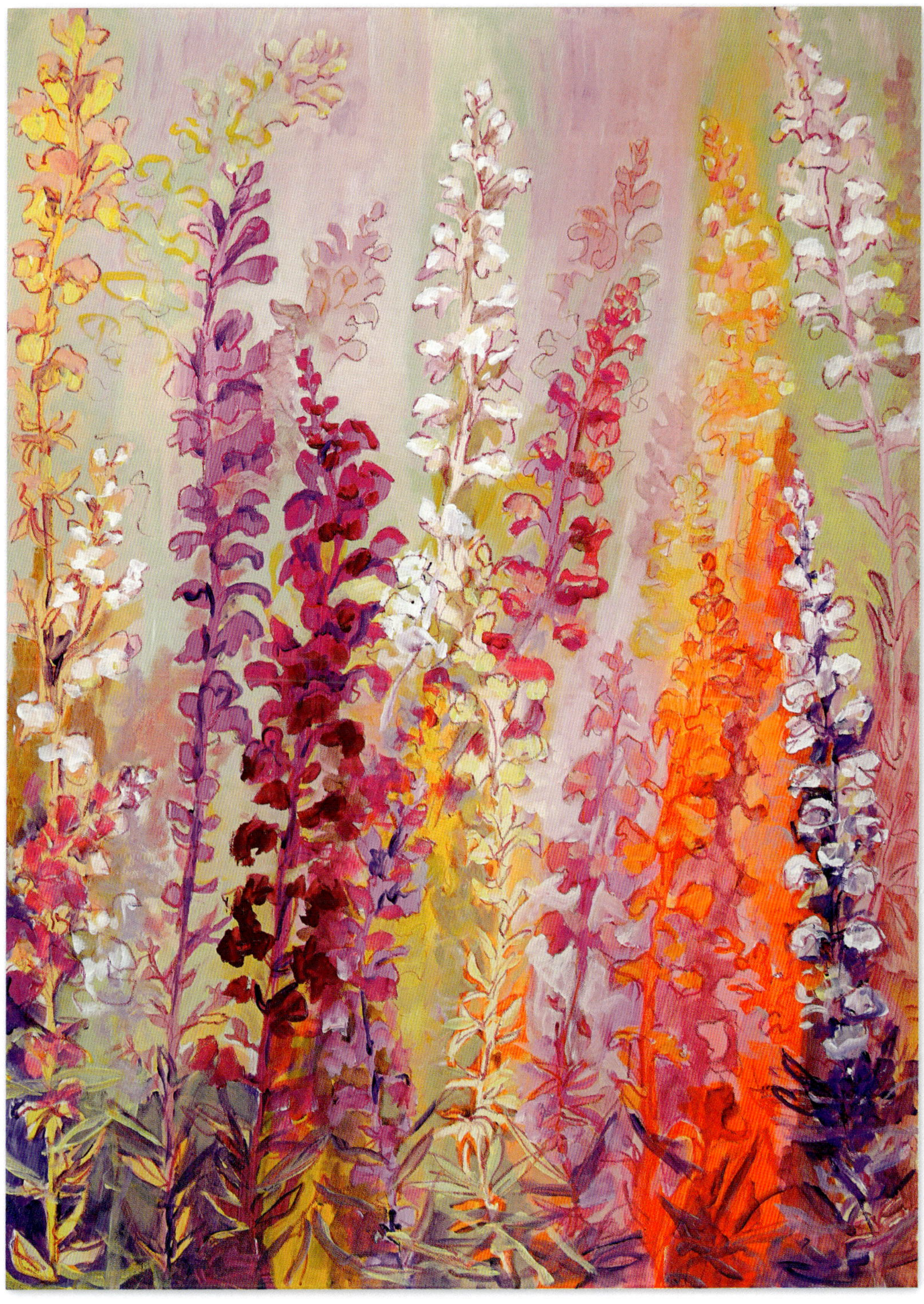

Finished Painting

Lighten up individual flowers with titanium white with irregular dabs to many flowers in the upper section of the picture. On the lower edge of the picture, intensify the straight, angular leaves to create a contrast to the soft petal shapes. Further darken the plants in the left section of the picture, using magenta and dark violet so that they are in starker contrast to the other lighter flower colors. In essence, the picture becomes lighter toward the top to show that snapdragons grow toward the light.

Flowering Lettuce

Materials:

- Canvas, 20 x 40 in.
- Acrylic paints in titanium white, cadmium yellow, cadmium red, cyan blue, turquoise light green, olive green, light umber, and burnt umber
- Flat synthetic bristle brush, size 50
- Angular brush, size 12
- Watercolor pencil in dark turquoise and dark green
- Smooth putty
- Palette knife with pointed blade
- Drawing ink in dark green
- Charcoal pencil
- Pipettes
- Water spray bottle
- Card scraper, oval with teeth (pottery tool)
- Rags
- Painter's palette

Material for the flower stamp:

- Thin cardboard
- Scissors
- Sticky tape

You may be familiar with many types of lettuce, but have you also seen flowering lettuce? They appear likes strange aliens in the garden, these bolted endives, these big and strange plants.

Putty is used to accentuate the fine feathery white flowers that grow on the zigzag stalks, while short, straight scratch marks add to the effect of the plant's jagged leaves.

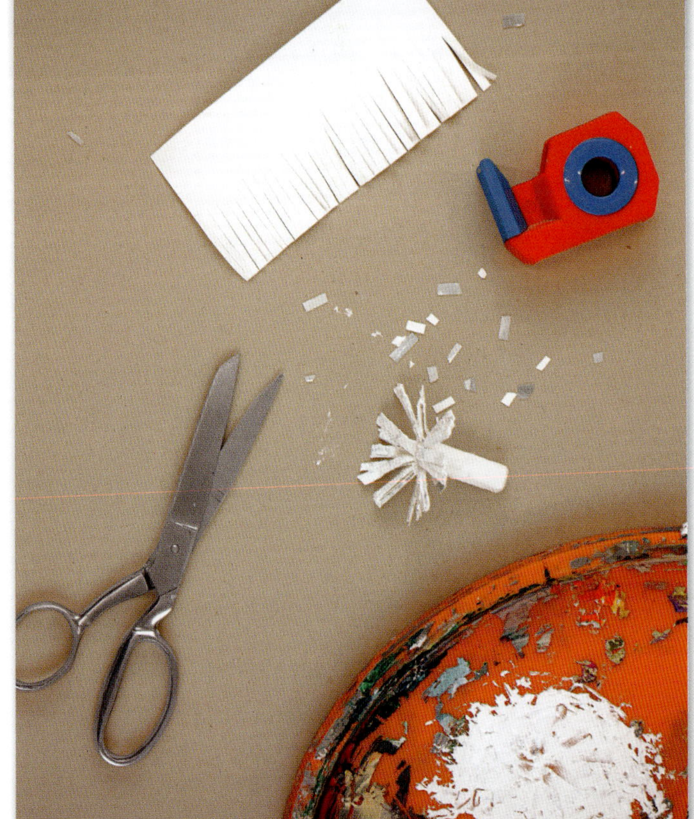

Step 1

DIY stamps make it easier to add the flowers. To create the stamp, cut two lengths from some thin cardboard. Cut in a fringe by snipping randomly in the edge. Roll up the length of card and stick together with sticky tape. Fold the fringe outward and cut so the petals are slightly different lengths. A printed flower often appears looser and more natural than painted flowers because the paint is fragmented.

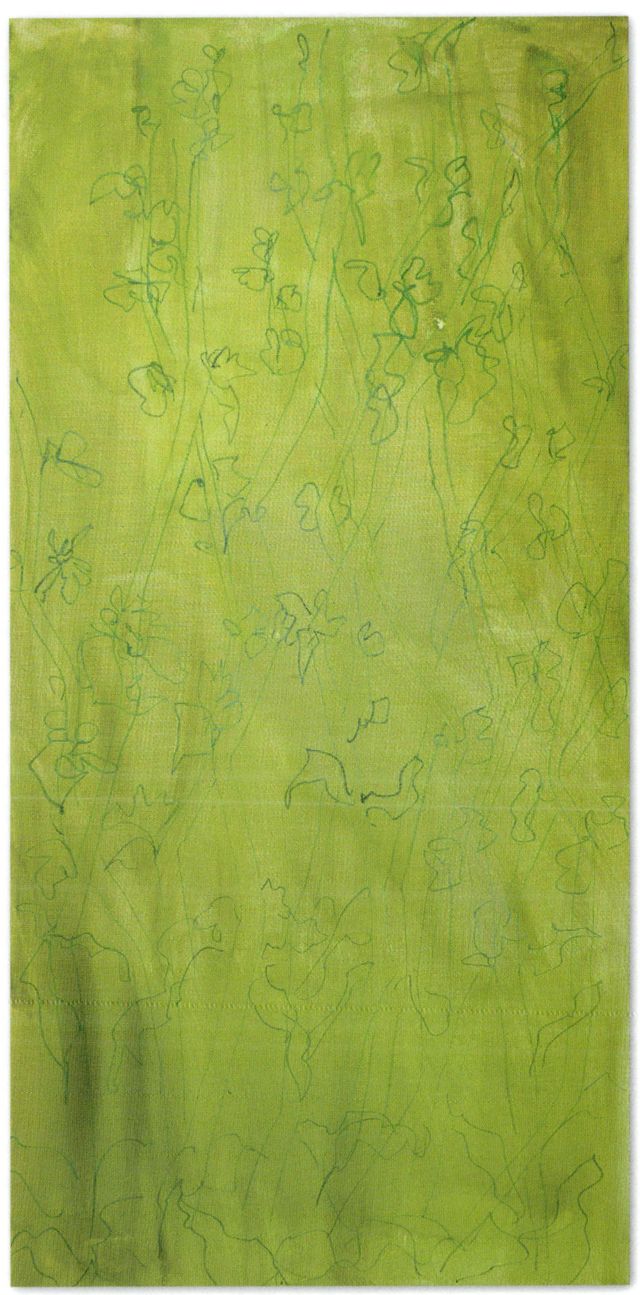

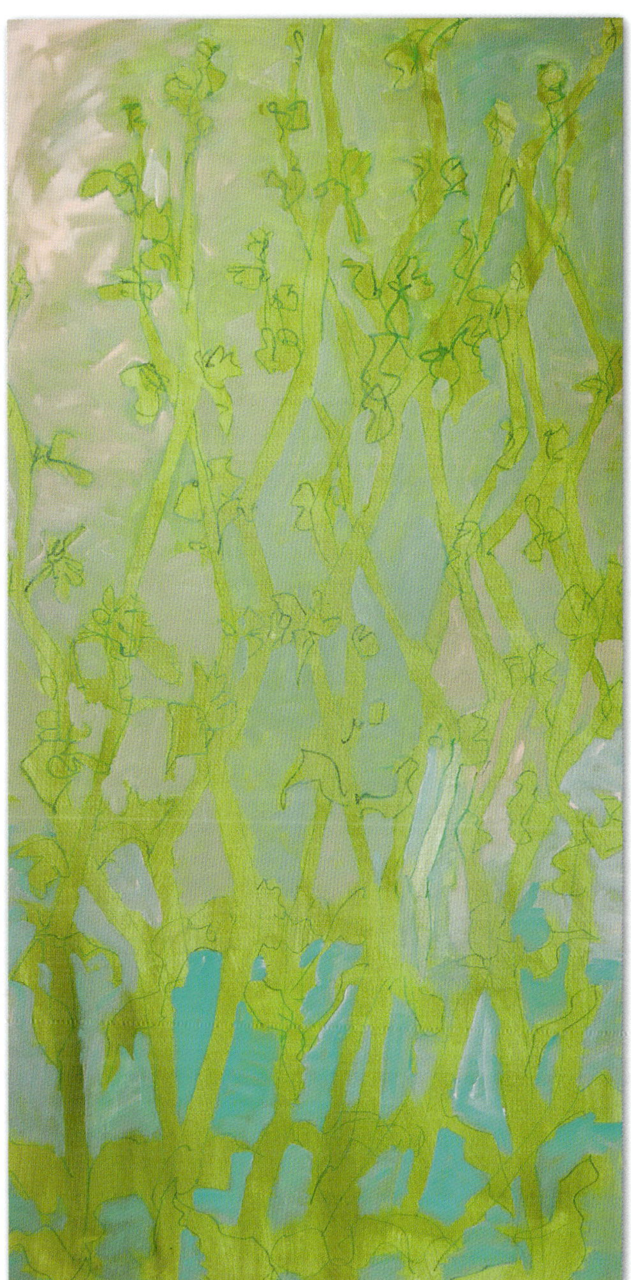

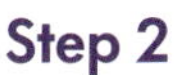

Step 2

Paint a base layer on the canvas, using a broad brush and slightly diluted acrylic paint in light green and olive green. Move the brush up and down vertically. Let dry. Use a dark-turquoise watercolor pencil to sketch the outlines. The zigzag stalks should overlap at random to create background areas of different sizes. Some of the stalks extend beyond the edge of the canvas, to highlight the bolting growth in terms of the picture's composition.

Step 3

Use a flat brush to paint the background with light umber and turquoise that has been lightened with titanium white. Use light umber primarily in the upper section and the turquoise preferably in the lower section of the picture. Create soft transitions so that a flowing color gradient appears. In places, keep going over the background until the shapes clearly emerge as green stalks. Fill large background areas randomly so that the paint appears slightly patchy.

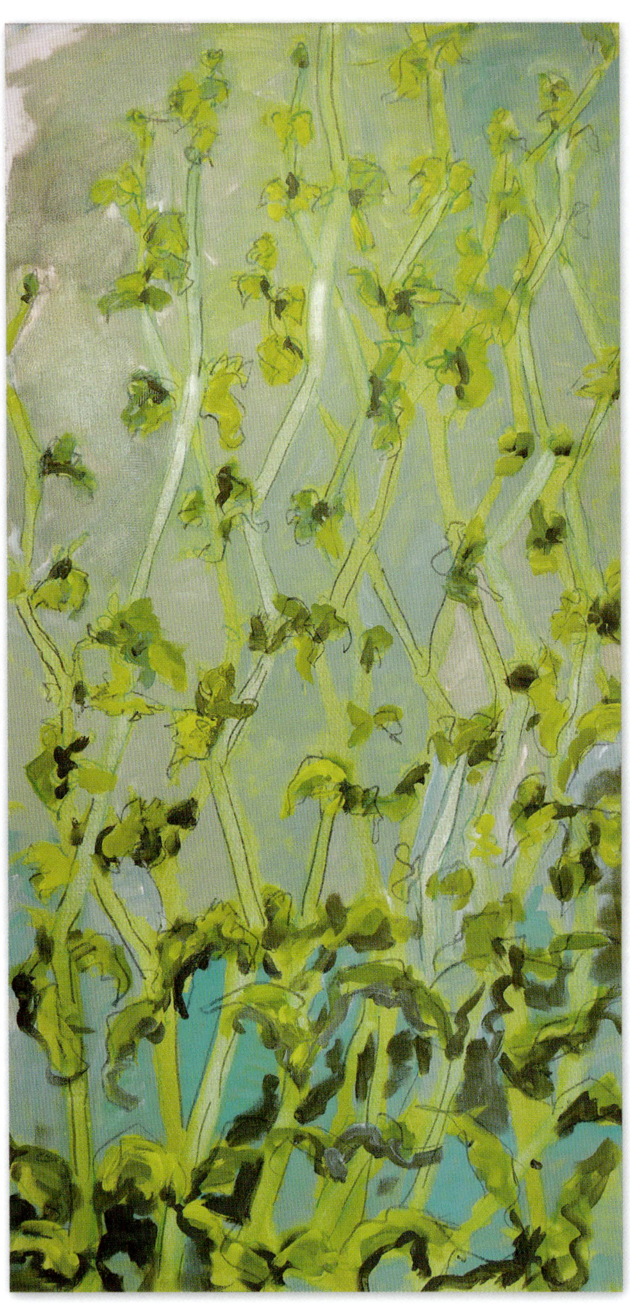

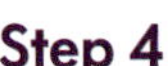

Step 4

Use a damp rag to gently wipe the paint off a few of the stalks. Trace some of the outlines with a dark-green watercolor pencil. Use a card scraper to make scratches in the background. Use a brush to add structure to the leaves in green shades mixed from light green, olive green, and burnt umber, with lighter shades at the top and darker shades toward the bottom. Add light, loose strokes without exactly defining the leaves. Use burnt umber to work in dark accents at the base of the leaves.

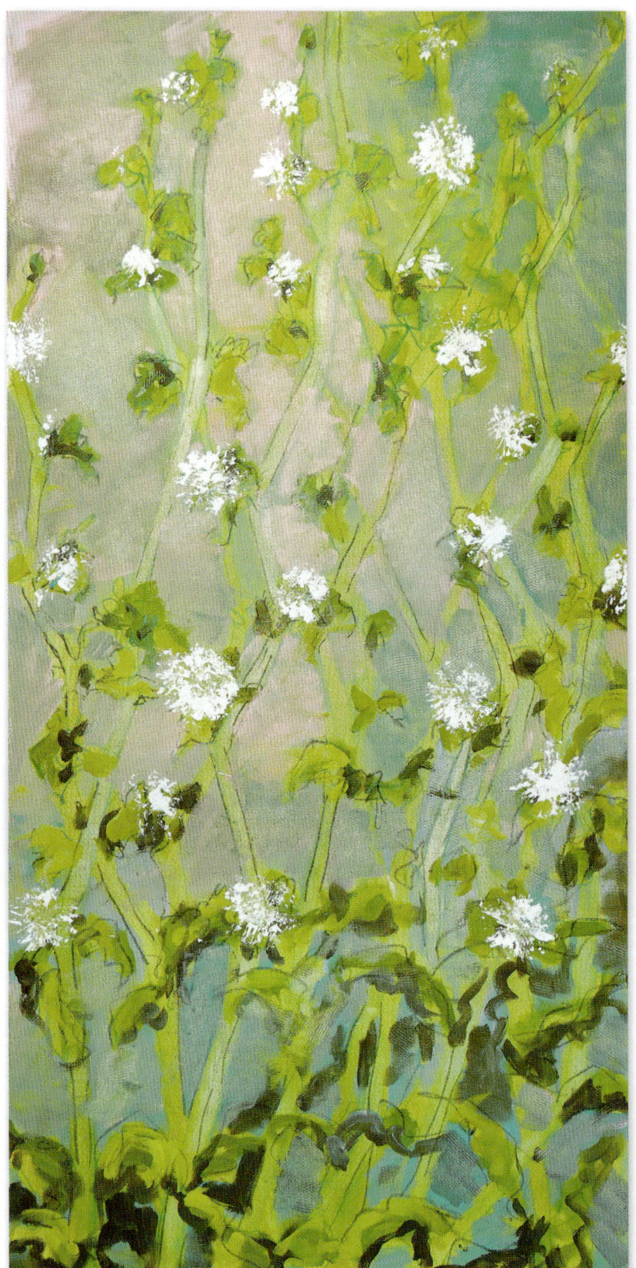

Step 5

Mix a different green color, using cadmium yellow, and set further accents with it. The vivacity of the subject comes from the multitude of different shades of green. In the central section, add some light umber. Keep going over the fresh paint with the card scraper. Loosely trace the outlines with the charcoal pencil. Print the flowers by using the DIY stamp and smooth putty. The larger flowers grow at the bottom. The upper flowers are smaller and partially still in bud.

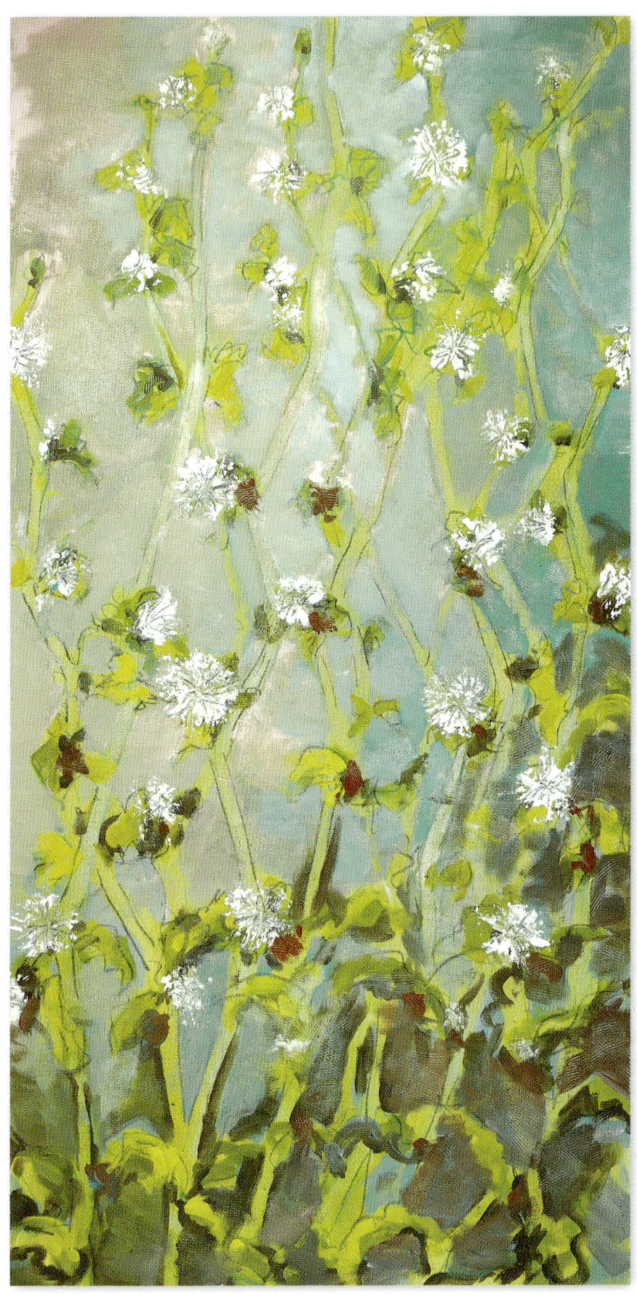

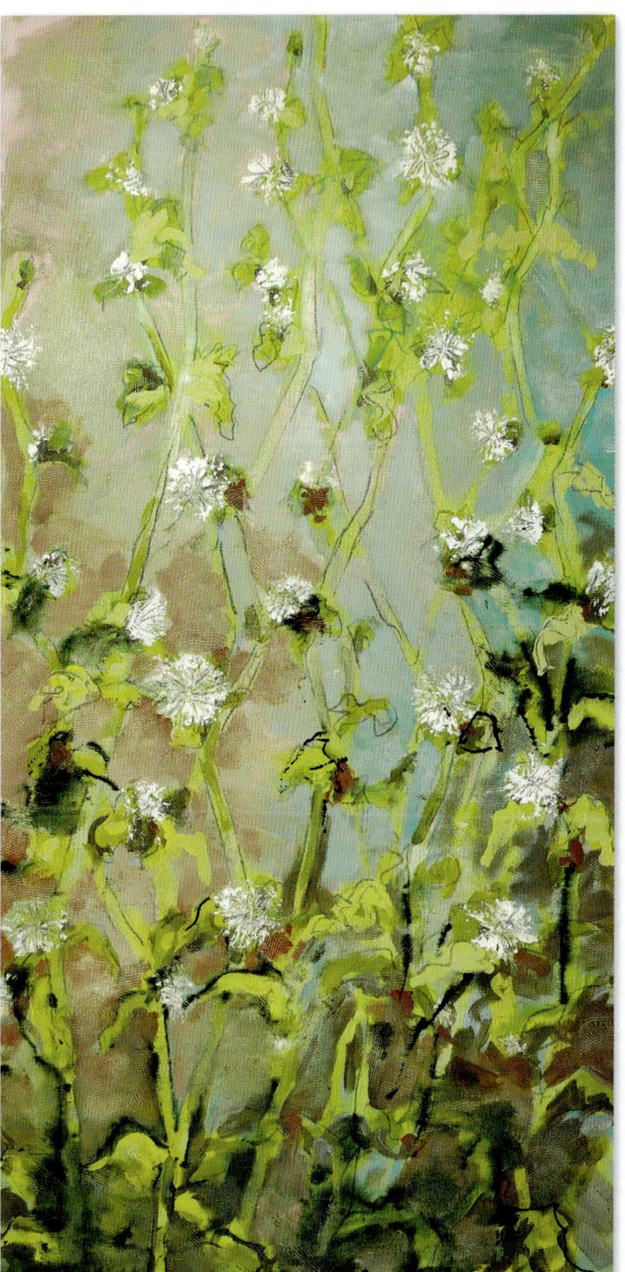

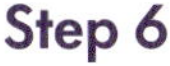

Step 6

In the background, add a light blue mixed from titanium white and cyan blue. Don't fully paint over the background areas. Let the paint under it show through by revealing it with the card scraper. Add burnt umber to the centers of the lower flowers. Increase the darkness in the background on the lower edge of the painting. Use the card scraper after every new layer of paint to create a fragmented surface of short lines.

Step 7

In the lower half of the picture, use a pipette to draw around some outlines with dark-green drawing ink. Spray with the water spray bottle. Use a brush to gently work the ink into the motif. Lighten the left side of background with burnt umber mixed with titanium white, and add details. Go over the surface with the card scraper while the paint is still wet, to partially reveal the layer of paint below.

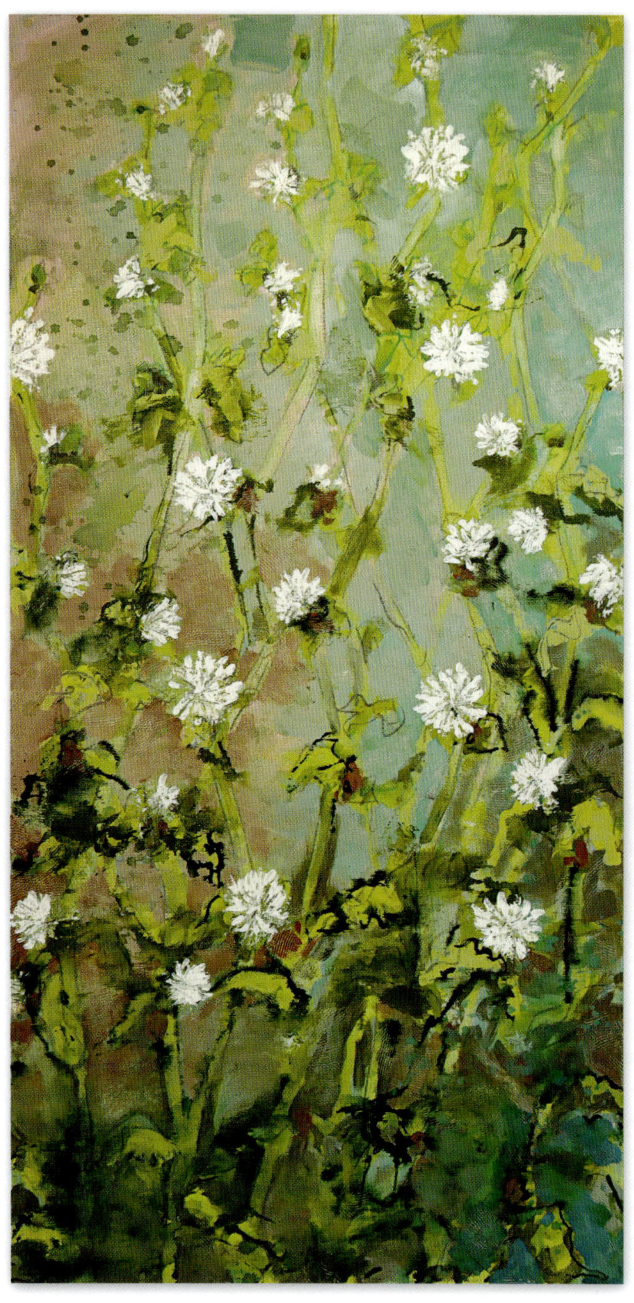

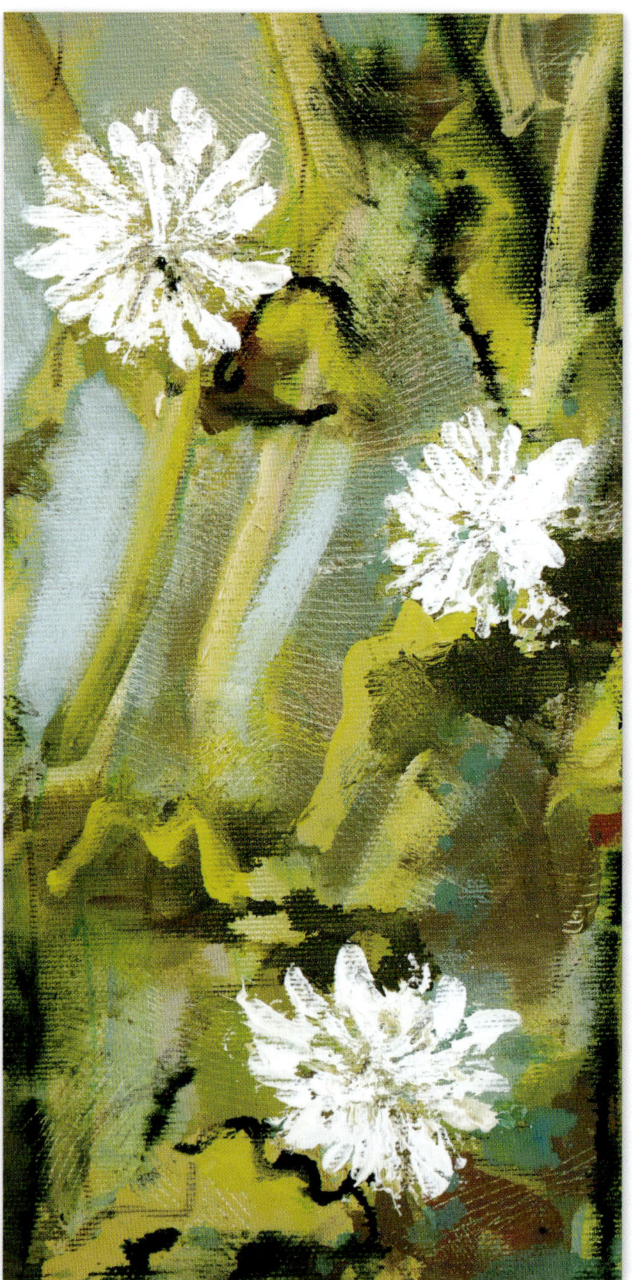

Step 8

Go over the flowers with fine putty and a palette knife with a pointed tip. Almost closed flowers are positioned next to fully opened ones. In the upper area of the picture, there are several small buds. Deliberately work loosely. Use a broad brush to add some olive-green splats to the left section of the picture only. It creates tension when sections of the picture have undergone their own individual processes. Add a bold dark turquoise to the lower right corner. Let dry.

Close Up

The flowers are almost see-through because of the fragmented coverage and the openings between the petals that allow the background to show through. This effect is mirrored by the card scraper on the background. By scratching the surfaces, the underlying layers of paint are partially revealed. The short, straight lines appear like the hatching on a drawing and add to the sketch-like style of many elements of the painting.

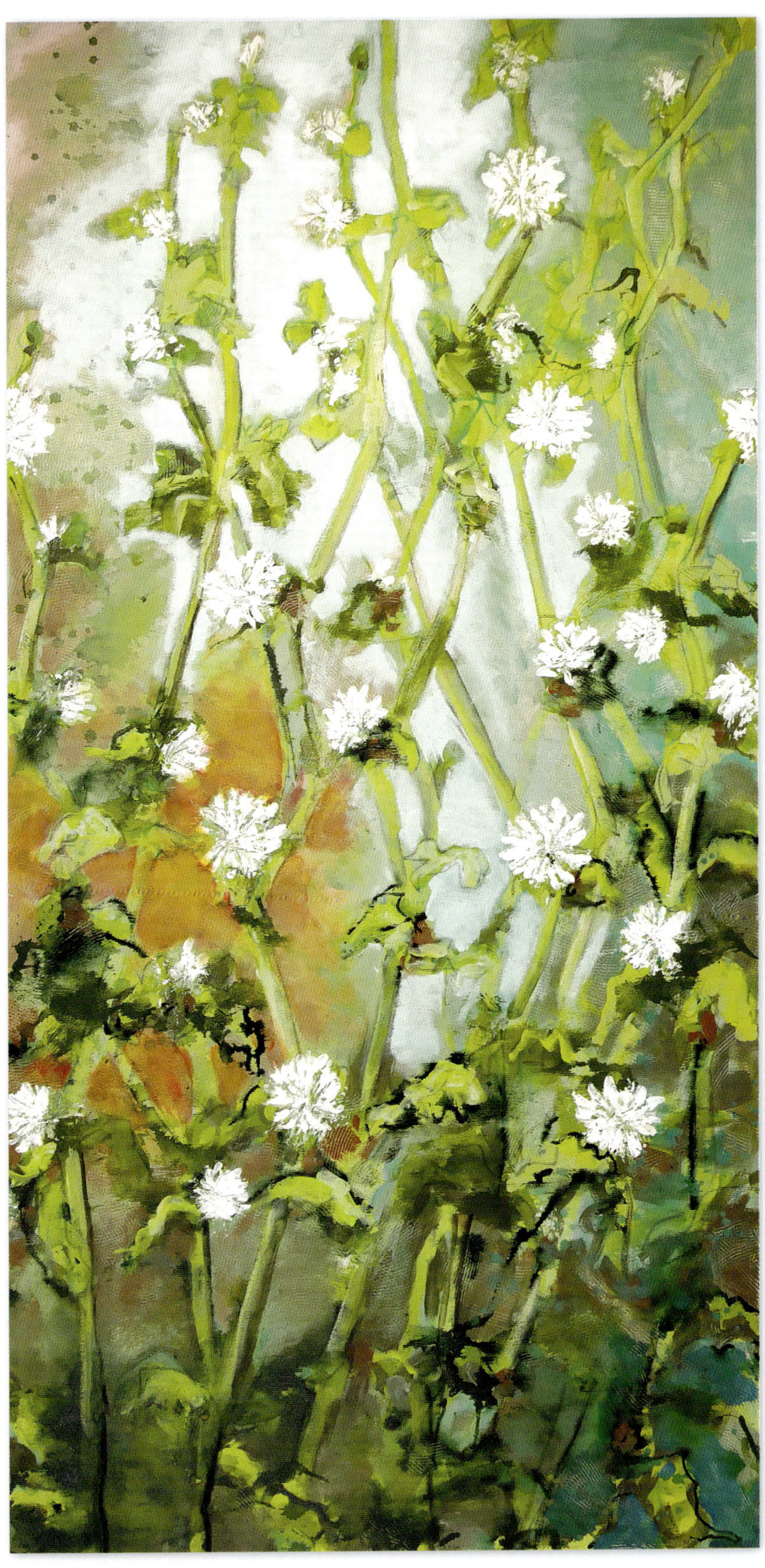

Finished Painting

Significantly lighten the central section of the background by using titanium white that has been mixed with a little cyan blue, but don't fully cover the shades underneath it. The multilayered color play creates vivacity. Add a slight shading to the stalks, using olive green on the right and light green on the left, so that they appear more three-dimensional. Finally, mix cadmium yellow, cadmium red, and burnt umber into a rust red and add it to the left section of the background. This red shade creates a complementary contrast to the predominantly green tones of the subject.

Asters

Materials:

- Canvas, 24 x 32 in.
- Acrylic paints in titanium white, cadmium yellow, orange, cadmium red, magenta, cyan blue, light violet, dark violet, burnt umber, and light gray
- Flat synthetic bristle brush, size 50
- Angular brush, sizes 8 and 10
- Binder
- Palette knife with long, thin blade
- Fine putty
- Jute sack
- Scissors
- Piece of charcoal, 0.75–1 in.
- Painter's palette

As all the leaves are turning yellow and wilting in the garden, the flowers of the violet aster open up and compete with the luminous yellows and oranges of fall.
The rough surface of the jute sack, which is used as the base, is reminiscent of fall and harvesttime. An unevenly cut and frayed fringe increases its rustic character. Fine putty is used as a base for the paint to cover over the jute sack's roughness. The bold interplay between orange and violet adds an intense contrast.

Step 1

It's particularly effective to use an unusual material—e.g., jute—stretched over a frame as the base. Since stretching can be tricky, a piece of material can alternatively be laid flat on the canvas and glued in place. To do so, cut the grain sack to the right size, but make sure the edges are not fully straight. Roughly fray a fringe.

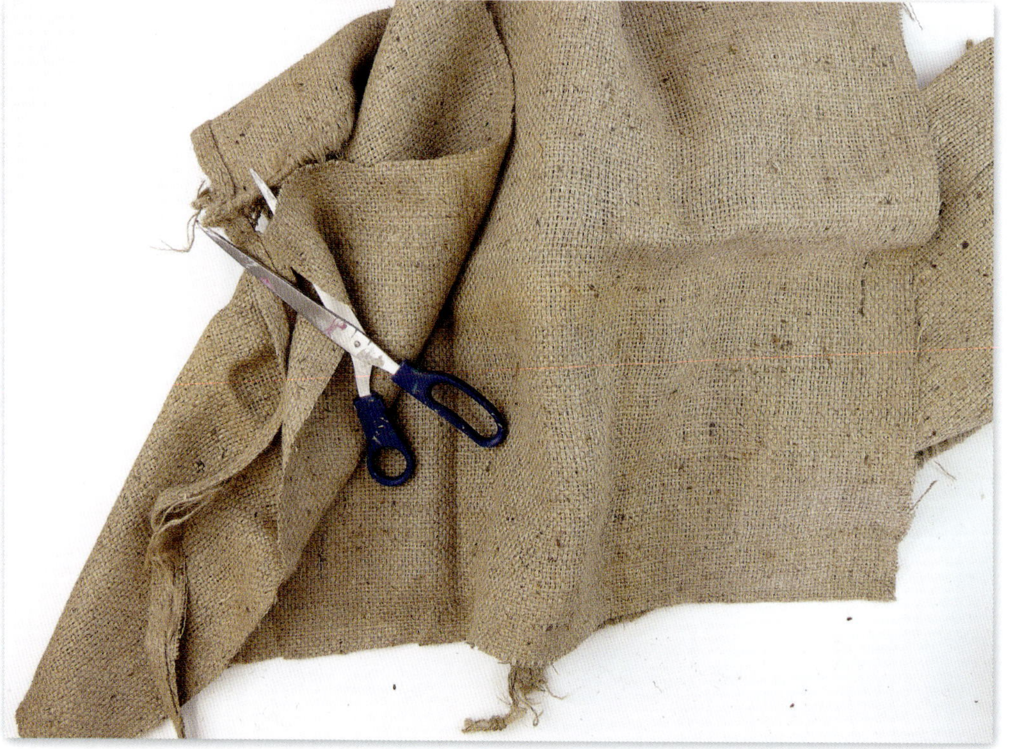

Step 2
Add a base of burned umber mixed with light gray around the edge of the canvas. Let dry. Generously apply the binder to the canvas, and spread using a broad brush. Place the jute sack on top of the canvas and stroke out any bubbles from the center so that the material lies flat on the canvas. Cover the top side of the jute with binder. The rustic appearance of the jute is accentuated by the unevenly cut edges and fringes. Allow to dry well.

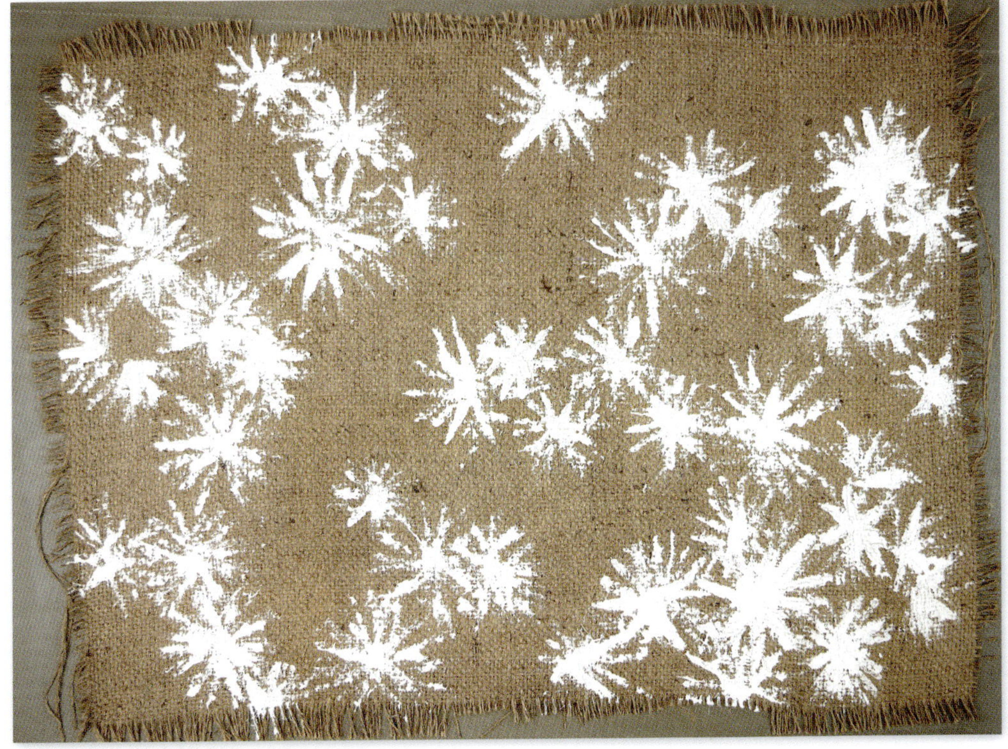

Step 3
Use the palette knife and the fine putty to model the flower heads. Make the individual petals in a flower different lengths and breadth, in no particular order. Combine large and small flowers. Some flowers should overlap. Create groups so that there are some empty spaces and the flower heads are not evenly distributed. Be sure to place only a small flower at the center of the canvas, because a large flower would be too dominant.

Step 4
Use a brush to paint the flowers with slightly diluted acrylic paint in various shades of violet mixed from light violet and dark violet. Thanks to the white putty base, bright violet shades with structure are created. Also use mixtures of magenta, light violet, and cyan blue. Each flower has its own main shade with slight color gradients. The paint may go beyond the putty base and run onto the jute sack.

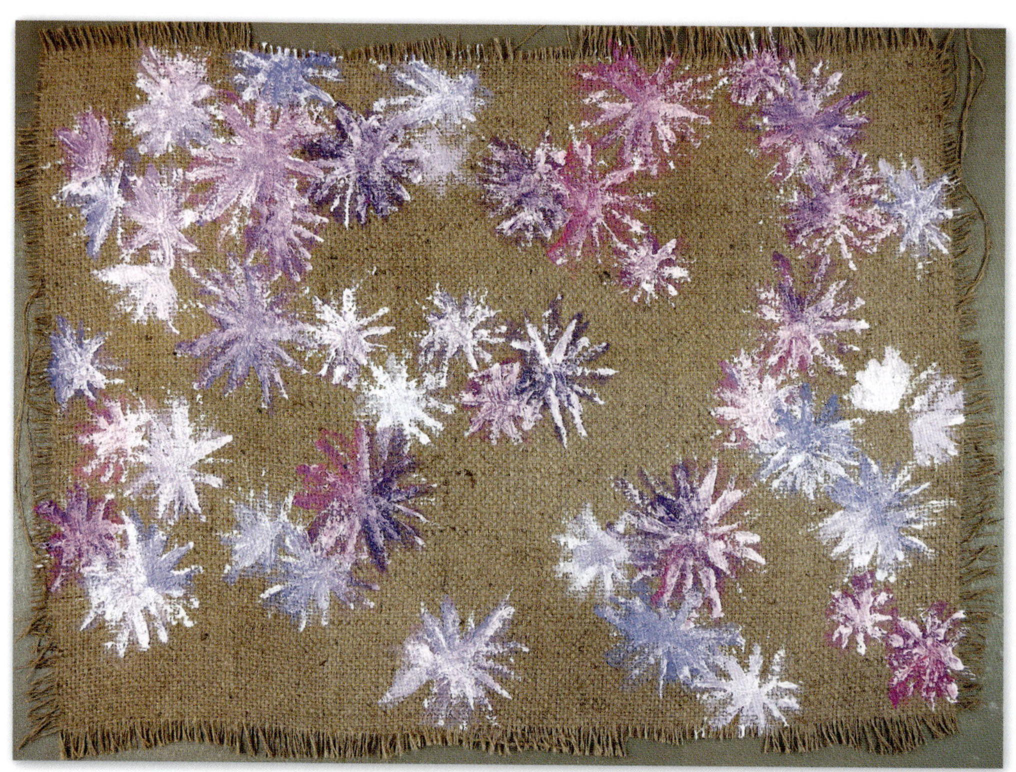

Step 5
Use a brush to add further detail to the flower heads by adding further petals in different shades of violet on the edges and in the centers. Work loosely so that a new shade is dabbed over only a third of the flower head, and use undiluted acrylic paint. The jute sack has been pretreated with binder so the acrylic paint can be applied to it. Otherwise, the paint would be absorbed by the material and drastically change in color.

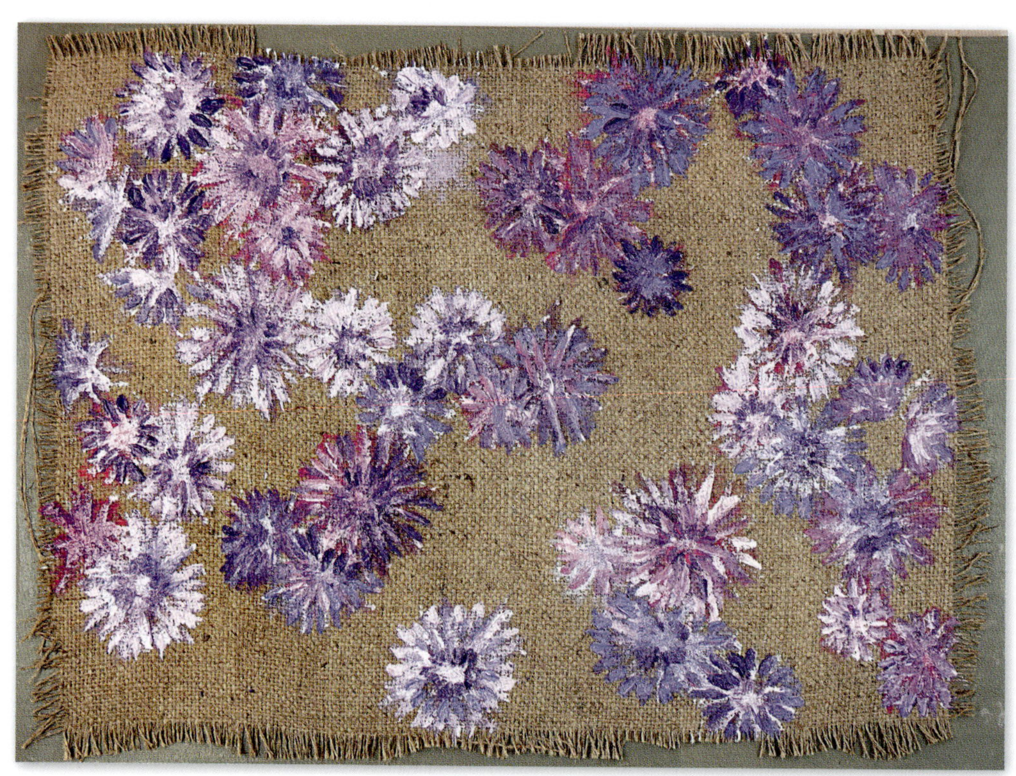

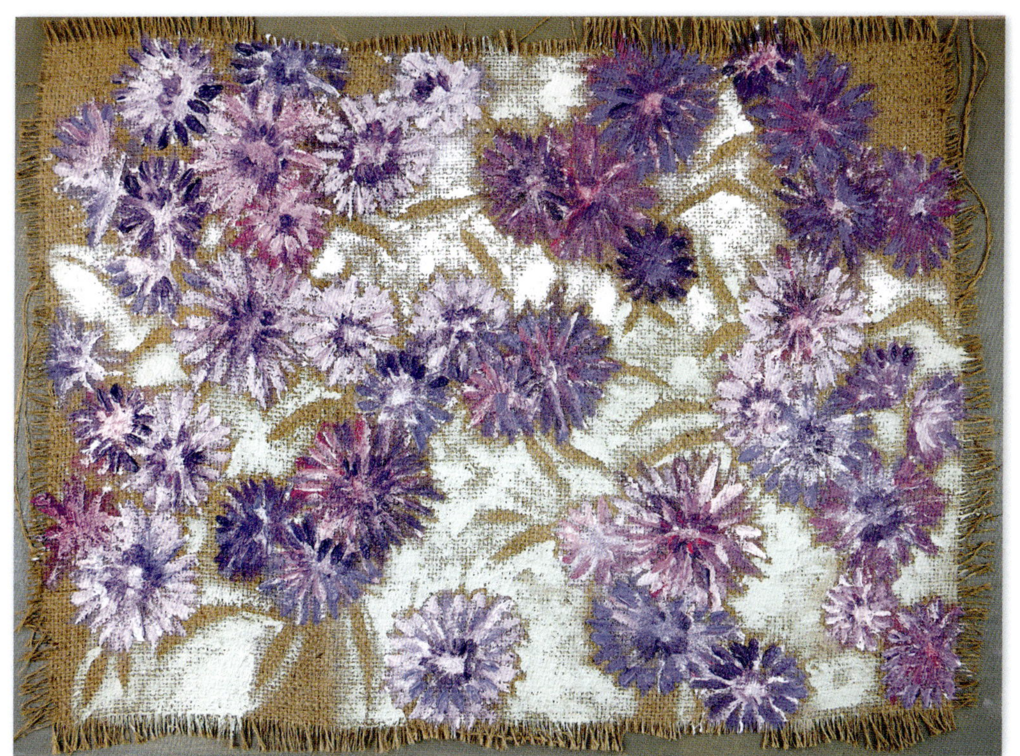

Step 6

Paint the background with a light shade mixed from titanium white, cadmium yellow, and light violet. Don't fully cover the background spaces, so that there is a thin border of the brown jute color around each flower. The thin leaves of the aster are created by leaving spaces when applying the paint. They would normally be green; however, in this picture they are the color of the jute. By not using green, the colors in the painting are reduced to a limited palette, which creates harmony.

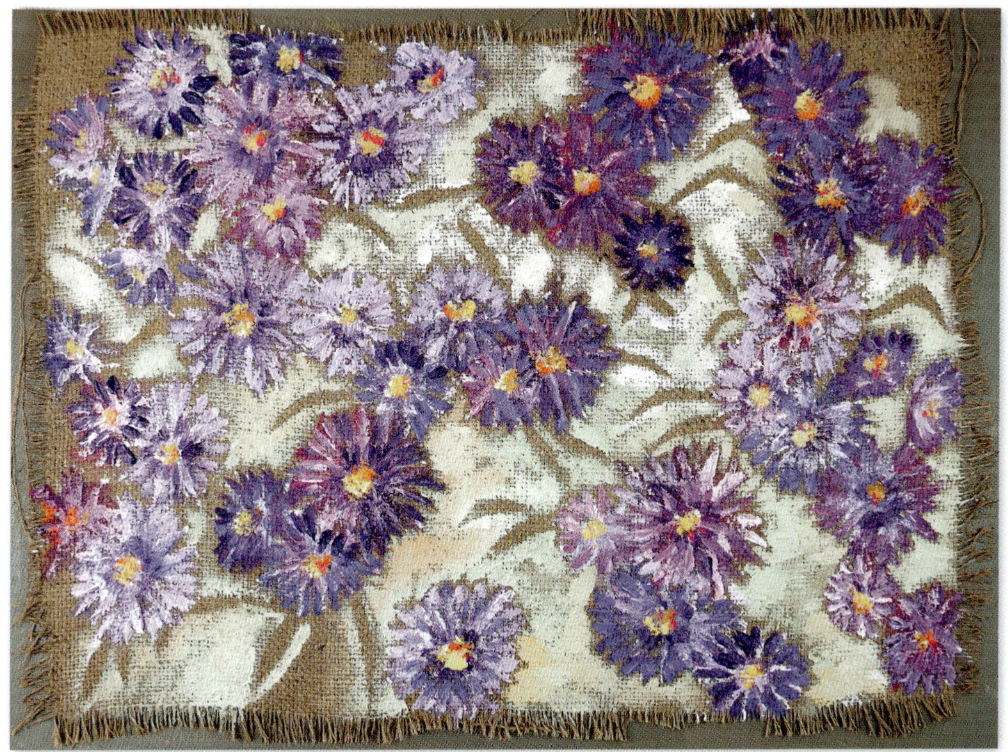

Step 7

In the centers of the flowers, dab cadmium yellow that has been lightened with titanium white as well as pure cadmium yellow. In some centers, add magenta, too. Give the background slight color nuances. Make the saturation of the acrylic paint uneven, so that some places are fully covered in paint, while in other places the structure of the jute is clearly visible. Just like in nature drawing, inconsistencies are important. Slight untidiness and imprecisions make the picture appear vivid.

Step 8

Use a thin piece of charcoal to draw loose outlines. In the background, add a few outlines of leaves with the charcoal. Due to the rough surface, the charcoal will crumble a little and leave fragmented lines of various widths. Remove the rough pieces of charcoal by standing up the canvas and beating it. Add to the base color of the background, using various shades of pale violet and pink that have been mixed from titanium white and a little magenta or dark violet.

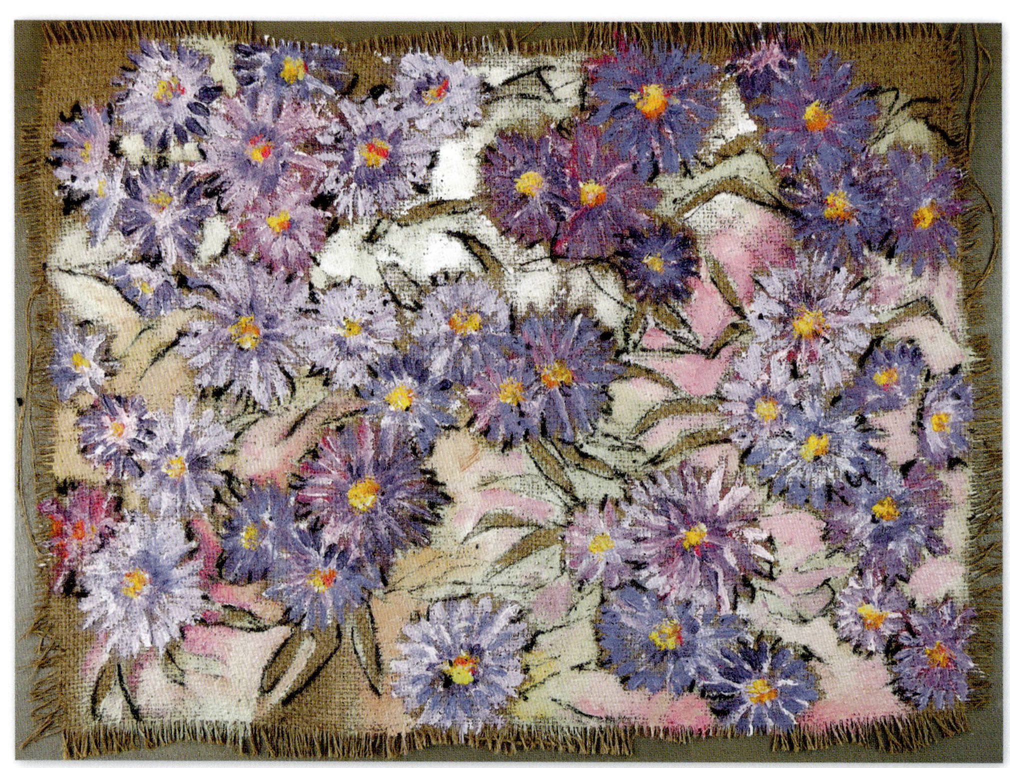

Close Up

The edge of the painting is an important design medium, and for that reason, framed pictures often look more impressive than unframed pictures. The unevenly cut fringe and the extremely rough woven structure of the jute sack give the painting a rustic character. The unpainted areas, where the woven structure remains clearly visible, and the loose application of paint, which allows the base to show through, increase this impression and add to the fall motif.

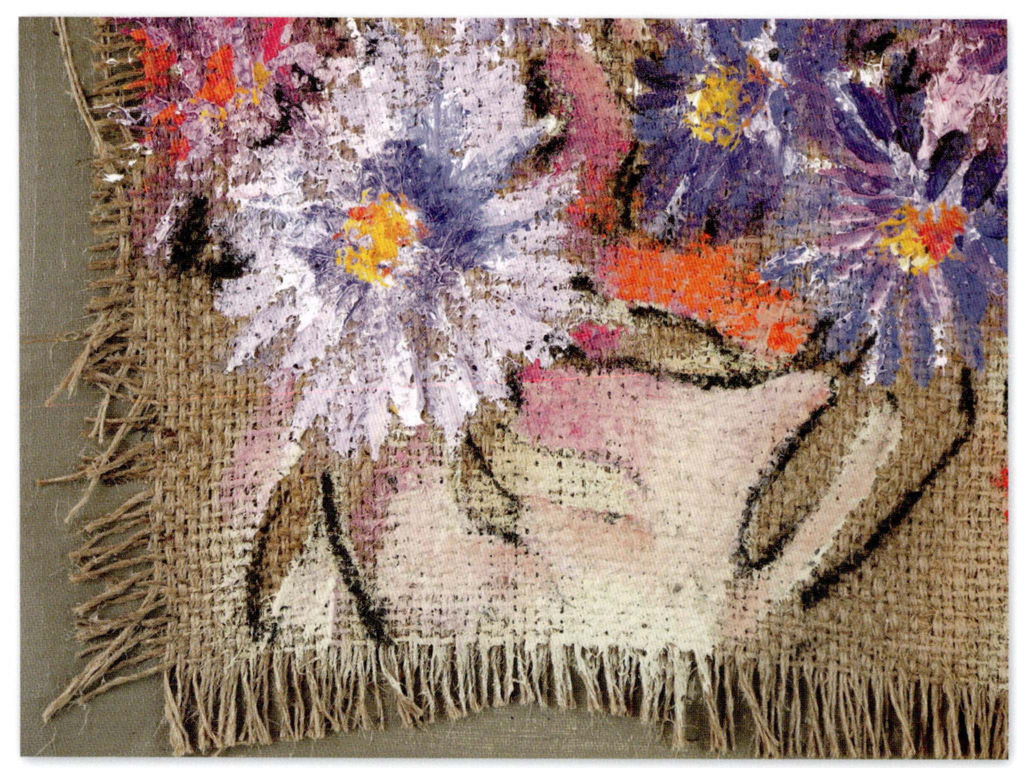

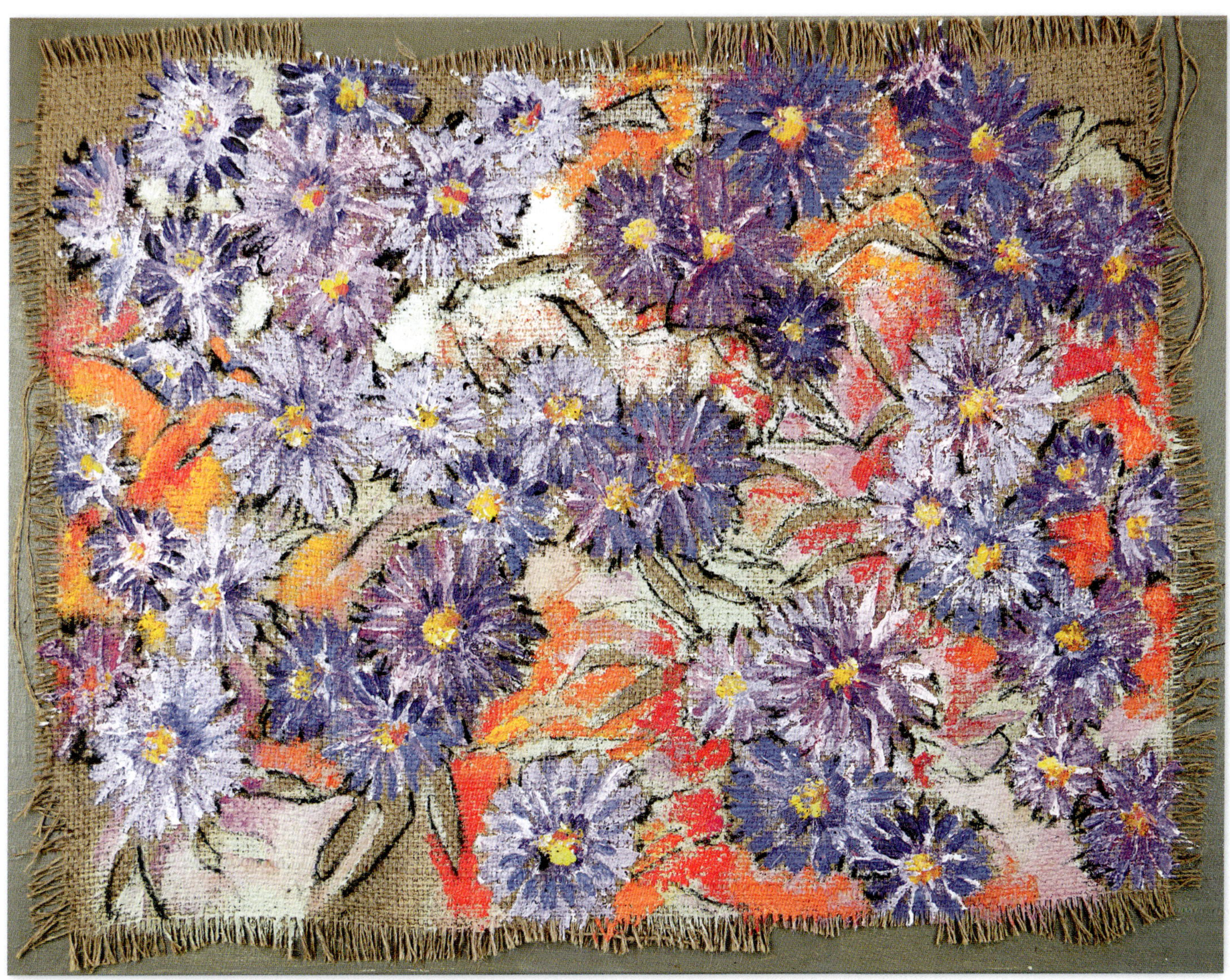

Finished Painting

Paint the background in undiluted acrylic paint in the flaming fall colors of cadmium yellow, orange, cadmium red, and magenta. Do so in such a way that the paint somewhat fragments due to the rough base. Don't fully fill the areas. Ensure that the underlying colors are visible at the edge of each area. In a few places, slightly paint over the charcoal. Leave a few background areas unworked, in particular those at the center of the canvas, allowing the lighter shades to be visible instead.

Poinsettia

Materials:

- Canvas, 32 x 32 in.
- Acrylic paints in titanium white, cadmium yellow, rose, magenta, pink, cyan blue, light green, grass green, and black
- Flat synthetic bristle brush, size 35
- Round natural hair brush, size 2
- Angular brush, size 12
- Watercolor pencils: in white and red
- Binder and container
- Drawing ink in white, yellow, and dark green
- Pipettes
- Water spray bottle
- Paper towels
- Painter's palette

If you have ever seen a tall poinsettia in its natural environment, you will never forget the sight of it. Originally from tropical Central America, it now also grows in the hotter regions of Europe—and Christmas wouldn't be Christmas without it. Its colors range from various red and rose shades right up to a bold pink. The unusual colors occur in the bracts or upper leaves, which are above the normal green leaves. This motif makes use of pink, a color that is otherwise seldomly used. Together with the bright green of the background, an intensive color play develops.

Step 1

Squeeze rose, magenta, and pink directly from the tubes onto the canvas. Use the flat synthetic brush to randomly distribute the paint on the canvas. Sketch the bracts with a white watercolor pencil. Use a flat brush to fill the dark areas in the background with water-diluted dark-green drawing ink. Use a pipette to outline the edges with white drawing ink.

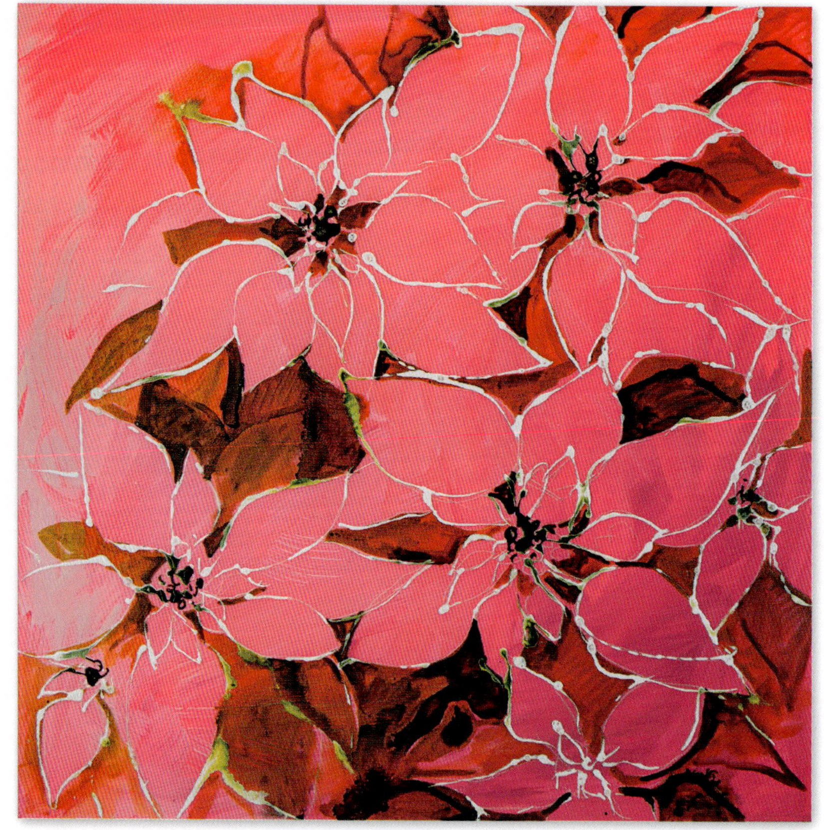

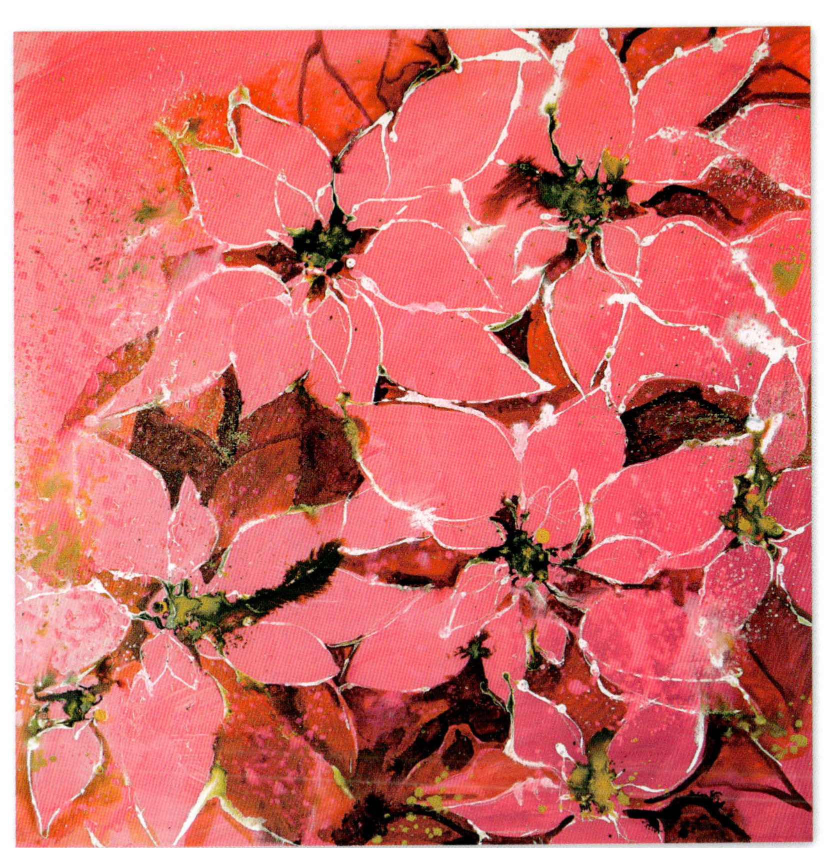

Step 2

Use dark-green drawing ink and a pipette to draw in the inflorescences. Spray with the water spray bottle so that some of the ink runs. The colors may run into each other to create a light green. Add light-green splats to the outer areas of the canvas. Use a pipette to add a few drops of yellow drawing ink to the still-wet centers to create starlike circle shapes as the ink runs. Let dry.

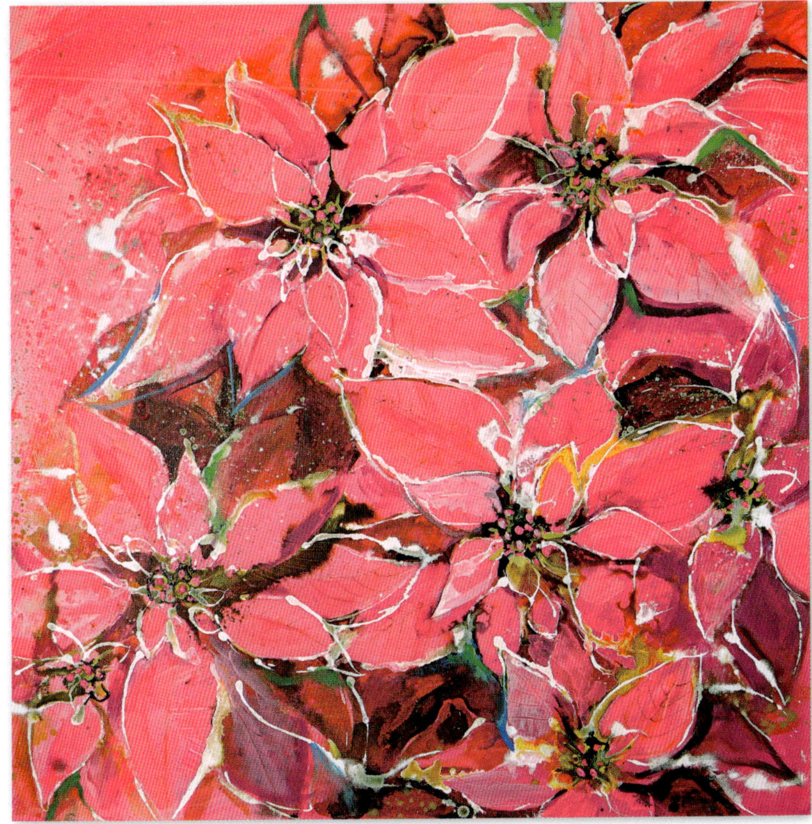

Step 3

Dip a red watercolor pen in the binder and draw in the veins on the bracts. Since the pencil is wet, the stroke will be thicker. Once dried, the watercolor pencil is fixed, thanks to the binder. Mix up a bright green from a lot of cadmium yellow and light green. Use a fine brush to go over the centers with this green and pink to highlight the circular inflorescences. Also use the bright green to add some accents on the edges of the bracts. Add further accents by using cyan blue and grass green.

Step 4

Use a brush to add a few splats of a mixture of titanium white and pink. Go over or add outlines by using a pipette and white drawing ink. Add outlines for small bracts in the centers. Spray lightly with a water spray bottle to create runs. Add a few splats of the white drawing ink. Use paper towels to wipe up any uncontrolled runs.

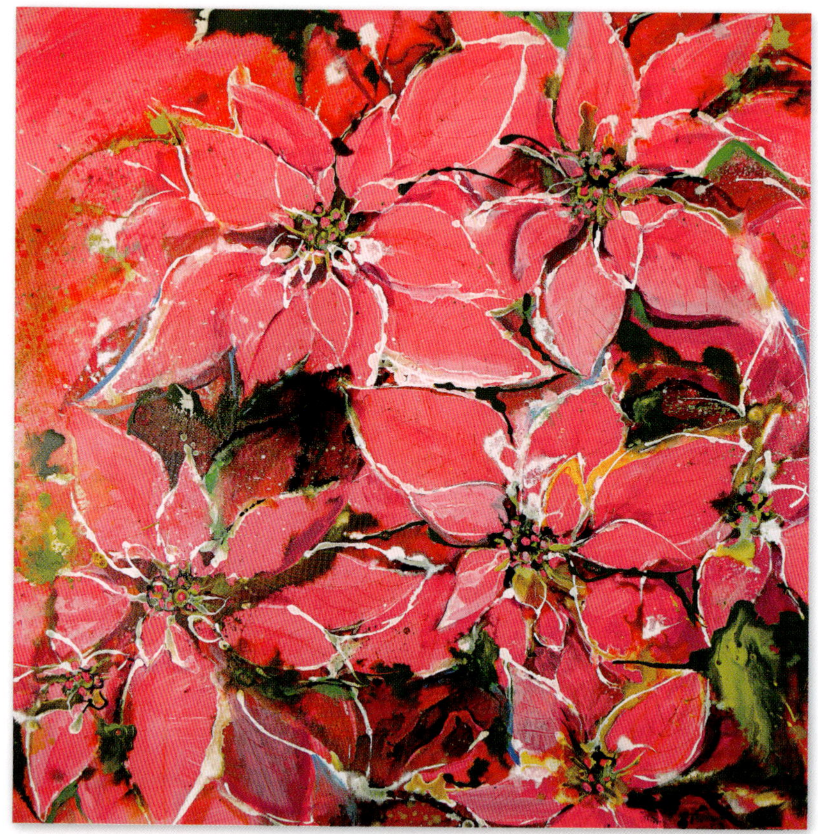

Step 5

Use a pipette to add the dark-green drawing ink—particularly to the background areas—and occasionally use a wet brush to spread it. When it combines with the still-wet white drawing ink, light-green runs occur. Use a brush to add a powerful bright green mixed from cadmium yellow and grass green throughout the whole painting, sometimes as areas in the background, and sometimes on broad outlines or as delicate lines in the inflorescences.

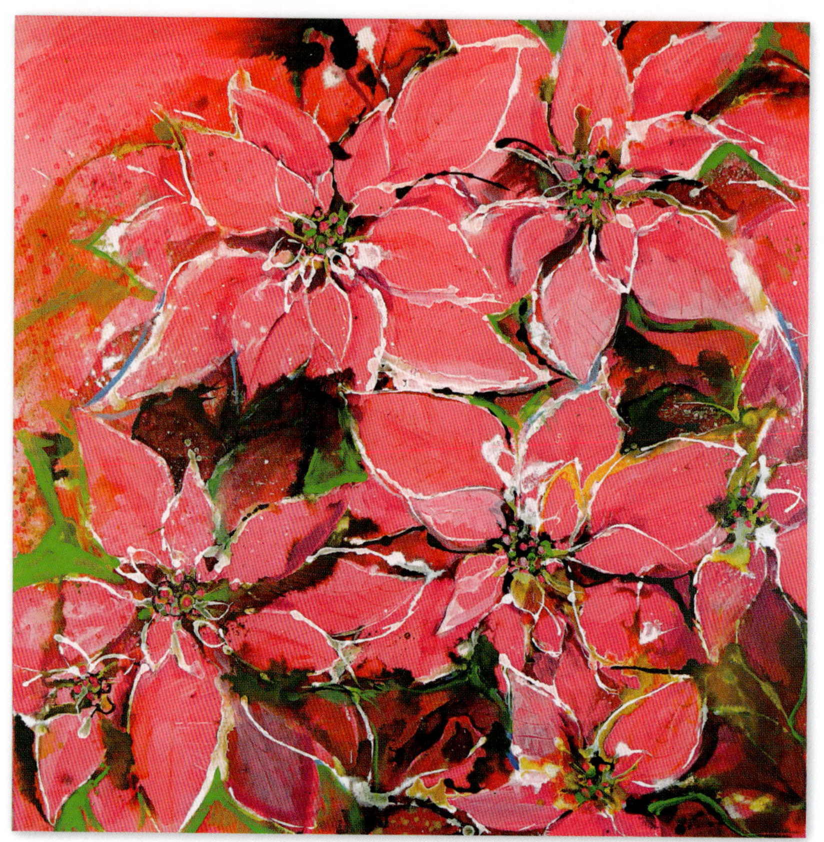

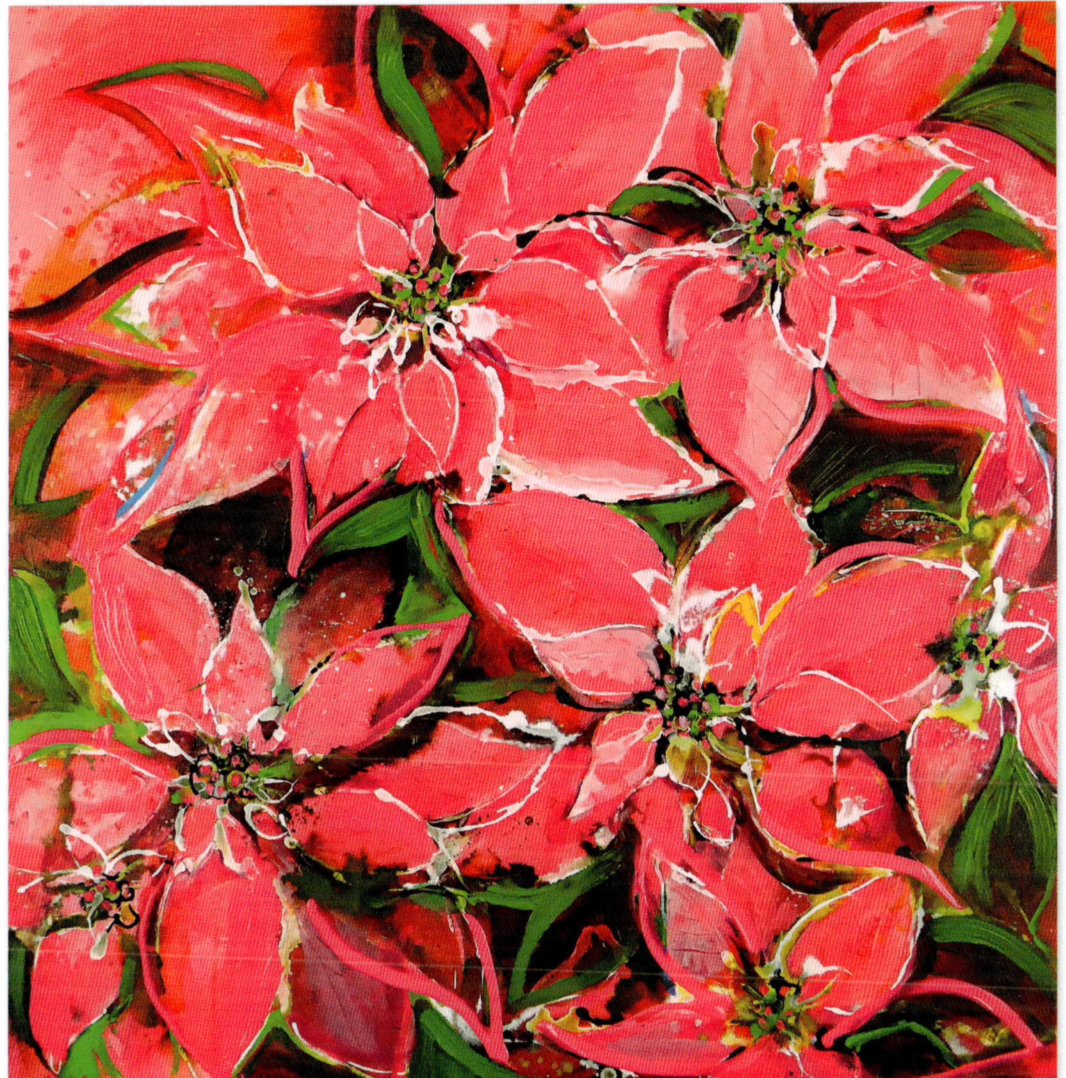

Finished Painting

Add further outlines by using acrylic paint directly from the tubes onto the canvas. Also add a few empty outlines in the dark background. Add patches of pink on a few of the bracts. Use a flat brush to go over the background areas in a mixture of black and grass green, using the shade as a glaze. The colors and shapes underneath it will show through. Add suggestions of leaf shapes, using a bold light green mixed from cadmium yellow and grass green.

Tip: The vividness of many subjects is derived from inaccuracies, unusual infusions, splats, and unfinished elements. However, every subject also needs calm zones and areas of uniform colors to contrast with unsettled sections with lots of detail. Many such decisions are often made only during the painting process. Therefore, it's advisable to frequently take a break and look at the subject with fresh eyes to be able to plan the next step better. It's also helpful to take photos on your phone of the various steps, since shrinking the picture in this way makes the contrasts clearly visible.

Postscript

Every painting has its own dynamic. I am often surprised at how different the pictures of the same plants are when I paint them again at a later point in time. Depending on my mood on the day, I sometimes experience the same plant more intensely and other times more subtly. I often don't know in advance which of the presented design techniques I'll use. Only a few, never all, can be used at once. Otherwise, the picture will be fussy. I'm usually inspired by something such as a new technique or a tool that I want to use. However, the picture has its own mind and does what it wants. And that's a good thing. The process of struggling is part of the work. I usually go through three phases: a short phase of inspiration, a long phase of struggling and intense work, and then the final phase of rising like a phoenix from the ashes. And if I'm lucky, something in me has changed through the struggle, something that I can't describe in words, something that has nothing to do with the painting, but solely with the artistic process. And this process is medicative. I wish you constant, always new transitions when struggling and working with your own pictures.

Ruth Alice Kosnick

Originally published as *Flower Power in Acryl*, ©2021 Christophorus Verlag / Christian Verlag GmbH, Munich
Translated from the German by Catherine Venner

Library of Congress Control Number: 2022944180

Cover design by Ashley Millhouse
Type set in Quincy/Futura
Photos and illustrations: Ruth Alice Kosnick

ISBN: 978-0-7643-6607-9
Printed in China

Published by Schiffer Publishing, Ltd.
4880 Lower Valley Road
Atglen, PA 19310
Phone: (610) 593-1777; Fax: (610) 593-2002
Email: Info@schifferbooks.com
Web: www.schifferbooks.com

For our complete selection of fine books on this and related subjects, please visit our website at www.schifferbooks.com. You may also write for a free catalog.

Schiffer Publishing's titles are available at special discounts for bulk purchases for sales promotions or premiums. Special editions, including personalized covers, corporate imprints, and excerpts, can be created in large quantities for special needs. For more information, contact the publisher.

We are always looking for people to write books on new and related subjects. If you have an idea for a book, please contact us at proposals@schifferbooks.com.

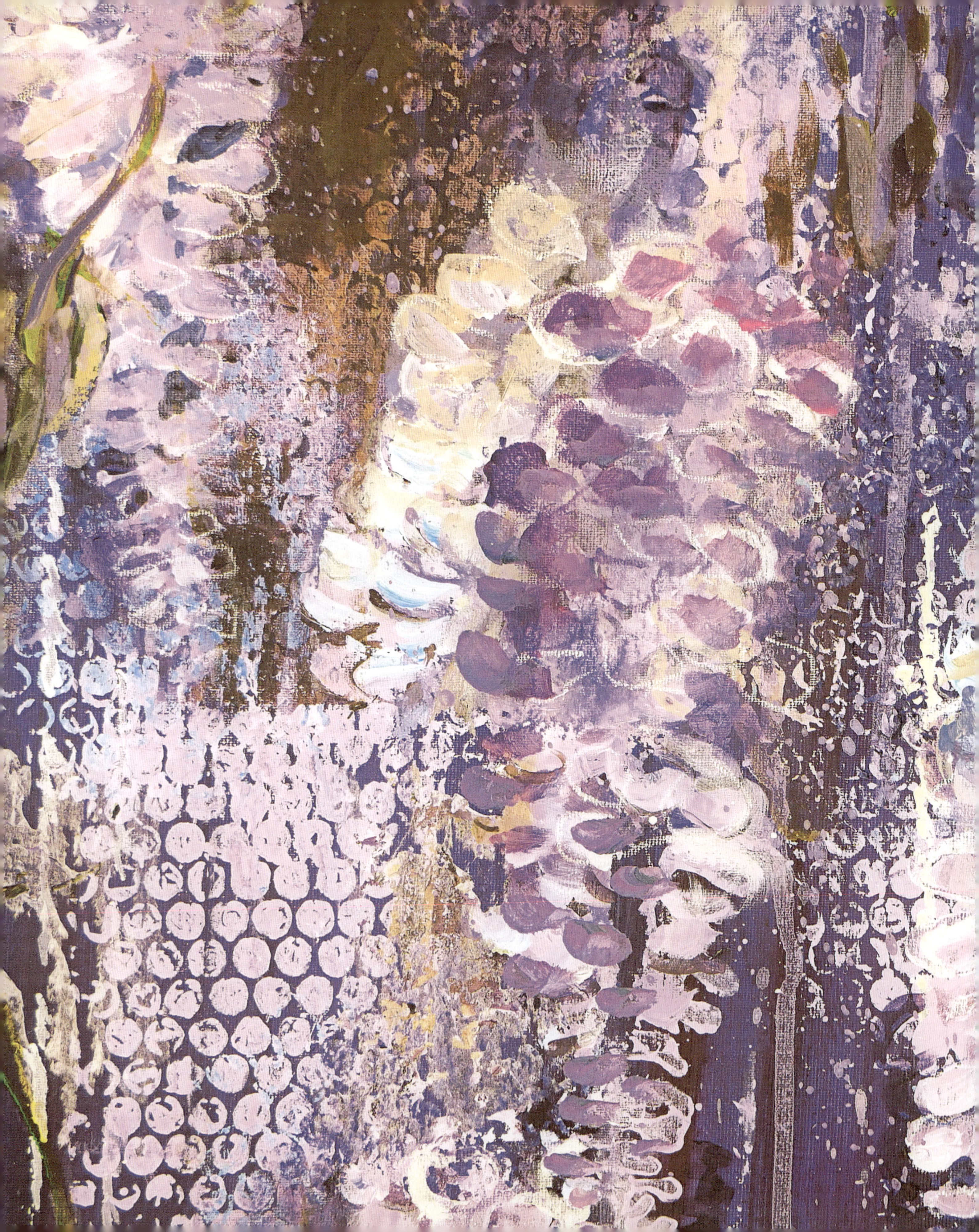